# PILLSBURY
## BAKING

### Pillsbury Editors

WILEY PUBLISHING, INC.

Published by Wiley Publishing, Inc., Hoboken, NJ

Published simultaneously in Canada

No part of this publication may be reproduced, stored in a retrieval system or transmitted in any form or by any means, electronic, mechanical, photocopying, recording, scanning or otherwise, except as permitted under Sections 107 or 108 of the 1976 United States Copyright Act, without either the prior written permission of the Publisher, or authorization through payment of the appropriate per-copy fee to the Copyright Clearance Center, 222 Rosewood Drive, Danvers, MA 01923, (978) 750-8400, fax (978) 750-4470. Requests to the Publisher for permission should be addressed to the Permissions Department, John Wiley & Sons, Inc., 111 River Street, Hoboken, NJ 07030, (201) 748-6011, fax (201) 748-6008, or online at http://www.wiley.com/go/permissions.

Trademarks: Wiley and the Wiley Publishing logo are trademarks or registered trademarks of John Wiley & Sons, Inc. and/or its affiliates. All other trademarks referred to herein are trademarks of General Mills. Wiley Publishing, Inc. is not associated with any product or vendor mentioned in this book.

Limit of Liability/Disclaimer of Warranty: While the publisher and author have used their best efforts in preparing this book, they make no representations or warranties with respect to the accuracy or completeness of the contents of this book and specifically disclaim any implied warranties of merchantability or fitness for a particular purpose. No warranty may be created or extended by sales representatives or written sales materials. The advice and strategies contained herein may not be suitable for your situation. You should consult with a professional where appropriate. Neither the publisher nor author shall be liable for any loss of profit or any other commercial damages, including but not limited to special, incidental, consequential, or other damages.

For general information on our other products and services or to obtain technical support, please contact our Customer Care Department within the United States at 800-762-2974, outside the United States at 317-572-3993 or fax 317-572-4002.

Wiley also publishes its books in a variety of electronic formats. Some content that appears in print may not be available in electronic books. For more information about Wiley products, visit our web site at www.wiley.com.

**Library of Congress Cataloging-in-Publication Data:**

Pillsbury baking / Pillsbury Editors.

    p. cm.

Includes index.

ISBN-13: 978-0-471-78088-5

ISBN-10: 0-471-78088-X

1. Baking.  2. Desserts.  I. Pillbury Company.

TX765.P5193 2006

641.8'15—dc22                    2006018001

**GENERAL MILLS**

Director, Book and Online Publishing: **Kim Walter**

Manager, Book Publishing: **Lois Tlusty**

Editor: **Cheri Olerud**

Recipe Development and Testing:
  **Betty Crocker Kitchens**

Photography:
  **General Mills Photography Studios**

Photographer: **Rudy Calin**

Food Stylists: **Cindy Syme and Kimberly Colburn**

**WILEY PUBLISHING, INC.**

Publisher: **Natalie Chapman**

Executive Editor: **Anne Ficklen**

Senior Production Editor: **Angela Riley**

Cover Design: **Suzanne Sunwoo**

Interior Design and Layout: **BTDNYC**

Photography Art Direction: **Sue Schultz**

Manufacturing Manager: **Kevin Watt**

*Home of the Pillsbury Bake-Off® Contest*

*Our recipes have been tested in the Pillsbury Kitchens and meet our standards of easy preparation, reliability and great taste.*

For more great recipes, visit pillsbury.com

# Welcome . . .

## FROM THE PILLSBURY KITCHENS
Home of the Pillsbury Bake-Off® Contest

Remember when you baked a favorite cookie or delicious pie for someone special? The reaction was, "Wow! You took the time to bake one of my favorite things. You're amazing!" Add to that rave the deep satisfaction you felt, and you'll agree, home-baked goodies are a great gift, memorable for giver and receiver alike.

Share the fun and your love of baking. Good times and good feelings are wrapped together in the form of baking. Even better, share your love of baking by enlisting the kids. Think of the fun they'll have learning the ropes as they get their little fingers (and faces) dirty and happy while baking with you. Give them memories that will last a lifetime!

If you're still learning or unsure in the kitchen, you'll be surprised at how easy and fun these recipes are. And if you want to learn more, there are challenging breads and inspiring new desserts to try. Inviting aromas and delicious flavors—and wonderful food—are right here waiting for you!

The Pillsbury Editors

# Contents

## Help! I Live in the Mountains

If you live at high altitude (over 3500 feet), you already know foods bake differently than at sea level. Changes are needed because:

Lower air pressure changes the way foods cook and bake.

Humidity is lower, so flour dries out more and absorbs more liquid in a recipe.

Water boils at a lower temperature and liquids evaporate faster, so foods take longer to cook.

Some foods become harder faster, so keeping baked goods tightly covered is a good idea.

Certain recipes may need to bake longer, and some baked goods may be drier or brown more quickly. The structure of breads may not be as strong, and yeast bread dough may rise too quickly. Biscuits, cookies and muffins usually need the fewest recipe changes.

Changes to a recipe depend on the kind of food and the proportion of ingredients. All of the recipes in this cookbook were tested at high altitude, so you can relax and simply follow the high altitude directions on each recipe for your best baking.

## Ingredients Common to Baking

Begin with the freshest ingredients to get off to a good start and guarantee baking success.

**Baking Powder:** Reacts with the liquids in a recipe and the heat of the oven to make cookies, pancakes, breads and muffins rise.

**Baking Soda:** Reacts instantly with liquids and acid ingredients like buttermilk, sour cream and yogurt to make baked goods rise.

**Butter or Margarine:** Adds flavor and tenderness; helps brown baked foods. For recipes that call for butter or margarine, either works equally well. But in some recipes, such as Browned Butter Frosting, only butter is listed because it works best.

**Eggs:** Provide structure, height or volume and bind ingredients together. The recipes have been tested with large eggs, so use that size.

**Flour:** The protein in flour provides the structure for baked goods. Use all-purpose flour (either bleached or unbleached) in any recipe in this cookbook. *__Whole wheat flour__* is a whole-grain flour that's milled from the complete wheat kernel (bran, germ and endosperm), which gives it a wheaty flavor and appearance.

**Milk:** Moistens ingredients and affects the consistency of the batter or dough. Recipes are written for 2% milk, but fat-free (skim) or whole milk can easily be used instead.

**Salt:** Adds flavor. Although there are other types of salt, table salt is what most people have on hand and is used in our recipes. Table salt is also needed in yeast breads to work with the yeast.

**Spices, Herbs and Seeds:** Provide that just-right touch of seasoning to baked goods. Dried herbs and spices last only so long and need to be replaced about every year. Store fresh herbs in the refrigerator.

**Sugar:** Flavors and tenderizes baked goods and gives them a golden brown crust. ***Brown sugar*** contains a small amount of molasses that keeps it moist and firm. ***Granulated sugar*** is white, all-purpose sugar. ***Powdered sugar*** is finely ground and is usually used in frosting.

**Yeast:** Used to make yeast breads rise, yeast is a living organism that is activated by warm water and sugar. Heat the liquid added to yeast only to the temperature called for in a recipe so the water doesn't kill the yeast.

## In a Pinch
Because the recipes were tested with the specific ingredients listed, it's really best to use those ingredients. If you happen to run out of something, you can substitute:

| If you don't have | You can use |
| --- | --- |
| Baking powder, 1 teaspoon | 1/4 teaspoon baking soda plus 1/2 teaspoon cream of tartar |
| Buttermilk, 1 cup | 1 tablespoon vinegar or lemon juice plus enough milk to make 1 cup |
| Chocolate, semisweet, 1 ounce | 1 ounce unsweetened baking chocolate plus 1 tablespoon sugar OR 3 tablespoons semisweet chocolate chips |
| Chocolate, unsweetened, 1 ounce | 3 tablespoons unsweetened baking cocoa plus 1 tablespoon shortening, butter or margarine |
| Cornstarch, 1 tablespoon | 2 tablespoons flour |
| Flour (for thickening), 1 tablespoon | 1 1/2 teaspoons cornstarch |
| Half-and-half, 1 cup | 7/8 cup (3/4 cup plus 2 tablespoons) milk plus 3 tablespoons butter |
| Honey, 1 cup | 1 1/4 cups sugar plus 1/4 cup liquid |
| Lemon, 1 medium (for fresh juice) | 2 to 3 tablespoons bottled lemon juice |
| Orange, 1 medium (for fresh juice) | 1/4 to 1/3 cup orange juice |
| Sour cream, 1 cup | 1 cup plain yogurt |
| Yogurt, plain, 1 cup | 1 cup sour cream |

## Get Ready, Get Set . . .
If you haven't baked before, start with an easy cookie recipe, like Old-Time Sugar Cookies, page 84. Before you take off, take a look at these pointers:

**Read It:** Read the entire recipe before you begin to avoid surprises at the end. You'll know just what ingredients and equipment are needed and how much time the recipe will take.

**Find It:** Find and measure ingredients and get out equipment in advance.

**Clean It:** Put containers away, wipe up spills and place dirty dishes in the sink. And keep distractions to a minimum so you don't accidentally skip a step or leave out an ingredient.

### Measuring Musts
Measuring carefully helps ensure that your baked goods will turn out just right.

**Butter:** The wrapper on sticks of butter or margarine shows tablespoon and cup markings; use a sharp knife to cut off the amount you need.

**Dry Ingredients:** Use standard dry-ingredient measuring cups that come in sets of 1/4, 1/3, 1/2 and 1 cup. Lightly spoon ingredient into measuring cup, then level it off with the straight edge of a spatula or knife.

**Brown Sugar and Shortening:** Firmly press ingredient into standard dry-ingredient measuring cup, then level it off with a spatula or knife.

**Spices and Dried Herbs:** Use standard measuring spoons that come in sets of 1/4 teaspoon, 1/2 teaspoon, 1 teaspoon and 1 tablespoon. For dry ingredients, fill the spoon, then level it off with a spatula or knife. For liquid ingredients, fill the spoon completely.

## The Scoop on Pans

You don't need expensive equipment or a lot of it, but having basic, good-quality tools makes your baking experience successful and enjoyable.

### Pan Types

**Shiny Metal:** Shiny aluminum, tin and stainless steel are the best metals for baking pans because they reflect heat and give the most tender, light brown crusts. Shiny metal is recommended by the Pillsbury Kitchens.

**Silicone:** The newest in bakeware, silicone pans brown foods evenly, can withstand extreme heat and are safe for the microwave, freezer and dishwasher. Silicone pans are soft and flexible and come in many colors, shapes and sizes.

**Dull-Finish, including Aluminum, Tin and Glass:** These pans absorb more heat, so baked goods brown more quickly. They are actually the pan of choice for the best pie crusts, but remember to reduce the oven temperature by 25 degrees.

**Black Steel:** These pans give breads a crisp, dark crust and are often used for French bread and breadsticks to give them their distinctive crunch.

### Pan Sizes

Pans come in standard sizes. If you use the standard size pan, you can be more confident that your baked goods will turn out well. The sizes of pans used in this cookbook are:

| | |
|---|---|
| 8- or 9-inch square pan | 9- or 10-inch tart pan |
| 8- or 9-inch round cake pan | 10-inch angel food (tube) cake pan |
| 8x4-inch loaf pan | 12-cup fluted tube cake pan |
| 9x5-inch loaf pan | Cookie sheets |
| 9-inch glass pie plate | 15x10x1-inch pan (or jelly roll pan) |
| 9- or 10-inch springform pan | Muffin pans |

### What If I Don't Have the Right Size Pan?

If a recipe calls for a pan you don't have, you can try using a pan you do have that is a similar size. Use the chart below to help you substitute.

| *If you don't have* | *You can use* |
|---|---|
| One 13x9-inch pan | Two 9-inch round cake pans OR |
| | Two 8-inch round cake pans OR |
| | Two 8-inch square pans |
| One 9-inch round cake pan | One 8-inch square pan |
| Two 9-inch round cake pans | Three 8-inch round cake pans |
| One 8x4-inch loaf pan | Two 5 1/2x3 1/4-inch loaf pans |
| One 9x5-inch loaf pan | Two 7 1/2x3 3/4-inch loaf pans OR |
| | Three 5 1/2x3 1/4-inch loaf pans |
| One 12-cup fluted tube cake pan | One 10-inch angel food (tube) cake pan |
| | OR Two 9x5-inch loaf pans |

Most recipes for baked goods (except cookies) call for the pan to be greased or be greased and floured. Prepare the pan before you begin to make the recipe.

**To Grease a Pan:**

Use solid vegetable shortening because it won't brown or add flavor to your baked goods.

Apply a thin, even layer of shortening to the pan with a paper towel or pastry brush.

**To Grease and Flour a Pan:**

Grease the pan using above technique. Add a tablespoonful of flour to the pan and shake so that flour sticks to all greased areas.

Turn the pan upside down and tap the bottom to remove excess flour.

To use cooking spray or a cooking spray and flour combination:

Spray on pan just before using, following package instructions.

## Prep the Oven

To make certain that your goodies bake in the time called for in a recipe, heat the oven for 10 to 15 minutes before baking. When baking cookies, cakes or pies, be sure to place the pan in the middle of the middle oven rack.

## . . . Go!

Recipe in hand, you're ready to get started. If you take your time and enjoy what you're doing, baking will be a pleasure.

~~~~~~~~~~

## The Pillsbury Kitchens Answer the Top Five Baking Questions

The experts behind the scenes at the Pillsbury Kitchens—the home economists and technicians who test the recipes to guarantee that you get the best baking results possible—answer the top five baking questions:

Q. *Where do I store flour for the best quality?*
A. Flour can usually be stored in an airtight container in a cool, dry place. For longer periods or during the summer, you can seal it tightly and place it in the refrigerator or freezer. Just let it warm to room temperature before using.

Q. *What's the best way to cut breads, cakes and other baked goods?*
A. To cut breads, use a serrated knife or electric knife and a light sawing motion to avoid tearing the bread. To cut frosted layer cakes, use a sharp, long, thin knife dipped in hot water; wipe it off with a damp paper towel between slices.

To cut pies, use a sharp, thin-bladed knife. Dip the knife in warm water when cutting meringue or ice cream pies, wiping it off between cuts.

To cut bars, use a table knife or plastic knife for soft bars and brownies to prevent "tearing" the bars. For harder bars or bars with nuts, use a sharp, thin knife.

Q. *How do I store my goodies after baking?*

A. Store breads tightly covered at room temperature or freeze.

Store cakes with a creamy powdered sugar frosting at room temperature, loosely covered with foil or waxed paper or in a "cake saver." Store cakes with a cream cheese or whipped frosting in the refrigerator. Freeze unfrosted cakes for up to 3 months.

Store crisp cookies in a loosely covered container at room temperature. Store chewy and soft cookies and bars tightly covered at room temperature or freeze.

Store fruit and pecan pies loosely covered at room temperature for up to 3 days. Store pumpkin and cream pies or any pies that contain eggs in the refrigerator and use within 3 days.

Q. *Some of the recipes make more than what I need. Is there any way to cut down the recipe?*

A. There are many reasons a recipe makes the yield it does, including pan size and ingredient size or quantity. All of this affects the way cakes, bars and other baked goods turn out. Most recipes are developed to bake a certain amount of finished goods, like 1 pan of bars, 3 dozen cookies, 12 muffins or 2 loaves of bread. Certain recipes can be halved successfully, especially cookies, but unless you are experienced at this, we don't recommend cutting the recipes in half. You can, though, make a few alterations in the way you use the recipes:

Check the recipes for tips and instructions for longer storage.

Make the full quantity of dough for cookies, but bake only half the amount and freeze the other half to bake later.

Bake the full recipe and freeze the finished breads, cookies, bars or cakes to use later.

Q. *Is it best to use butter, margarine or blends in baking? Can I use shortening or olive oil if I have that on hand?*

A. The recipes in this cookbook call for butter first, then margarine. You can use margarine instead of butter with satisfactory results, except for recipes where only butter is recommended for flavor and the way it melts (Browned Butter Frosting, page 72). When using margarine, use the stick form for baking. Margarines in tubs have added air and water, so the amount of fat has been reduced and the baked good will not be tender or flavorful. Butter-margarine blends sold in sticks can also be used for baking, but don't use the blends sold in tubs because the added air and water change the finished baked product.

Shortening can be used as a substitute for butter, but the finished product will not have as much flavor because butter imparts a superior flavor to baked goods. Unless a recipe calls for oil, it's best not to substitute oil for butter because both flavor and texture will be affected. If a recipe calls for oil, as in a muffin, you can use any type, including olive oil. In kitchen tests, no difference in flavor or texture in the finished baked goods was found among different kinds of oils.

*Just bread? Not with these enticing recipes!*

# CHEDDAR-CHIVE DROP BISCUITS

→ PREP TIME: 15 mins
START TO FINISH: 30 mins

**18 biscuits**

~~~~~~~~~~~~~~~~~~~~~~~~~~~~

2 cups all-purpose flour
3 teaspoons baking powder
1 teaspoon salt
1/2 cup shortening
1 1/4 cups plain yogurt
1 cup shredded Cheddar cheese
  (4 oz.)
1/4 cup chopped fresh chives

**1.** Heat oven to 450°F. Grease large cookie sheet with shortening or cooking spray. In large bowl, mix flour, baking powder and salt. With pastry blender or fork, cut in shortening until mixture resembles coarse crumbs. Stir in yogurt, cheese and chives just until moistened.

**2.** Drop dough by generous tablespoonfuls onto cookie sheet.

**3.** Bake 9 to 12 minutes or until light golden brown. Serve warm.

**High Altitude (3500–6500 ft): Decrease baking powder to 2 teaspoons. Bake 10 to 12 minutes.**

**1 Biscuit:** Calories 140 (Calories from Fat 70); Total Fat 8g (Saturated Fat 3g; Trans Fat 1g); Cholesterol 10mg; Sodium 260mg; Total Carbohydrate 12g (Dietary Fiber **0g; S**ugars 1g); Protein 4g

% Daily Value: Vitamin A 2%; Vitamin C 0%; Calcium 10%; Iron 4%

Exchanges: 1 Starch, 1 1/2 Fat

Carbohydrate Choices: 1

**BAKING TIP:**
*Stir gently and work quickly to get the most tender biscuits. Stirring just until all the dry ingredients are moistened keeps the biscuits from becoming tough.*

# BAKING POWDER BISCUITS

→ **PREP TIME:** 15 mins
**START TO FINISH:** 30 mins

**14 biscuits**

~~~~~~~~~~~~~~~~~~~~~~~~

2 cups all-purpose flour
3 teaspoons baking powder
1/2 teaspoon salt
1/2 cup shortening
3/4 to 1 cup milk

**1.** Heat oven to 450°F. In large bowl, mix flour, baking powder and salt. With pastry blender or fork, cut in shortening until mixture resembles coarse crumbs. Stirring with fork, add enough milk until mixture leaves sides of bowl and forms a soft, moist dough.

**2.** On floured work surface, knead dough lightly until no longer sticky. Roll or press dough to 1/2-inch thickness. Cut with floured 2-inch round cutter; place on ungreased cookie sheet.

**3.** Bake 8 to 12 minutes or until light golden brown. Serve warm.

**High Altitude (3500–6500 ft): Decrease baking powder to 2 1/2 teaspoons.**

**1 Biscuit:** Calories 140 (Calories from Fat 70); Total Fat 8g (Saturated Fat 2g; Trans Fat 1.5g); Cholesterol 0mg; Sodium 200mg; Total Carbohydrate 15g (Dietary Fiber 0g; Sugars 0g); Protein 2g

% Daily Value: Vitamin A 0%; Vitamin C 0%; Calcium 8%; Iron 6%

Exchanges: 1 Starch, 1 1/2 Fat

Carbohydrate Choices: 1

## VARIATIONS:

**Buttermilk Biscuits:** Add 1/4 teaspoon baking soda to flour. Substitute buttermilk for milk.

**Cheese Biscuits:** Stir 1 cup shredded Cheddar cheese (4 oz.) into flour-shortening mixture. Bake on greased cookie sheet.

**Drop Biscuits:** Increase milk to 1 1/4 cups. Drop dough by spoonfuls onto greased cookie sheet.

**Soft-Sided Biscuits:** Place biscuits in 9-inch round or square pan or on cookie sheet with sides touching. Bake 12 to 14 minutes.

**Southern-Style Biscuits:** Decrease shortening to 1/4 cup.

**Thin-Crispy Biscuits:** Roll dough to 1/4-inch thickness. Cut biscuits with floured 3-inch round cutter.

# APRICOT-ORANGE CREAM SCONES

→ PREP TIME: 15 mins
START TO FINISH: 30 mins

**8 scones**

~~~~~~~~~~~~~~~~~~~~~~~~~~~

2 cups all-purpose flour

3 tablespoons granulated sugar

3 teaspoons baking powder

2 teaspoons grated orange peel

1/2 teaspoon salt

1/2 cup chopped dried apricots

1/2 cup white vanilla baking chips

1 1/3 cups whipping (heavy) cream

1 cup powdered sugar

2 to 3 tablespoons orange juice

**1.** Heat oven to 400°F. Lightly grease cookie sheet with shortening or cooking spray. In large bowl, mix flour, granulated sugar, baking powder, orange peel and salt. Stir in apricots and baking chips. Add whipping cream all at once; stir just until dry ingredients are moistened.

**2.** On lightly floured work surface, knead dough 6 or 7 times until smooth. Divide dough in half. Pat each half into 6-inch round; cut each into 4 wedges. Place 2 inches apart on cookie sheet.

**3.** Bake 10 to 13 minutes or until light golden brown. Remove from cookie sheet; place on wire rack. Cool 5 minutes. Meanwhile, in small bowl, blend powdered sugar and enough orange juice until drizzling consistency. Drizzle icing over warm scones. Serve warm.

**High Altitude (3500–6500 ft): Increase flour to 2 1/4 cups; decrease whipping cream to 1 cup and add 1/3 cup water. Cut each 6-inch round of dough into 6 wedges. 12 scones.**

**1 Scone:** Calories 390 (Calories from Fat 140); Total Fat 16g (Saturated Fat 10g; Trans Fat 0g); Cholesterol 45mg; Sodium 360mg; Total Carbohydrate 57g (Dietary Fiber 2g; Sugars 32g); Protein 5g

% Daily Value: Vitamin A 15%; Vitamin C 2%; Calcium 15%; Iron 10%

Exchanges: 1 1/2 Starch, 2 1/2 Other Carbohydrate, 3 Fat

Carbohydrate Choices: 4

# CINNAMON-OAT SCONES

PREP TIME: 15 mins
START TO FINISH: 45 mins

**8 scones**

## SCONES
1 1/2 cups all-purpose flour
3/4 cup oats
1/4 cup packed brown sugar
2 teaspoons baking powder
1/2 teaspoon salt
1/2 teaspoon ground cinnamon
1/2 cup butter or margarine
1/2 cup milk

## TOPPING
1 tablespoon butter or
    margarine, melted
1 tablespoon granulated sugar
1/4 teaspoon ground cinnamon

**1.** Heat oven to 375°F. Lightly grease cookie sheet with shortening or cooking spray. In medium bowl, mix flour, oats, brown sugar, baking powder, salt and 1/2 teaspoon cinnamon. With pastry blender or fork, cut in 1/2 cup butter until mixture is crumbly. Add milk all at once; stir just until dry ingredients are moistened.

**2.** On floured work surface, gently knead dough 5 or 6 times. Place on cookie sheet; press into 6-inch round, about 1 inch thick. Brush top with melted butter.

**3.** In small bowl, mix granulated sugar and 1/4 teaspoon cinnamon. Sprinkle over top. Cut into 8 wedges; separate slightly.

**4.** Bake 20 to 30 minutes or until golden brown. Serve warm.

**High Altitude (3500–6500 ft): No change.**

**1 Scone:** Calories 270 (Calories from Fat 130); Total Fat 14g (Saturated Fat 7g; Trans Fat 1g); Cholesterol 35mg; Sodium 370mg; Total Carbohydrate 32g (Dietary Fiber 2g; Sugars 9g); Protein 4g

% Daily Value: Vitamin A 10%; Vitamin C 0%; Calcium 10%; Iron 10%

Exchanges: 1 1/2 Starch, 1/2 Other Carbohydrate, 2 1/2 Fat

Carbohydrate Choices: 2

> **BAKING TIP:**
> *We like it hot—scones are best served warm. Freshen individual room-temperature scones by heating in the microwave on High for 10 to 15 seconds. If frozen, heat scones on High for 25 to 50 seconds.*

# MUFFINS

**12 muffins**

〜〜〜〜〜〜〜〜〜〜〜〜〜〜

2 cups all-purpose flour
1/2 cup sugar
3 teaspoons baking powder
1/2 teaspoon salt
3/4 cup milk
1/3 cup vegetable oil
1 egg

**1.** Heat oven to 400°F. Grease bottoms only of 12 regular-size muffin cups with shortening or cooking spray, or line with paper baking cups. In medium bowl, mix flour, sugar, baking powder and salt.

**2.** In small bowl, beat milk, oil and egg until well blended. Add to flour mixture all at once; stir just until dry ingredients are moistened (batter will be lumpy). Divide batter evenly among muffin cups.

**3.** Bake 20 to 25 minutes or until toothpick inserted in center comes out clean. Cool 1 minute; remove from muffin cups. Serve warm.

**High Altitude (3500–6500 ft): Decrease baking powder to 2 teaspoons.**

**1 Muffin:** Calories 180 (Calories from Fat 60); Total Fat 7g (Saturated Fat 1g; Trans Fat 0g); Cholesterol 20mg; Sodium 230mg; Total Carbohydrate 25g (Dietary Fiber 0g; Sugars 9g); Protein 3g

% Daily Value: Vitamin A 0%; Vitamin C 0%; Calcium 8%; Iron 6%

Exchanges: 1 Starch, 1/2 Other Carbohydrate, 1 1/2 Fat

Carbohydrate Choices: 1 1/2

## VARIATIONS:

**Apple Muffins:** Decrease sugar to 1/4 cup; add 1 teaspoon ground cinnamon to flour. Stir 1 cup finely chopped, peeled apple into dry ingredients. Substitute apple juice for milk. Bake 18 to 22 minutes.

**Blueberry Muffins:** Stir 1 cup fresh or frozen blueberries (do not thaw) and 1 teaspoon grated lemon or orange peel into dry ingredients.

**Lemon Muffins:** Stir 1 tablespoon grated lemon peel into flour mixture.

**Orange Muffins:** Stir 1 tablespoon grated orange peel into flour mixture; substitute orange juice for milk.

**Whole Wheat Muffins:** Use 1 cup all-purpose flour and 1 cup whole wheat flour.

# PUMPKIN STREUSEL MUFFINS

→ PREP TIME: 20 mins
START TO FINISH: 45 mins

**12 muffins**

~~~~~~~~~~~~~~~~~~~~~~~~~~

## MUFFINS
1/2 cup milk
1/2 cup canned pumpkin (not
    pumpkin pie mix)
1/3 cup vegetable oil
1 egg
1 3/4 cups all-purpose flour
1/2 cup granulated sugar
2 1/2 teaspoons baking powder
3/4 teaspoon salt
1/2 teaspoon ground cinnamon
1/4 teaspoon ground nutmeg
1 package (3 oz.) cream cheese

## TOPPING
1/4 cup packed brown sugar
1/4 cup finely chopped nuts
1/2 teaspoon ground cinnamon
1 tablespoon butter or margarine

**1.** Heat oven to 400°F. Grease bottoms only of 12 regular-size muffin cups with shortening or cooking spray, or line with paper baking cups. In medium bowl, beat milk, pumpkin, oil and egg until well blended. Add flour, granulated sugar, baking powder, salt, 1/2 teaspoon cinnamon and the nutmeg; stir just until dry ingredients are moistened (batter will be lumpy).

**2.** Fill each muffin cup 1/2 full, reserving remaining batter. Cut cream cheese into 12 equal pieces; place 1 piece on batter in each cup. Top with reserved batter, filling each cup about 3/4 full.

**3.** In small bowl, mix topping ingredients; sprinkle evenly over batter in muffin cups.

**4.** Bake 18 to 22 minutes or until golden brown. Immediately remove from muffin cups. Serve warm. Store in refrigerator.

**High Altitude (3500–6500 ft): Decrease baking powder to 1 3/4 teaspoons.**

**1 Muffin:** Calories 240 (Calories from Fat 110); Total Fat 12g (Saturated Fat 3.5g; Trans Fat 0g); Cholesterol 30mg; Sodium 290mg; Total Carbohydrate 29g (Dietary Fiber 1g; Sugars 14g); Protein 4g

% Daily Value: Vitamin A 35%; Vitamin C 0%; Calcium 8%; Iron 8%

Exchanges: 1 Starch, 1 Other Carbohydrate, 2 Fat

Carbohydrate Choices: 2

> **BAKING TIP:**
> *Get attractive, rounded muffin tops by preheating the oven for 10 to 15 minutes before baking muffins. The creamy surprise in the center of these muffins adds extra flavor.*

●

# BANANA BREAD

→ PREP TIME: 15 mins
START TO FINISH: 2 hrs 20 mins

**1 loaf; 16 slices**

3/4 cup sugar
1/2 cup butter or margarine,
    softened
2 eggs
1 cup mashed ripe bananas (2
    medium)
1/3 cup milk
1 teaspoon vanilla
2 cups all-purpose flour
1/2 cup chopped nuts, if desired
1 teaspoon baking soda
1/2 teaspoon salt

**1.** Heat oven to 350°F. Grease bottom only of 9x5- or 8x4-inch loaf pan with shortening or cooking spray. In large bowl, beat sugar and butter with spoon until light and fluffy. Beat in eggs. Stir in bananas, milk and vanilla until well blended.

**2.** In small bowl, mix flour, nuts, baking soda and salt. Add to banana mixture all at once; stir just until dry ingredients are moistened. Pour into pan.

**3.** Bake 50 to 60 minutes or until toothpick inserted in center comes out clean. Cool 5 minutes; remove from pan. Cool completely, about 1 hour. Wrap tightly and store in refrigerator.

**High Altitude (3500–6500 ft): Heat oven to 375°F.**

**1 Slice:** Calories 170 (Calories from Fat 60); Total Fat 7g (Saturated Fat 3g; Trans Fat 0g); Cholesterol 40mg; Sodium 200mg; Total Carbohydrate 25g (Dietary Fiber 0g; Sugars 11g); Protein 3g

% Daily Value: Vitamin A 6%; Vitamin C 0%; Calcium 0%; Iron 4%

Exchanges: 1 Starch, 1/2 Other Carbohydrate, 1 1/2 Fat

Carbohydrate Choices: 1 1/2

**VARIATIONS:**

**Applesauce Bread:** Substitute 1 cup applesauce for mashed bananas; stir 3/4 teaspoon ground cinnamon into flour mixture.

**Berry-Banana Bread:** Stir 1/2 cup sweetened dried cranberries into flour mixture.

**Currant-Banana Bread:** Stir 1/2 cup dried currants into flour mixture.

# NUT BREAD

**1 loaf; 16 slices**

~~~~~~~~~~~~~~~~~~~~~~~

3/4 cup sugar
1/2 cup butter or margarine,
    softened
1 cup buttermilk
2 eggs
2 cups all-purpose flour
1 cup chopped nuts
1/2 teaspoon baking powder
1/2 teaspoon baking soda
1/2 teaspoon salt

**1.** Heat oven to 350°F. Grease bottom only of 9x5- or 8x4-inch loaf pan with shortening or cooking spray. In large bowl, beat sugar and butter with spoon until light and fluffy. Stir in buttermilk and eggs until well blended.

**2.** In small bowl, mix flour, nuts, baking powder, baking soda and salt. Add to buttermilk mixture; stir just until dry ingredients are moistened. Pour into pan.

**3.** Bake 55 to 65 minutes or until toothpick inserted in center comes out clean. Cool 15 minutes; remove from pan. Cool completely, about 1 hour. Wrap tightly and store in refrigerator.

**High Altitude (3500–6500 ft): Heat oven to 375°F. Increase flour to 2 cups plus 1 tablespoon. Bake 50 to 60 minutes.**

**1 Slice:** Calories 210 (Calories from Fat 100); Total Fat 11g (Saturated Fat 3.5g; Trans Fat 0g); Cholesterol 40mg; Sodium 190mg; Total Carbohydrate 23g (Dietary Fiber 0g; Sugars 10g); Protein 4g

% Daily Value: Vitamin A 6%; Vitamin C 0%; Calcium 4%; Iron 6%

Exchanges: 1 Starch, 1/2 Other Carbohydrate, 2 Fat

Carbohydrate Choices: 1 1/2

> **BAKING TIP:**
> *To substitute for buttermilk, use 1 tablespoon vinegar or lemon juice plus milk to make 1 cup.*

**VARIATIONS:**

**Date Bread:** Substitute packed brown sugar for sugar; decrease nuts to 1/2 cup. Stir in 1 cup chopped dates and 1 teaspoon grated orange peel after flour addition.

**Pocket of Streusel Bread:** For filling, mix 1/2 cup packed brown sugar, 1/2 cup chopped walnuts, 1 teaspoon ground cinnamon and 1 tablespoon butter or margarine, melted. For batter, substitute packed brown sugar for sugar; decrease nuts to 1/2 cup. Spread half of batter in greased and floured 9x5-inch loaf pan. Spoon filling down center of batter; spread to within 1/2 inch of sides. Carefully spoon remaining batter over filling, spreading gently to cover. Bake 50 to 55 minutes.

# APPLE STREUSEL COFFEE CAKE

→ PREP TIME: 20 mins
START TO FINISH: 1 hr 5 mins

**8 servings**

## COFFEE CAKE

1 cup all-purpose flour
1 teaspoon baking powder
1/4 teaspoon baking soda
1/8 teaspoon salt
1/4 cup butter or margarine,
  softened
1/2 cup granulated sugar
1 egg
1 teaspoon vanilla
3 tablespoons plain yogurt
2 cups thinly sliced, unpeeled
  apples (3 medium)

## TOPPING

1/4 cup all-purpose flour
2 tablespoons packed brown
  sugar
1/2 teaspoon ground cinnamon
2 tablespoons butter or
  margarine

**1.** Heat oven to 350°F. Grease 9-inch round or 8-inch square pan with shortening or cooking spray. In small bowl, mix 1 cup flour, the baking powder, baking soda and salt; set aside.

**2.** In large bowl, beat 1/4 cup butter and the granulated sugar with spoon until light and fluffy. Beat in egg and vanilla. Alternately add flour mixture and yogurt to butter mixture, beating well after each addition. Spread batter in pan. Arrange apple slices over batter.

**3.** In small bowl, mix topping ingredients except butter. With pastry blender or fork, cut in 2 tablespoons butter until crumbly; sprinkle evenly over apples.

**4.** Bake 30 to 35 minutes or until toothpick inserted in center comes out clean. Cool 10 minutes. If desired, remove from pan. Serve warm.

**High Altitude (3500–6500 ft): No change.**

**1 Serving:** Calories 240 (Calories from Fat 90); Total Fat 10g (Saturated Fat 4.5g; Trans Fat 0.5g); Cholesterol 50mg; Sodium 210mg; Total Carbohydrate 36g (Dietary Fiber 1g; Sugars 19g); Protein 3g

% Daily Value: Vitamin A 8%; Vitamin C 0%; Calcium 6%; Iron 6%

Exchanges: 1 Starch, 1 1/2 Other Carbohydrate, 2 Fat

Carbohydrate Choices: 2 1/2

> **BAKING TIP:**
> *If you don't keep plain yogurt on hand, try one of the flavored yogurts for a twist. Vanilla, Key lime pie or apple yogurt would all make a great-tasting coffee cake—or use sour cream or reduced-fat sour cream in place of the yogurt.*

# RASPBERRY–CREAM CHEESE COFFEE CAKE

→ PREP TIME: 25 mins
START TO FINISH: 1 hr 35 mins

**16 servings**

~~~~~~~~~~~~~~~~~~~~~~~~~~

2 1/4 cups all-purpose flour
1 cup sugar
3/4 cup butter or margarine
1/2 teaspoon baking powder
1/2 teaspoon baking soda
1/4 teaspoon salt
3/4 cup sour cream
1 teaspoon almond extract
2 eggs
1 package (8 oz.) cream cheese,
    softened
1/2 cup raspberry preserves
1/2 cup sliced almonds

**1.** Heat oven to 350°F. Grease bottom and side of 9- or 10-inch spring-form pan with shortening or cooking spray; lightly flour. In large bowl, mix flour and 3/4 cup of the sugar. With pastry blender or fork, cut in butter until mixture resembles coarse crumbs. Reserve 1 cup of crumb mixture.

**2.** To remaining crumb mixture, stir in baking powder, baking soda, salt, sour cream, almond extract and 1 of the eggs until well blended. Spread batter in bottom and 2 inches up side (about 1/4 inch thick) of pan.

**3.** In another small bowl, beat cream cheese, remaining 1/4 cup sugar and 1 egg until well blended. Pour into batter-lined pan. Carefully spoon preserves evenly over cream cheese mixture. In another small bowl, mix reserved crumb mixture and sliced almonds; sprinkle over preserves.

**4.** Bake 45 to 55 minutes or until cream cheese filling is set and crust is deep golden brown. Cool 15 minutes. Remove side of pan; leave coffee cake on pan bottom. Serve warm or cool. Store in refrigerator.

**High Altitude (3500–6500 ft): No change.**

**1 Serving:** Calories 320 (Calories from Fat 160); Total Fat 18g (Saturated Fat 9g; Trans Fat 0.5g); Cholesterol 70mg; Sodium 210mg; Total Carbohydrate 34g (Dietary Fiber 1g; Sugars 18g); Protein 5g

% Daily Value: Vitamin A 15%; Vitamin C 0%; Calcium 4%; Iron 8%

Exchanges: 1 1/2 Starch, 1 Other Carbohydrate, 3 1/2 Fat

Carbohydrate Choices: 2

# WHOLE WHEAT BREAD

→ PREP TIME: 35 mins
START TO FINISH: 3 hrs 50 mins

**2 loaves; 16 slices each**

~~~~~~~~~~~~~~~~~~~~~~~~~

2 packages regular active dry yeast
1/4 cup warm water (105°F to 115°F)
1/2 cup packed brown sugar or honey
1/4 cup butter or margarine
3 teaspoons salt
2 1/2 cups hot water
4 1/2 cups whole wheat flour
2 3/4 to 3 3/4 cups all-purpose flour

**1.** In small bowl, dissolve yeast in warm water. In large bowl, mix brown sugar, butter, salt and hot water; cool 5 minutes.

**2.** To cooled brown sugar mixture, beat in 3 cups of the whole wheat flour with electric mixer on low speed until moistened, scraping bowl frequently. Beat on medium speed 3 minutes, scraping bowl frequently. Beat in remaining 1 1/2 cups whole wheat flour and the dissolved yeast. With spoon, stir in 2 1/4 to 2 3/4 cups of the all-purpose flour until dough pulls cleanly away from side of bowl.

**3.** On floured work surface, knead in remaining 1/2 to 1 cup all-purpose flour until dough is smooth and elastic, 10 to 15 minutes. Grease large bowl with shortening or cooking spray. Place dough in bowl; cover loosely with plastic wrap and cloth towel. Let rise in warm place (80°F to 85°F) 30 to 45 minutes or until light and doubled in size.

**4.** Generously grease 2 (8x4- or 9x5-inch) loaf pans with shortening or cooking spray. Gently push fist into dough to deflate; divide in half. On lightly floured work surface, roll out each half of dough with rolling pin into 18x8-inch rectangle. Starting with one 8-inch side, roll up dough tightly, pressing with thumbs to seal after each turn. Pinch edge of dough into roll to seal; press each end with side of hand to seal. Fold ends under loaf; place seam side down in pan. Cover; let rise in warm place 30 to 45 minutes or until light and doubled in size.

**5.** Heat oven to 375°F. Uncover dough; bake 30 minutes. Reduce oven temperature to 350°F; bake 10 to 15 minutes longer or until loaves sound hollow when lightly tapped. Immediately remove from pans; place on wire racks. Cool completely, about 1 hour.

**High Altitude (3500–6500 ft): No change.**

**1 Slice:** Calories 130 (Calories from Fat 15); Total Fat 2g (Saturated Fat 1g; Trans Fat 0g); Cholesterol 0mg; Sodium 230mg; Total Carbohydrate 24g (Dietary Fiber 2g; Sugars 3g); Protein 4g

% Daily Value: Vitamin A 0%; Vitamin C 0%; Calcium 0%; Iron 8%

Exchanges: 1 1/2 Starch

Carbohydrate Choices: 1 1/2

**BAKING TIP:**
*Whole wheat flour adds a nutty flavor, hearty texture and higher fiber content, and best of all, adds good-for-you whole grains in a tasty way.*

# CRACKED WHEAT–RAISIN BREAD

→ **PREP TIME: 40 mins**
**START TO FINISH: 4 hrs 25 mins**

**2 loaves; 20 slices each**

~~~~~~~~~~~~~~~~~~~~~~~~~

1 1/2 cups uncooked cracked
   wheat
1 cup raisins
1/2 cup packed brown sugar
2 teaspoons salt
3 tablespoons butter or
   margarine
2 cups boiling water
2 packages regular active dry
   yeast
2/3 cup warm water (105°F to
   115°F)
5 to 6 cups all-purpose flour
1 egg, beaten

**1.** In large bowl, mix cracked wheat, raisins, brown sugar, salt, butter and boiling water; cool to 105°F to 115°F.

**2.** In small bowl, dissolve yeast in warm water. Add dissolved yeast and 2 cups of the flour to cracked wheat mixture; beat with electric mixer on low speed until moistened, scraping bowl frequently. Beat on medium speed 2 minutes, scraping bowl frequently. With spoon, stir in 2 1/2 to 3 cups of the flour until dough pulls cleanly away from side of bowl.

**3.** On floured work surface, knead in remaining 1/2 to 1 cup flour until dough is smooth and elastic, about 10 minutes. Grease large bowl with shortening or cooking spray. Place dough in bowl; cover loosely with greased plastic wrap and cloth towel. Let rise in warm place (80°F to 85°F) 45 to 60 minutes or until light and doubled in size.

**4.** Grease large cookie sheet with shortening or cooking spray. Gently push fist into dough to deflate; divide in half. Shape each half into ball; place on cookie sheet. Cover; let rise in warm place 45 to 60 minutes or until light and doubled in size.

**5.** Heat oven to 350°F. With sharp knife, slash a 1/2-inch-deep lattice design on top of each loaf. Brush with beaten egg. Bake 35 to 45 minutes or until loaves sound hollow when lightly tapped. Immediately remove from cookie sheet; place on wire racks. Cool completely, about 1 hour.

**High Altitude (3500–6500 ft): No change.**

**1 Slice:** Calories 110 (Calories from Fat 10); Total Fat 1.5g (Saturated Fat 0.5g; Trans Fat 0g); Cholesterol 10mg; Sodium 125mg; Total Carbohydrate 21g (Dietary Fiber 1g; Sugars 5g); Protein 3g
% Daily Value: Vitamin A 0%; Vitamin C 0%; Calcium 0%; Iron 6%
Exchanges: 1 1/2 Starch
Carbohydrate Choices: 1 1/2

# DELICIOUS WHITE BREAD

➜ PREP TIME: 35 mins
START TO FINISH: 4 hrs

**2 loaves; 18 slices each**

5 to 6 cups all-purpose flour
3 tablespoons sugar
2 teaspoons salt
2 packages regular active dry
   yeast
2 cups water
1/4 cup vegetable oil or
   shortening
1 tablespoon butter or
   margarine, melted

**1.** In large bowl, mix 2 cups of the flour, the sugar, salt and yeast. In 1-quart saucepan, heat water and oil until very warm (120°F to 130°F). Add warm liquid to flour mixture; beat with electric mixer on low speed until moistened, scraping bowl frequently. Beat on medium speed 3 minutes, scraping bowl frequently. With spoon, stir in 2 1/2 to 3 cups of the flour until dough pulls cleanly away from side of bowl.

**2.** On floured work surface, knead in remaining 1/2 to 1 cup flour until dough is smooth and elastic, about 5 minutes. Grease large bowl with shortening or cooking spray. Place dough in bowl; cover loosely with greased plastic wrap and cloth towel. Let rise in warm place (80°F to 85°F) 45 to 60 minutes or until light and doubled in size.

**3.** Grease 2 (8x4- or 9x5-inch) loaf pans with shortening or cooking spray. Gently push fist into dough to deflate; divide in half. On lightly floured work surface, roll out each half of dough with rolling pin into 16x8-inch rectangle. Starting with one 8-inch side, roll up dough tightly, pressing with thumbs to seal after each turn. Pinch edge of dough into roll to seal; press each end with side of hand to seal. Fold ends under loaf; place seam side down in pan. Cover; let rise in warm place 30 to 35 minutes or until dough fills pans and tops of loaves are about 1 inch above pan edges.

**4.** Heat oven to 375°F. Uncover dough; bake 40 to 50 minutes or until loaves sound hollow when lightly tapped. Immediately remove from pans; place on wire racks. Brush with melted butter. Cool completely, about 1 hour.

**High Altitude (3500–6500 ft): No change.**

**1 Slice:** Calories 80 (Calories from Fat 20); Total Fat 2g (Saturated Fat 0g; Trans Fat 0g); Cholesterol 0mg; Sodium 135mg; Total Carbohydrate 14g (Dietary Fiber 0g; Sugars 1g); Protein 2g
% Daily Value: Vitamin A 0%; Vitamin C 0%; Calcium 0%; Iron 4%
Exchanges: 1 Starch
Carbohydrate Choices: 1

**VARIATION:**
**Raisin Bread:** Add 1/2 teaspoon ground cinnamon with the salt and stir in 1 cup raisins after beating step. Continue as directed.

# QUICK SOURDOUGH FRENCH BREAD

**2 loaves; 17 slices each**

4 to 5 cups all-purpose flour
2 tablespoons wheat germ
1 tablespoon sugar
2 teaspoons salt
1/2 teaspoon ground ginger
2 packages fast-acting dry yeast
1 cup very warm water (120°F to 130°F)
1 cup sour cream, room temperature
2 tablespoons vinegar
1 egg white
1 tablespoon water
2 teaspoons poppy seed

**1.** In large bowl, mix 1 1/2 cups of the flour, the wheat germ, sugar, salt, ginger and yeast. Beat in very warm water, sour cream and vinegar with electric mixer on low speed until moistened, scraping bowl frequently. Beat on medium speed 3 minutes, scraping bowl frequently. With spoon, stir in 2 to 2 1/2 cups of the flour until dough pulls cleanly away from side of bowl.

**2.** On floured work surface, knead in remaining 1/2 to 1 cup flour until dough is smooth and elastic, about 3 minutes. Grease large bowl with shortening or cooking spray. Place dough in bowl; cover loosely with plastic wrap and cloth towel. Let rise in warm place (80°F to 85°F) 20 to 30 minutes or until light and doubled in size.

**3.** Grease large cookie sheet with shortening or cooking spray. Gently push fist into dough to deflate; divide in half. On lightly floured work surface, roll out each half of dough with rolling pin into 14x8-inch rectangle. Starting with one 14-inch side, roll up; pinch edge of dough into roll to seal. Place both loaves seam side down on cookie sheet; taper ends to a point. With sharp knife, make 5 (1/4-inch-deep) diagonal slashes on top of each loaf. Cover; let rise in warm place about 15 minutes or until light and doubled in size.

**4.** Heat oven to 375°F. Uncover dough; bake 25 minutes. In small bowl, beat egg white and water. Brush loaves with egg white mixture; sprinkle with poppy seed. Bake 5 to 10 minutes longer or until loaves sound hollow when lightly tapped. Immediately remove from cookie sheet; place on wire rack. Cool completely, about 1 hour.

**High Altitude (3500–6500 ft): No change.**

**1 Slice:** Calories 70 (Calories from Fat 15); Total Fat 1.5g (Saturated Fat 1g; Trans Fat 0g); Cholesterol 0mg; Sodium 140mg; Total Carbohydrate 12g (Dietary Fiber 0g; Sugars 0g); Protein 2g
% Daily Value: Vitamin A 0%; Vitamin C 0%; Calcium 0%; Iron 4%
Exchanges: 1 Starch
Carbohydrate Choices: 1

**BAKING TIP:**
*A blending of two favorites—sourdough and French bread. Try it— you won't believe how easy it is to make and how good it tastes!*

# HERBED OATMEAL PAN BREAD

→ PREP TIME: 15 mins
START TO FINISH: 1 hr 45 mins

**16 servings**

## BREAD
2 cups water
1 cup oats
3 tablespoons butter
3 3/4 to 4 3/4 cups all-purpose
  flour
1/4 cup sugar
2 teaspoons salt
2 packages regular active dry
  yeast
1 egg
6 tablespoons butter, melted

## HERB BUTTER
1 tablespoon grated Parmesan
  cheese
1/2 teaspoon dried basil leaves
1/4 teaspoon dried oregano
  leaves
1/4 teaspoon garlic powder

**1.** In 2-quart saucepan, heat water to boiling. Stir in oats. Remove from heat. Stir in 3 tablespoons butter. Cool to 120°F to 130°F. In large bowl, mix 1 1/2 cups of the flour, the sugar, salt and yeast. Beat in cooled oats mixture and egg with electric mixer on low speed until moistened, scraping bowl frequently. Beat on medium speed 3 minutes, scraping bowl frequently. With spoon, stir in 1 3/4 cups to 2 1/2 cups of the flour to form a stiff dough.

**2.** On floured work surface, knead in remaining 1/2 to 3/4 cup flour until dough is smooth and elastic, about 5 minutes. Shape dough into ball; cover with large bowl. Let rest 15 minutes.

**3.** Grease 13x9-inch pan with shortening or cooking spray. Gently push fist into dough to deflate. Press dough evenly in pan. With very sharp knife, cut diagonal lines 1 1/2 inches apart, cutting completely through dough; repeat in opposite direction creating diamond pattern. Cover loosely with greased plastic wrap and cloth towel. Let rise in warm place (80°F to 85°F) about 45 minutes or until light and doubled in size.

**4.** Heat oven to 375°F. Redefine cuts by poking tip of knife into cuts until knife hits bottom of pan; do not pull knife through dough. Spoon 4 tablespoons of the melted butter over cut dough. Bake 15 minutes.

**5.** Meanwhile, in small bowl, mix Parmesan cheese, basil, oregano and garlic powder; set aside.

**6.** Brush partially baked bread with remaining 2 tablespoons butter; sprinkle with cheese-herb mixture. Bake 10 to 15 minutes longer or until golden brown. Serve warm or cool.

**High Altitude (3500–6500 ft): No change.**

**1 Serving:** Calories 200 (Calories from Fat 70); Total Fat 8g (Saturated Fat 3.5g; Trans Fat 0g); Cholesterol 30mg; Sodium 350mg; Total Carbohydrate 29g (Dietary Fiber 2g; Sugars 3g); Protein 5g
% Daily Value: Vitamin A 6%; Vitamin C 0%; Calcium 0%; Iron 10%
Exchanges: 2 Starch, 1 Fat
Carbohydrate Choices: 2

**BAKING TIP:**
*Cutting through the dough before baking makes this tasty bread easy to break into pieces after baking.*

# DINNER ROLLS

**32 rolls**

～～～～～～～～～

5 3/4 to 6 3/4 cups all-purpose
    flour
1/4 cup sugar
2 teaspoons salt
2 packages regular active dry
    yeast
1 cup water
1 cup milk
1/2 cup butter or margarine
1 egg
Melted butter or margarine,
    if desired

**1.** In large bowl, mix 2 cups of the flour, the sugar, salt and yeast. In 1-quart saucepan, heat water, milk and 1/2 cup butter until very warm (120°F to 130°F). Beat warm liquid and egg into flour mixture with electric mixer on low speed until moistened, scraping bowl frequently. Beat on medium speed 3 minutes, scraping bowl frequently. With spoon, stir in 2 1/2 to 3 cups of the flour until dough pulls cleanly away from side of bowl.

**2.** On floured work surface, knead in remaining 1 1/4 to 1 3/4 cups flour until dough is smooth and elastic, 8 to 10 minutes. Grease large bowl with shortening or cooking spray. Place dough in bowl; cover loosely with greased plastic wrap and cloth towel. Let rise in warm place (80°F to 85°F) 45 to 60 minutes or until light and doubled in size.

**3.** Gently push fist into dough to deflate; divide in half. To make Pan Rolls, lightly grease 2 (13x9-inch) pans with shortening or cooking spray. Divide each half of dough into 16 equal pieces. Shape each into ball, pulling edges under to make smooth top. Place 16 balls, smooth side up, in each pan. Cover; let rise in warm place 20 to 30 minutes or until light and doubled in size.

**4.** Heat oven to 400°F. Uncover dough; bake 16 to 20 minutes or until golden brown. Immediately remove rolls from pans; place on wire racks. Cool 15 minutes. Brush with melted butter. Serve warm or cool.

**High Altitude (3500–6500 ft): No change.**

**1 Roll:** Calories 120 (Calories from Fat 30); Total Fat 3.5g (Saturated Fat 1.5g; Trans Fat 0g); Cholesterol 15mg; Sodium 170mg; Total Carbohydrate 19g (Dietary Fiber 0g; Sugars 2g); Protein 3g

% Daily Value: Vitamin A 2%; Vitamin C 0%; Calcium 0%; Iron 6%

Exchanges: 1 Starch, 1/2 Fat

Carbohydrate Choices: 1

**VARIATIONS:**

**Bow Knot Rolls:** Lightly grease cookie sheets with shortening or cooking spray. Using half of dough, divide into 16 equal pieces. On lightly floured surface, roll each piece into 9-inch rope. Tie each into a loose knot; place 2 to 3 inches apart on cookie sheets. After rising, bake 12 to 15 minutes or until golden brown. 16 rolls

**Cloverleaf Rolls:** Lightly grease 12 regular-size muffin cups with shortening or cooking spray. Using half of dough, divide into 12 equal pieces; divide each into 3 portions. Shape each portion into ball, pulling edges under to make a smooth top. Place 3 balls, smooth side up, in each muffin cup. After rising, bake 14 to 18 minutes or until golden brown. 12 rolls

**Crescent Rolls:** Lightly grease cookie sheets with shortening or cooking spray. Using half of dough, divide in half again; shape each half into ball. On lightly floured surface, roll out each ball into 12-inch round. Spread each round with 1 tablespoon softened butter or margarine. Cut each round into 12 wedges. Starting with shortest side of wedge, roll up toward point. Place point side down 2 to 3 inches apart on cookie sheets; curve ends to form crescent shape. After rising, bake 12 to 15 minutes or until golden brown. 24 rolls

**Crown Rolls:** Lightly grease 12 regular-size muffin cups with shortening or cooking spray. Using half of dough, divide into 12 equal pieces. Shape each piece into ball, pulling edges under to make smooth top; place 1 ball, smooth side up, in each muffin cup. Using kitchen scissors dipped in flour, cut balls of dough into quarters almost to bottom. After rising, bake 14 to 18 minutes or until golden brown. 12 rolls

**Swirl Rolls:** Lightly grease cookie sheets with shortening or cooking spray. Using half of dough, divide into 16 equal pieces. On lightly floured surface, roll each piece into 8-inch rope. Starting at center, make loose swirl or coil with each rope, tucking end under; place 2 to 3 inches apart on cookie sheets. After rising, bake 12 to 15 minutes or until golden brown. 16 rolls

# EASY CHEESE BATTER BREAD

**1 loaf; 18 slices**

~~~~~~~~~~~~~~~~~~~~~~~~

2 1/2 cups all-purpose flour
2 teaspoons sugar
1 1/2 teaspoons salt
1 package regular active dry
  yeast
1 cup shredded Cheddar cheese
  (4 oz.)
3/4 cup milk
1/2 cup butter or margarine
3 eggs

**1.** In large bowl, mix 1 1/2 cups of the flour, the sugar, salt and yeast. Stir in cheese.

**2.** In 1-quart saucepan, heat milk and butter until very warm (120°F to 130°F). Add warm liquid and eggs into flour mixture; beat with electric mixer on low speed until moistened, scraping bowl frequently. Beat on medium speed 3 minutes, scraping bowl frequently. With spoon, stir in remaining 1 cup flour. Cover loosely with plastic wrap and cloth towel; let rise in warm place (80°F to 85°F) 45 to 60 minutes or until light and doubled in size.

**3.** Generously grease 1 1/2- or 2-quart casserole or 9x5-inch loaf pan with shortening or cooking spray. Gently push fist into dough to deflate. Turn dough into casserole. Cover; let rise in warm place 20 to 25 minutes or until light and doubled in size.

**4.** Heat oven to 350°F. Uncover dough; bake 40 to 45 minutes or until deep golden brown. Immediately remove from casserole; place on wire rack. Cool at least 30 minutes before serving.

**High Altitude (3500–6500 ft):** Heat oven to 375°F. Bake 40 to 45 minutes.

**1 Slice:** Calories 150 (Calories from Fat 80); Total Fat 8g (Saturated Fat 4.5g; Trans Fat 0g); Cholesterol 55mg; Sodium 290mg; Total Carbohydrate 15g (Dietary Fiber 0g; Sugars 1g); Protein 5g
% Daily Value: Vitamin A 6%; Vitamin C 0%; Calcium 6%; Iron 6%
Exchanges: 1 Starch, 1 1/2 Fat
Carbohydrate Choices: 1

> **BAKING TIP:**
> *Batter breads are so simple because they don't need to be kneaded or shaped. Another bonus? This moist, cheesy bread is even better the second day.*

# DOUBLE-CHOCOLATE BATTER BREAD

→ **PREP TIME: 30 mins**
**START TO FINISH: 2 hrs 40 mins**

**1 loaf; 12 slices**

〰〰〰〰〰〰〰〰〰〰〰

3 1/2 cups all-purpose flour
1/3 cup unsweetened baking
   cocoa
1/3 cup sugar
1/4 teaspoon salt
1/4 teaspoon baking soda
1 package regular active dry
   yeast
1 1/2 cups buttermilk
1/4 cup butter
2 eggs
1 bag (12 oz.) semisweet chocolate chips (2 cups)
2 teaspoons vegetable oil

**1.** Generously grease 12-cup fluted tube cake pan with shortening. In large bowl, mix 2 1/2 cups of the flour, the cocoa, sugar, salt, baking soda and yeast.

**2.** In 1-quart saucepan, heat buttermilk and butter until very warm (120°F to 130°F). Add warm liquid and eggs to flour mixture; beat with electric mixer on low speed until moistened, scraping bowl frequently. Beat on high speed 3 minutes, scraping bowl frequently. With spoon, stir in remaining 1 cup flour and 1 1/2 cups of the chocolate chips. Spoon dough evenly into pan. Cover with plastic wrap and cloth towel; let rise in warm place (80°F to 85°F) 30 to 40 minutes or until light and doubled in size.

**3.** Heat oven to 350°F. Uncover dough; bake 35 to 45 minutes or until toothpick inserted near center comes out clean. Immediately place wire rack upside down on top of pan; turn rack and pan over. Remove pan. Cool completely, about 45 minutes.

**4.** In small resealable freezer plastic bag, place remaining 1/2 cup chocolate chips and the oil; seal bag. Knead bag to evenly distribute oil. Microwave on High 30 to 60 seconds or until melted. Cut small hole in bottom corner of bag; squeeze bag to drizzle melted chocolate over cooled bread.

**High Altitude (3500–6500 ft): No change.**

**1 Slice:** Calories 380 (Calories from Fat 130); Total Fat 15g (Saturated Fat 8g; Trans Fat 0g); Cholesterol 45mg; Sodium 150mg; Total Carbohydrate 54g (Dietary Fiber 4g; Sugars 22g); Protein 8g

% Daily Value: Vitamin A 4%; Vitamin C 0%; Calcium 6%; Iron 15%

Exchanges: 2 1/2 Starch, 1 Other Carbohydrate, 2 1/2 Fat

Carbohydrate Choices: 3 1/2

> **BAKING TIP:**
> *To substitute for buttermilk, use 1 tablespoon and 1 1/2 teaspoons vinegar or lemon juice plus milk to make 1 1/2 cups.*

# CORNMEAL BREADSTICKS

→ PREP TIME: 30 mins
START TO FINISH: 1 hr 10 mins

**24 breadsticks**

〜〜〜〜〜〜〜〜〜〜〜〜〜〜

1 3/4 to 2 1/4 cups all-purpose
   flour
1 cup cornmeal
1/4 cup sugar
1 teaspoon salt
1 package fast-acting dry yeast
1 cup water
1/4 cup butter or margarine
2 tablespoons butter or
   margarine, melted
2 tablespoons cornmeal

**1.** In large bowl, mix 1 cup of the flour, 1 cup cornmeal, the sugar, salt and yeast. In 1-quart saucepan, heat water and 1/4 cup butter until hot (120°F to 130°F). Add hot liquid to flour mixture; beat with electric mixer on low speed until moistened, scraping bowl frequently. Beat on medium speed 2 minutes, scraping bowl frequently. With spoon, stir in 1/2 to 1 cup of the flour until dough pulls away from side of bowl.

**2.** On floured work surface, knead in remaining 1/4 cup flour until dough is smooth and elastic, about 2 minutes. Grease large bowl with shortening or cooking spray. Place dough in bowl; cover loosely with plastic wrap and cloth towel. Let rise in warm place (80°F to 85°F) about 10 minutes or until light and doubled in size.

**3.** Grease 2 large cookie sheets with shortening or cooking spray; sprinkle with cornmeal. Gently push fist into dough to deflate; divide dough into 24 pieces. Roll each piece into 10-inch rope; place on cookie sheets. Cover; let rise in warm place about 10 minutes or until light and doubled in size.

**4.** Heat oven to 375°F. Uncover dough. Carefully brush sticks with 2 tablespoons melted butter; sprinkle with 2 tablespoons cornmeal. Bake 12 to 16 minutes or until bottoms are golden brown. Immediately remove from cookie sheets. Serve warm or cool.

**High Altitude (3500–6500 ft): No change.**

**1 Breadstick:** Calories 90 (Calories from Fat 30); Total Fat 3g (Saturated Fat 1.5g; Trans Fat 0g); Cholesterol 10mg; Sodium 120mg; Total Carbohydrate 14g (Dietary Fiber 0g; Sugars 2g); Protein 2g

% Daily Value: Vitamin A 2%; Vitamin C 0%; Calcium 0%; Iron 4%

Exchanges: 1 Starch, 1/2 Fat

Carbohydrate Choices: 1

> **BAKING TIP:**
> *Fast-acting yeast is a time-saver because it reduces the rising time by about half. Serve these easy breadsticks with any soup, stew or salad.*

# HERB FOCACCIA

→ PREP TIME: 25 mins
START TO FINISH: 1 hr 35 mins

**1 loaf; 16 slices**

~~~~~~~~~~~~~~~~~~~~~~~~~~~~~~~

3 1/2 cups all-purpose flour
1 teaspoon sugar
1 teaspoon salt
1 package fast-acting dry yeast
1 cup water
2 tablespoons vegetable oil
1 egg
3 to 4 tablespoons olive oil
1 teaspoon dried rosemary or
    basil leaves, crushed

**1.** In large bowl, mix 1 cup of the flour, the sugar, salt and yeast. In 1-quart saucepan, heat water and vegetable oil until very warm (120°F to 130°F). Add warm liquid and egg to flour mixture; beat with electric mixer on low speed until moistened, scraping bowl frequently. Beat on medium speed 2 minutes, scraping bowl frequently. With spoon, stir in 1 3/4 cups of the flour until dough pulls cleanly away from side of bowl.

**2.** On floured work surface, knead in remaining 3/4 cup flour until dough is smooth and elastic, about 5 minutes. Shape dough into ball; cover with large bowl. Let rest 5 minutes.

**3.** Grease cookie sheet with shortening or cooking spray. Place dough on cookie sheet. With rolling pin or hands, roll or press dough into 12-inch round. Cover loosely with greased plastic wrap and cloth towel; let rise in warm place (80°F to 85°F) about 30 minutes or until light and doubled in size.

**4.** Heat oven to 400°F. Uncover dough. With fingers or handle of wooden spoon, poke holes in dough at 1 inch intervals. Drizzle olive oil over top of dough; sprinkle evenly with rosemary.

**5.** Bake 17 to 27 minutes or until golden brown. Immediately remove from cookie sheet; place on wire rack. Cool 10 minutes. Serve warm or cool.

**High Altitude (3500–6500 ft): No change.**

1 **Slice:** Calories 140 (Calories from Fat 45); Total Fat 5g (Saturated Fat 0.5g; Trans Fat 0g); Cholesterol 15mg; Sodium 150mg; Total Carbohydrate 21g (Dietary Fiber 0g; Sugars 0g); Protein 3g

% Daily Value: Vitamin A 0%; Vitamin C 0%; Calcium 0%; Iron 8%

Exchanges: 1 1/2 Starch, 1/2 Fat

Carbohydrate Choices: 1 1/2

> **BAKING TIP:**
> *Make two smaller loaves by using two cookie sheets and dividing the dough in half. Roll or press each half into an 8-inch round and continue as directed in the recipe. Bake 10 to 20 minutes.*

# SWEET ROLL DOUGH

→ PREP TIME: 30 mins
START TO FINISH: 1 hr 35 mins

~~~~~~~~~~~~~~~~~~~~~~

6 to 7 cups all-purpose flour
1/2 cup sugar
2 teaspoons salt
2 packages regular active dry
   yeast
1 cup water
1 cup milk
1/2 cup butter or margarine
1 egg

**1.** In large bowl, mix 2 cups of the flour, the sugar, salt and yeast. In 1-quart saucepan, heat water, milk and butter until very warm (120°F to 130°F). Add warm liquid and egg to flour mixture; beat with electric mixer on low speed until moistened, scraping bowl frequently. Beat on medium speed 3 minutes, scraping bowl frequently. With spoon, stir in 3 cups of the flour until dough pulls cleanly away from side of bowl.

**2.** On floured work surface, knead in remaining 1 to 2 cups flour until dough is smooth and elastic, 8 to 10 minutes. Grease large bowl with shortening or cooking spray. Place dough in bowl; cover loosely with plastic wrap and cloth towel. Let rise in warm place (80°F to 85°F) 45 to 60 minutes or until light and doubled in size.

**3.** Gently push fist into dough to deflate. Divide dough in half; shape as directed in the following recipes.

**High Altitude (3500–6500 ft): No change.**

> **BAKING TIP:**
> *To make this dough a day ahead of time, after the first rise time, cover and refrigerate the dough overnight. The next day, shape the dough and let it rise as directed in the recipe.*

**VARIATIONS:**
**Basic Whole Wheat Sweet Roll Dough:** Use 3 to 3 1/2 cups all-purpose flour and 3 to 3 1/2 cups whole wheat flour.

# CARAMEL-NUT ROLLS

→ PREP TIME: 50 mins
START TO FINISH: 3 hrs 5 mins

**8 rolls**

~~~~~~~~~~~~~~~~~~~~

**TOPPING**
1/2 cup packed brown sugar
1/2 cup butter or margarine,
  softened
2 tablespoons light corn syrup
1/4 cup chopped nuts

**ROLLS**
1/2 recipe Sweet Roll Dough
(page 39)

**FILLING**

2 tablespoons butter or
  margarine, softened
1/4 cup sugar
1 teaspoon ground cinnamon

**1.** Generously grease 13x9-inch pan with shortening or cooking spray. In small bowl, mix brown sugar, 1/2 cup butter and the corn syrup until well blended. Drop mixture by spoonfuls into pan; spread evenly. Sprinkle with nuts.

**2.** On lightly floured work surface, roll out 1/2 recipe Sweet Roll Dough with rolling pin into 18x12-inch rectangle. Spread with 2 tablespoons butter. In small bowl, mix 1/4 cup sugar and the cinnamon. Sprinkle evenly over dough.

**3.** Starting with 18-inch side, roll up tightly, pressing edges to seal. Cut into 18 slices; place cut side down in pan. Cover; let rise in warm place (80°F to 85°F) 35 to 45 minutes or until light and doubled in size.

**4.** Heat oven to 375°F. Uncover dough; bake 25 to 30 minutes or until deep golden brown. Cool rolls in pan 1 minute. Place wire rack upside down over pan; turn rack and pan over. Remove pan. Serve warm.

**High Altitude (3500–6500 ft): No change.**

**1 Roll:** Calories 230 (Calories from Fat 90); Total Fat 11g (Saturated Fat 5g; Trans Fat 0.5g); Cholesterol 30mg; Sodium 200mg; Total Carbohydrate 30g (Dietary Fiber 0g; Sugars 13g); Protein 3g

% Daily Value: Vitamin A 8%; Vitamin C 0%; Calcium 2%; Iron 8%

Exchanges: 1 Starch, 1 Other Carbohydrate, 2 Fat

Carbohydrate Choices: 2

# CINNAMON ROLLS

→ PREP TIME: 45 mins
START TO FINISH: 3 hrs

**18 rolls**

### ROLLS
1/2 recipe Sweet Roll Dough
(page 39)

### FILLING
2 tablespoons butter or
    margarine, softened
1/2 cup sugar or packed brown
    sugar
2 teaspoons ground cinnamon

### GLAZE
1 cup powdered sugar
1 tablespoon butter or
    margarine, softened
1/2 teaspoon vanilla
1 to 2 tablespoons milk

**1.** Generously grease 13x9-inch pan with shortening or cooking spray. On lightly floured work surface, roll out 1/2 recipe Sweet Roll Dough with rolling pin into 18x12-inch rectangle. Spread with 2 tablespoons butter. In small bowl, mix 1/4 cup sugar and the cinnamon. Sprinkle evenly over dough.

**2.** Starting with 18-inch side, roll up tightly, pressing edges to seal. Cut into 18 slices. Arrange slices, cut side down, in pan. Cover; let rise in warm place (80°F to 85°F) 35 to 45 minutes or until light and doubled in size.

**3.** Heat oven to 375°F. Uncover dough; bake 25 to 30 minutes or until golden brown. Immediately remove rolls from pan; place on wire rack. Cool 5 minutes.

**4.** In small bowl, mix glaze ingredients until smooth, adding enough milk for desired drizzling consistency; drizzle over warm rolls. Serve warm.

**High Altitude (3500–6500 ft): No change.**

**1 Roll:** Calories 190 (Calories from Fat 60); Total Fat 6g (Saturated Fat 3g; Trans Fat 0g); Cholesterol 20mg; Sodium 180mg; Total Carbohydrate 32g (Dietary Fiber 0g; Sugars 15g); Protein 3g

% Daily Value: Vitamin A 4%; Vitamin C 0%; Calcium 0%; Iron 6%

Exchanges: 1 Starch, 1 Other Carbohydrate, 1 Fat

Carbohydrate Choices: 2

> **BAKING TIP:**
> *It's easy to cut even slices of "everyone's favorite" rolls if you use a sharp, serrated knife.*

*J*azz up your cake, create a whole new look, and then eat it too!

# BASIC WHITE CAKE

→ PREP TIME: 15 mins
START TO FINISH: 2 hrs

**12 servings**

〜〜〜〜〜〜〜〜〜〜

2 cups all-purpose flour
1 1/2 cups sugar
3 teaspoons baking powder
1/2 teaspoon salt
1 cup milk
1/2 cup shortening
1 teaspoon vanilla or 1/2
  teaspoon almond extract
5 egg whites

**1.** Heat oven to 350°F. Grease 2 (8- or 9-inch) round cake pans with shortening; lightly flour.

**2.** In large bowl, beat flour, sugar, baking powder, salt, milk, shortening and vanilla with electric mixer on low speed until moistened, scraping bowl occasionally. Beat on medium speed 2 minutes, scraping bowl occasionally. Add egg whites; beat 2 minutes longer, scraping bowl occasionally. Pour batter evenly into pans.

**3.** Bake 8-inch pans 30 to 38 minutes (9-inch pans 27 to 35 minutes) or until toothpick inserted in center comes out clean. Cool in pans 10 minutes. Remove from pans; place on wire racks. Cool completely, about 1 hour. Fill and frost as desired.

**High Altitude (3500–6500 ft): Decrease sugar to 1 1/4 cups; decrease baking powder to 2 teaspoons. Bake 8-inch pans 33 to 38 minutes (9-inch pans 30 to 35 minutes).**

**1 Serving:** Calories 270 (Calories from Fat 80); Total Fat 9g (Saturated Fat 2.5g; Trans Fat 1.5g); Cholesterol 0mg; Sodium 250mg; Total Carbohydrate 42g (Dietary Fiber 0g; Sugars 26g); Protein 4g

% Daily Value: Vitamin A 0%; Vitamin C 0%; Calcium 10%; Iron 6%

Exchanges: 1 Starch, 2 Other Carbohydrate, 1 1/2 Fat

Carbohydrate Choices: 3

> **BAKING TIP:**
> *If you'd like, bake this cake in a greased and floured 13x9-inch pan for 33 to 40 minutes—easy to frost and easy to carry!*

**VARIATIONS:**

**Coconut Cake:** Stir 1 cup flaked coconut into batter before pouring into pans.

**Poppy Seed Cake:** Mix 1/4 cup poppy seed with an additional 1/4 cup milk; let stand 30 minutes. Add to batter with vanilla and egg whites.

# BASIC YELLOW CAKE

→ **PREP TIME:** 10 mins
**START TO FINISH:** 1 hr 55 mins

**12 servings**

~~~~~~~~~~~~~~~~~~~~~~

2 1/2 cups all-purpose flour
3 teaspoons baking powder
1/4 teaspoon salt
1 1/4 cups sugar
3/4 cup butter or margarine,
    softened
1 teaspoon vanilla
3 eggs
1 cup milk

**1.** Heat oven to 350°F. Grease 2 (8- or 9-inch) round cake pans with shortening; lightly flour. In medium bowl, mix flour, baking powder and salt.

**2.** In large bowl, beat sugar and butter with electric mixer on medium speed until light and fluffy, scraping bowl occasionally. Beat in vanilla and eggs until well blended. Alternately add flour mixture and milk, beating well and scraping bowl after each addition. Pour batter evenly into pans.

**3.** Bake 27 to 35 minutes or until toothpick inserted in center comes out clean. Cool in pans 10 minutes. Remove from pans; place on wire racks. Cool completely, about 1 hour. Fill and frost as desired.

**High Altitude (3500–6500 ft): Decrease baking powder to 1 3/4 teaspoons.**

**1 Serving:** Calories 310 (Calories from Fat 120); Total Fat 13g (Saturated Fat 6g; Trans Fat 0.5g); Cholesterol 85mg; Sodium 270mg; Total Carbohydrate 42g (Dietary Fiber 0g; Sugars 22g); Protein 5g

% Daily Value: Vitamin A 10%; Vitamin C 0%; Calcium 10%; Iron 8%

Exchanges: 1 1/2 Starch, 1 1/2 Other Carbohydrate, 2 1/2 Fat

Carbohydrate Choices: 3

> **BAKING TIP:**
> *Just like Basic White Cake, you can bake this cake in a greased and floured 13x9-inch pan for 33 to 40 minutes—it's a time saver, and just as tasty.*

# DEVIL'S FOOD CAKE

→ PREP TIME: 15 mins
START TO FINISH: 2 hrs

**12 servings**

2 cups all-purpose flour
1 teaspoon baking soda
1/2 teaspoon salt
1 1/2 cups packed brown sugar
1/2 cup butter or margarine,
     softened
1 teaspoon vanilla
3 eggs
4 oz. unsweetened baking
     chocolate, cut into pieces,
     melted
1 1/4 cups water

**1.** Heat oven to 350°F. Grease 2 (8- or 9-inch) round cake pans with shortening; lightly flour. In medium bowl, mix flour, baking soda and salt.

**2.** In large bowl, beat brown sugar and butter with electric mixer on medium speed until well blended, scraping bowl occasionally. Beat in vanilla and eggs. Beat in melted chocolate until blended, scraping bowl occasionally. Alternately add flour mixture and water, beating well and scraping bowl after each addition. Pour batter evenly into pans.

**3.** Bake 8-inch pans 28 to 38 minutes (9-inch pans 25 to 35 minutes) or until toothpick inserted in center comes out clean. Cool in pans 10 minutes. Remove from pans; place on wire racks. Cool completely, about 1 hour. Fill and frost as desired.

**High Altitude (3500–6500 ft): Decrease brown sugar to 1 1/4 cups. Bake 8-inch pans 32 to 38 minutes (9-inch pans 30 to 35 minutes).**

**1 Serving:** Calories 330 (Calories from Fat 130); Total Fat 14g (Saturated Fat 7g; Trans Fat 0g); Cholesterol 75mg; Sodium 280mg; Total Carbohydrate 46g (Dietary Fiber 2g; Sugars 27g); Protein 5g

% Daily Value: Vitamin A 8%; Vitamin C 0%; Calcium 4%; Iron 10%

Exchanges: 2 Starch, 1 Other Carbohydrate, 2 1/2 Fat

Carbohydrate Choices: 3

**BAKING TIP:**
*For an easy spin on the classic Boston Cream Pie—yellow cake filled with custard and glazed with chocolate—spread instant vanilla pudding between the chocolate layers and top the cake with creamy chocolate ready-to-spread frosting.*

# GERMAN CHOCOLATE CAKE WITH COCONUT-PECAN FROSTING

→ **PREP TIME:** 30 mins
**START TO FINISH:** 2 hrs 50 mins

**16 servings**

### CAKE

4 oz. sweet baking chocolate,
   cut into pieces
1/2 cup water
2 cups sugar
1 cup butter or margarine,
   softened
4 eggs
2 1/2 cups all-purpose flour
1 teaspoon baking soda
1/2 teaspoon salt
1 cup buttermilk
1 teaspoon vanilla

### FROSTING

1 cup sugar
1 cup evaporated milk
1/2 cup butter or margarine
3 eggs, beaten
1 1/3 cups flaked coconut
1 cup chopped pecans or walnuts
1 teaspoon vanilla

**1.** Heat oven to 350°F. Grease 3 (9-inch) round cake pans with shortening; lightly flour. In 1-quart saucepan, melt chocolate with water over low heat, stirring frequently. Cool.

**2.** In large bowl, beat 2 cups sugar and 1 cup butter with electric mixer on medium speed until light and fluffy, scraping bowl occasionally. Add 4 eggs, one at a time, beating and scraping well after each addition. Beat in chocolate mixture. On low speed, beat in remaining cake ingredients until well blended, scraping bowl occasionally. Pour batter evenly into pans.

**3.** Bake 35 to 45 minutes or until toothpick inserted in center comes out clean. Cool in pans 5 minutes. Remove from pans; place on wire racks. Cool completely, about 1 hour.

**4.** In 2-quart saucepan, cook 1 cup sugar, the evaporated milk, 1/2 cup butter and 3 eggs over medium heat, stirring constantly, until mixture begins to bubble. Remove saucepan from heat. Stir in coconut, pecans and 1 teaspoon vanilla. Cool completely, about 30 minutes.

**5.** Place 1 cake layer, top side down, on serving plate. Spread with 1/3 of frosting. Repeat with remaining cake layers and frosting, ending with frosting.

**High Altitude (3500–6500 ft):** Heat oven to 375°F. Decrease sugar in cake to 1 3/4 cups; decrease baking soda to 3/4 teaspoon. Bake 25 to 30 minutes.

**1 Serving:** Calories 560 (Calories from Fat 270); Total Fat 30g (Saturated Fat 14g; Trans Fat 1g); Cholesterol 145mg; Sodium 340mg; Total Carbohydrate 63g (Dietary Fiber 2g; Sugars 46g); Protein 8g

% Daily Value: Vitamin A 15%; Vitamin C 0%; Calcium 8%; Iron 10%

Exchanges: 2 Starch, 2 Other Carbohydrate, 6 Fat

Carbohydrate Choices: 4

**BAKING TIP:**

*To substitute for buttermilk, use 1 tablespoon vinegar or lemon juice plus milk to make 1 cup.*

# COOKIES 'N CREAM CAKE

→ **PREP TIME: 25 mins**
**START TO FINISH: 2 hrs 5 mins**

**12 servings**

~~~~~~~~~~~~~~~~~~~~~~~~

## CAKE
1 box (1 lb. 2.25 oz.) white cake
 mix with pudding
1 1/4 cups water
1/4 cup vegetable oil
3 egg whites
1 cup coarsely crushed
 creme-filled chocolate
 sandwich cookies

## FROSTING
3 cups powdered sugar
3/4 cup shortening
1/4 cup milk
1 teaspoon vanilla

**1.** Heat oven to 350°F. Grease 13x9-inch pan with shortening or cooking spray.

**2.** In large bowl, beat cake mix, water, oil and egg whites with electric mixer on low speed 30 seconds or until moistened, scraping bowl occasionally. Beat on medium speed 2 minutes, scraping bowl occasionally. With spoon, stir in crushed cookies. Spread batter evenly in pan.

**3.** Bake 30 to 40 minutes or until toothpick inserted in center comes out clean. Cool completely, about 1 hour.

**4.** In medium bowl, beat frosting ingredients with spoon until smooth. Spread frosting over cooled cake. Garnish as desired.

**High Altitude (3500–6500 ft): No change.**

**1 Serving:** Calories 510 (Calories from Fat 210); Total Fat 24g (Saturated Fat 6g; Trans Fat 3g); Cholesterol 0mg; Sodium 370mg; Total Carbohydrate 71g (Dietary Fiber 0g; Sugars 59g); Protein 3g

% Daily Value: Vitamin A 0%; Vitamin C 0%; Calcium 6%; Iron 6%

Exchanges: 1 Starch, 4 Other Carbohydrate, 4 1/2 Fat

Carbohydrate Choices: 5

> **BAKING TIP:**
> *Here's the perfect take-along cake—just cover and take to a potluck supper, school party or birthday celebration—no special carrier needed.*

# CHOCOLATE-SOUR CREAM CAKE

→ PREP TIME: 25 mins
START TO FINISH: 2 hrs 15 mins

**12 servings**

~~~~~~~~~~~~~~~~~~~~~~~~

## CAKE

2 cups all-purpose flour
2 cups granulated sugar
1 1/4 teaspoons baking soda
1 teaspoon salt
1/2 teaspoon baking powder
1 cup water
3/4 cup sour cream
1/4 cup shortening
1 teaspoon vanilla
2 eggs
4 oz. unsweetened baking
   chocolate, cut into pieces,
   melted and cooled

## FROSTING

3 cups powdered sugar
1/4 cup sour cream
1/4 cup butter or margarine,
   softened
3 tablespoons milk
1 teaspoon vanilla
3 oz. unsweetened baking
   chocolate, cut into pieces,
   melted and cooled

**1.** Heat oven to 350°F. Grease 2 (8- or 9-inch) round cake pans with shortening; lightly flour. Line bottom of pans with waxed paper. In medium bowl, mix flour, granulated sugar, baking soda, salt and baking powder; set aside.

**2.** In large bowl, beat remaining cake ingredients with electric mixer on medium speed until well blended, scraping bowl occasionally. On low speed, beat in flour mixture until moistened, scraping bowl occasionally. Beat on high speed 3 minutes, scraping bowl occasionally. Pour batter evenly into pans.

**3.** Bake 30 to 40 minutes or until toothpick inserted in center comes out clean. Cool in pans 10 minutes. Remove from pans; place on wire racks. Cool completely, about 1 hour.

**4.** In small bowl, beat frosting ingredients with electric mixer on low speed until moistened. Beat on high speed until smooth and creamy. Place 1 cake layer, top side down, on serving plate. Spread evenly with about 1/4 of frosting. Top with remaining cake layer, top side up. Spread sides and top of cake with remaining frosting.

**High Altitude (3500–6500 ft): Heat oven to 375°F. Decrease sugar to 1 3/4 cups; omit baking powder. Bake 25 to 35 minutes.**

**1 Serving:** Calories 560 (Calories from Fat 200); Total Fat 22g (Saturated Fat 11g; Trans Fat 1g); Cholesterol 60mg; Sodium 400mg; Total Carbohydrate 85g (Dietary Fiber 3g; Sugars 63g); Protein 6g

% Daily Value: Vitamin A 6%; Vitamin C 0%; Calcium 6%; Iron 10%

Exchanges: 2 Starch, 3 1/2 Other Carbohydrate, 4 Fat

Carbohydrate Choices: 5 1/2

> **BAKING TIP:**
> *Wow your friends! Garnish this moist chocolate cake with chocolate curls and a sprinkling of unsweetened baking cocoa for a dramatic look. Or just make a simple topping of grated chocolate for an easy but impressive look.*

CHOICE CAKES

●

# DIXIE SPICE CAKE WITH CARAMEL FROSTING

→ PREP TIME: 30 mins
START TO FINISH: 2 hrs 15 mins

**12 servings**

CAKE
2 1/4 cups all-purpose flour
1 1/4 cups packed brown sugar
1/2 cup granulated sugar
1 teaspoon baking soda
1/2 teaspoon salt
1/2 teaspoon ground nutmeg
1/2 teaspoon ground allspice
1 cup buttermilk
2/3 cup shortening
1 teaspoon vanilla
3 eggs
1 cup chopped walnuts or pecans

FROSTING
1/2 cup butter or margarine
1 cup packed brown sugar
1/4 cup milk
3 cups powdered sugar
1/2 teaspoon vanilla

**1.** Heat oven to 350°F. Generously grease bottom only of 13x9-inch pan with shortening or cooking spray; lightly flour.

**2.** In large bowl, beat all cake ingredients except walnuts with electric mixer on low speed until moistened, scraping bowl occasionally. Beat on medium speed 3 minutes, scraping bowl occasionally. Stir in walnuts. Spread batter evenly in pan.

**3.** Bake 40 to 45 minutes or until top springs back when touched lightly in center. Cool completely, about 1 hour.

**4.** In 2-quart saucepan, melt butter. Stir in brown sugar. Cook over low heat 2 minutes, stirring constantly. Add milk; cook until mixture comes to a rolling boil. Remove from heat. Gradually beat in powdered sugar and vanilla until smooth. If needed, add a few drops of milk for desired spreading consistency. Spread over cooled cake.

High Altitude (3500–6500 ft): Heat oven to 375°F. Increase flour to 2 1/2 cups; decrease sugar to 1/4 cup. Increase buttermilk to 1 1/4 cups. In step 2, after beating on low speed, beat on medium speed 2 minutes. Bake 35 to 40 minutes.

1 **Serving:** Calories 670 (Calories from Fat 250); Total Fat 27g (Saturated Fat 8g; Trans Fat 2.5g); Cholesterol 75mg; Sodium 310mg; Total Carbohydrate 99g (Dietary Fiber 1g; Sugars 79g); Protein 6g

% Daily Value: Vitamin A 8%; Vitamin C 0%; Calcium 8%; Iron 15%

Exchanges: 2 Starch, 4 1/2 Other Carbohydrate, 5 Fat

Carbohydrate Choices: 6 1/2

BAKING TIP:
*To substitute for buttermilk, use 1 tablespoon vinegar or lemon juice plus milk to make 1 cup.*

VARIATION:
**Dixie Spice Cupcakes:** Place paper baking cups in each of 24 to 30 regular-size muffin cups. Fill each 2/3 full with batter. Bake at 350°F 20 to 25 minutes. Spread with frosting.

# OLD-FASHIONED OATMEAL CAKE WITH BROILED TOPPING

→ **PREP TIME: 30 mins**
**START TO FINISH: 2 hrs 15 mins**

**16 servings**

## CAKE
1 1/2 cups quick-cooking oats
1 1/4 cups boiling water
1 cup granulated sugar
1 cup packed brown sugar
1/2 cup butter or margarine,
   softened
1 teaspoon vanilla
3 eggs
1 1/2 cups all-purpose flour
1 teaspoon baking soda
1/2 teaspoon baking powder
1/2 teaspoon salt
1 1/2 teaspoons ground cinnamon
1/2 teaspoon ground nutmeg

## TOPPING
2/3 cup packed brown sugar
1/4 cup butter or margarine,
   melted
3 tablespoons half-and-half or
   milk
1 cup coconut
1/2 cup chopped nuts

**1.** In small bowl, mix oats and boiling water; let stand 20 minutes. Meanwhile, heat oven to 350°F. Grease 13x9-inch pan with shortening or cooking spray; lightly flour.

**2.** In large bowl, beat granulated sugar, 1 cup brown sugar and 1/2 cup butter with electric mixer on medium speed until light and fluffy, scraping bowl occasionally. Beat in vanilla and eggs. Beat in oat mixture and remaining cake ingredients until well blended, scraping bowl occasionally. Spread batter evenly in pan.

**3.** Bake 35 to 45 minutes or until toothpick inserted in center comes out clean.

**4.** Set oven control to broil. In small bowl, beat 2/3 cup brown sugar, 1/4 cup butter and the half-and-half with electric mixer on high speed until smooth. Stir in coconut and nuts. Spoon over warm cake; spread to cover.

**5.** Broil 4 to 6 inches from heat 1 to 2 minutes or until bubbly and light golden brown. Cool completely, about 1 hour.

**High Altitude (3500–6500 ft): Heat oven to 375°F. Decrease sugar to 3/4 cup; increase flour to 1 3/4 cups. Bake 30 to 40 minutes.**

**1 Serving:** Calories 360 (Calories from Fat 130); Total Fat 15g (Saturated Fat 7g; Trans Fat 0.5g); Cholesterol 65mg; Sodium 260mg; Total Carbohydrate 52g (Dietary Fiber 2g; Sugars 37g); Protein 4g

% Daily Value: Vitamin A 8%; Vitamin C 0%; Calcium 6%; Iron 10%

Exchanges: 1 Starch, 2 1/2 Other Carbohydrate, 3 Fat

Carbohydrate Choices: 3 1/2

**BAKING TIP:**
*Make it truly old-fashioned by using old-fashioned oats in place of the quick-cooking ones—you'll get a more oaty look and flavor. In baking, the two ingredients are usually interchangeable.*

# BANANA SNACK CAKE

→ PREP TIME: 10 mins
START TO FINISH: 45 mins

**16 servings**

~~~~~~~~~~~~~~~~~~~~~~

1 cup sugar
1 cup butter or margarine,
    softened
2 eggs
1/2 cup buttermilk
1 cup mashed ripe bananas
    (2 medium)
1 teaspoon vanilla
2 cups all-purpose flour
1 cup quick-cooking oats
1 1/2 teaspoons baking soda
1/2 teaspoon salt
1 cup semisweet chocolate chips
    (6 oz.)
1/2 cup chopped nuts

**1.** Heat oven to 350°F. Grease 13x9-inch pan with shortening or cooking spray. In large bowl, mix sugar, butter and eggs with spoon until combined. Stir in buttermilk, bananas and vanilla until well blended.

**2.** Stir in flour, oats, baking soda and salt until well combined. Fold in chocolate chips. Spread batter evenly in pan. Sprinkle nuts evenly over top.

**3.** Bake 30 to 35 minutes or until toothpick inserted in center comes out clean. Serve warm or cool.

**High Altitude (3500–6500 ft): No change.**

**1 Serving:** Calories 340 (Calories from Fat 170); Total Fat 18g (Saturated Fat 8g; Trans Fat 0.5g); Cholesterol 55mg; Sodium 290mg; Total Carbohydrate 39g (Dietary Fiber 2g; Sugars 20g); Protein 5g

% Daily Value: Vitamin A 10%; Vitamin C 0%; Calcium 2%; Iron 8%

Exchanges: 1 1/2 Starch, 1 Other Carbohydrate, 3 1/2 Fat

Carbohydrate Choices: 2 1/2

**BAKING TIP:**
*The flavor secret to this yummy cake is very ripe bananas. To speed the ripening, place the bananas in a perforated brown paper bag.*

# MISSISSIPPI MUD CAKE

→ **PREP TIME:** 20 mins
**START TO FINISH:** 1 hr 55 mins

**15 servings**

## CAKE

1 box (1 lb. 2.25 oz.) devil's food
   cake mix with pudding
1 1/4 cups water
1/2 cup vegetable oil
3 eggs
1 cup chopped pecans
1 jar (7 oz.) marshmallow creme
   (1 1/2 cups)

## FROSTING

1 container (1 lb.) chocolate
   creamy ready-to-spread
   frosting
2 tablespoons milk

**1.** Heat oven to 350°F. Grease bottom only of 13x9-inch pan with shortening or cooking spray; lightly flour.

**2.** In large bowl, beat cake mix, water, oil and eggs with electric mixer on low speed until moistened, scraping bowl occasionally. Beat on high speed 1 minute, scraping bowl occasionally. Spread batter evenly in pan. Sprinkle pecans evenly over top.

**3.** Bake 30 to 40 minutes or until toothpick inserted in center comes out clean. Spoon marshmallow creme evenly over top of hot cake; return to oven for 30 to 60 seconds or until soft. Carefully spread marshmallow creme to cover cake.

**4.** In small bowl, mix frosting and enough milk until smooth and spreading consistency. Drop frosting by spoonfuls onto cake; spread gently to cover, then lightly swirl to marble. Cool cake completely, about 1 hour.

**High Altitude (3500–6500 ft):** Follow High Altitude cake mix directions for 13x9-inch pan.

**1 Serving:** Calories 460 (Calories from Fat 220); Total Fat 24g (Saturated Fat 8g; Trans Fat 0.5g); Cholesterol 45mg; Sodium 330mg; Total Carbohydrate 57g (Dietary Fiber 3g; Sugars 44g); Protein 4g

% Daily Value: Vitamin A 0%; Vitamin C 0%; Calcium 6%; Iron 8%

Exchanges: 1 Starch, 3 Other Carbohydrate, 4 1/2 Fat

Carbohydrate Choices: 4

> **BAKING TIP:**
> *You can use 2 cups miniature marshmallows in place of the marshmallow creme. Just sprinkle them evenly over the top of the cake. Return it to the oven for 1 to 2 minutes or until the marshmallows have puffed. Immediately frost the cake as directed in the recipe.*

# CHOCOLATE CHIP–ZUCCHINI CAKE

→ PREP TIME: 15 mins
START TO FINISH: 2 hrs

**16 servings**

1 1/2 cups sugar

1/2 cup butter or margarine, softened

1/4 cup vegetable oil

1 teaspoon vanilla

2 eggs

2 1/2 cups all-purpose flour

1/4 cup unsweetened baking cocoa

1 teaspoon baking soda

1/2 cup buttermilk

2 cups shredded zucchini (1 medium)

1/2 to 1 cup semisweet chocolate chips (3 to 6 oz.)

1/2 cup chopped nuts, if desired

**1.** Heat oven to 350°F. Grease 13x9-inch pan with shortening or cooking spray; lightly flour. In large bowl, beat sugar, butter, oil, vanilla and eggs with spoon until well blended.

**2.** Stir in flour, cocoa, baking soda and buttermilk until well combined. Fold in zucchini, chocolate chips and, if desired, nuts. Spread batter evenly in pan.

**3.** Bake 35 to 45 minutes or until toothpick inserted in center comes out clean. Cool completely, about 1 hour. If desired, frost cooled cake.

**High Altitude (3500–6500 ft): Heat oven to 375°F. Bake 35 to 40 minutes.**

**1 Serving:** Calories 280 (Calories from Fat 110); Total Fat 12g (Saturated Fat 4.5g; Trans Fat 0g); Cholesterol 40mg; Sodium 135mg; Total Carbohydrate 39g (Dietary Fiber 2g; Sugars 22g); Protein 4g

% Daily Value: Vitamin A 8%; Vitamin C 0%; Calcium 2%; Iron 8%

Exchanges: 1 Starch, 1 1/2 Other Carbohydrate, 2 1/2 Fat

Carbohydrate Choices: 2 1/2

**BAKING TIP:**
*To substitute for buttermilk, use 1 1/2 teaspoons vinegar or lemon juice plus milk to make 1/2 cup.*

# CHOCOLATE CARROT CAKE

→ PREP TIME: 15 mins
START TO FINISH: 2 hrs

**12 servings**

~~~~~~~~~~~~~~~~~~~~~~~

1 (1 lb. 2.25-oz.) pkg. pudding-included devil's food cake mix
1 teaspoon cinnamon
1/4 teaspoon cloves
3 cups shredded carrots
  (5 medium)
1/2 cup buttermilk
1/3 cup oil
3 eggs
1/2 cup chopped nuts
1/2 cup semisweet chocolate
  chips

**1.** Heat oven to 350°F. Grease and flour 13x9-inch pan. In large bowl, combine cake mix, cinnamon, cloves, carrots, buttermilk, oil and eggs; beat at low speed until moistened. Beat 2 minutes at high speed. Pour into greased and floured pan. Sprinkle with nuts and chocolate chips.

**2.** Bake at 350°F for 35 to 40 minutes or until toothpick inserted in center comes out clean. Cool 1 hour or until completely cooled.

**High Altitude (3500–6500 ft): Add 2 tablespoons flour to dry cake mix. Bake at 375°F for 30 to 40 minutes.**

**1 Serving:** Calories 330 (Calories from Fat 150); Total Fat 17g (Saturated Fat 4g; Trans Fat 0); Cholesterol 55mg; Sodium 360mg; Total Carbohydrate 40g (Dietary Fiber 3g; Sugars 25g); Protein 5g

% Daily Value: Vitamin A 44%; Vitamin C 2%; Calcium 15%; Iron 15%

Exchanges: 2 Starch, 1/2 Fruit, 2 1/2 Other Carbohydrate, 3 Fat

Carbohydrate Choices: 2 1/2

# PINEAPPLE UPSIDE-DOWN CAKE

→ PREP TIME: 20 mins
START TO FINISH: 1 hr

**6 servings**

~~~~~~~~~~~~~~~~~~~~~~

1/2 cup firmly packed brown
   sugar
1/4 cup margarine or butter,
   melted
6 canned pineapple slices,
   drained
6 maraschino cherries
2 eggs, separated
1/2 cup sugar
3/4 cup all-purpose or
   unbleached flour
1/2 teaspoon baking powder
1/4 teaspoon salt
1/4 cup pineapple juice
Whipped cream

**1.** Heat oven to 350°F. In small bowl, combine brown sugar and margarine; blend well. Spread in bottom of ungreased 9-inch round cake pan. Arrange pineapple slices and maraschino cherries over brown sugar mixture. Set aside.

**2.** In small bowl, beat egg yolks until thick and lemon colored. Gradually add sugar; beat well. Lightly spoon flour into measuring cup; level off. Add flour, baking powder, salt and pineapple juice; mix well.

**3.** In another small bowl, beat egg whites until stiff peaks form. Fold into batter. Pour batter evenly over pineapple slices and cherries.

**4.** Bake at 350°F for 30 to 35 minutes or until toothpick inserted in center comes out clean. Cool upright in pan 2 minutes. Invert cake onto serving plate. Serve warm with whipped cream.

**High Altitude (3500–6500 ft): Increase flour to 3/4 cup plus 3 tablespoons. Bake at 375°F for 30 to 35 minutes.**

**1 Serving:** Calories 370 (Calories from Fat 140); Total Fat 15g (Saturated Fat 5g; Trans Fat 0); Cholesterol 90mg; Sodium 250mg; Total Carbohydrate 55g (Dietary Fiber 1g; Sugars 43g); Protein 4g

% Daily Value: Vitamin A 15%; Vitamin C 6%; Calcium 8%; Iron 10%

Exchanges: 1 Starch, 2 1/2 Fruit, 3 1/2 Other Carbohydrate, 3 Fat

Carbohydrate Choices: 3 1/2

# JELLY ROLL

**10 servings**

~~~~~~~~~~~~~~~~~~~~~~~

2 tablespoons powdered sugar
4 eggs
3/4 cup granulated sugar
1/4 cup cold water
1 teaspoon vanilla
1 cup all-purpose flour
1 teaspoon baking powder
1/4 teaspoon salt
3/4 cup any flavor jelly or
   preserves

**1.** Heat oven to 375°F. Line 15x10x1-inch pan with foil; generously grease foil with shortening. Sprinkle clean towel with powdered sugar; set aside.

**2.** In large bowl, beat eggs with electric mixer on high speed 5 minutes or until thick and lemon colored, scraping bowl occasionally. Gradually beat in granulated sugar until light and fluffy, scraping bowl occasionally. Beat in water and vanilla. On low speed, beat in flour, baking powder and salt just until smooth, scraping bowl occasionally. Spread batter evenly in pan.

**3.** Bake 8 to 12 minutes or until cake springs back when touched lightly in center.

**4.** Immediately loosen cake from edges of pan; turn upside down onto towel sprinkled with powdered sugar. Remove pan and foil. While cake is hot and starting with one short side, carefully roll up cake and towel; place on wire rack. Cool completely, about 1 hour.

**5.** Carefully unroll cake; remove towel. Spread jelly over cake; loosely roll up cake. Wrap in foil or waxed paper; refrigerate 30 minutes. If desired, sprinkle with powdered sugar just before serving; cut into 1-inch slices.

**High Altitude (3500–6500 ft): No change.**

**1 Serving:** Calories 200 (Calories from Fat 20); Total Fat 2.5g (Saturated Fat 0.5g; Trans Fat 0g); Cholesterol 85mg; Sodium 140mg; Total Carbohydrate 42g (Dietary Fiber 0g; Sugars 28g); Protein 4g

% Daily Value: Vitamin A 2%; Vitamin C 0%; Calcium 4%; Iron 6%

Exchanges: 1 Starch, 2 Other Carbohydrate, 1/2 Fat

Carbohydrate Choices: 3

# CHOCOLATE POUND CAKE

→ PREP TIME: 20 mins
START TO FINISH: 4 hrs 10 mins

**16 servings**

~~~~~~~~~~~~~~~~~~

### CAKE

3 cups all-purpose flour

1/4 cup unsweetened baking
   cocoa

1/2 teaspoon baking powder

1/2 teaspoon salt

3 cups granulated sugar

1 cup butter or margarine,
   softened

1/2 cup shortening

1 teaspoon vanilla

5 eggs

1 cup milk

### GLAZE

2 tablespoons unsweetened
   baking cocoa

1 tablespoon water

1 tablespoon light corn syrup

2 tablespoons butter or
   margarine

1/4 teaspoon vanilla

1/2 cup powdered sugar

**1.** Heat oven to 350°F. Grease 10-inch angel food (tube) cake pan with shortening; lightly flour. In medium bowl, mix flour, 1/4 cup cocoa, the baking powder and salt.

**2.** In large bowl, beat granulated sugar, 1 cup butter, the shortening and 1 teaspoon vanilla with electric mixer on medium speed until light and fluffy, scraping bowl occasionally. Add eggs, one at a time, beating well and scraping bowl after each addition. Alternately add flour mixture and milk to sugar mixture, beginning and ending with flour mixture, beating and scraping after each addition. Pour batter evenly into pan.

**3.** Bake 1 hour 10 minutes to 1 hour 25 minutes or until toothpick inserted in center comes out clean. Cool upright in pan 25 minutes. Place serving plate upside down over pan; turn plate and pan over. Remove pan. Cool completely, about 2 hours.

**4.** In 1-quart saucepan, mix 2 tablespoons cocoa, the water, corn syrup and 2 tablespoons butter. Cook over low heat, stirring constantly, until mixture thickens. Remove from heat. Beat in 1/4 teaspoon vanilla and the powdered sugar with spoon until smooth. Spread glaze over top of cooled cake, allowing some to run down sides.

**High Altitude (3500–6500 ft): Heat oven to 375°F. Increase flour to 3 1/4 cups. Bake 1 hour 10 minutes to 1 hour 20 minutes.**

**1 Serving:** Calories 470 (Calories from Fat 200); Total Fat 22g (Saturated Fat 9g; Trans Fat 2g); Cholesterol 100mg; Sodium 200mg; Total Carbohydrate 62g (Dietary Fiber 1g; Sugars 43g); Protein 5g

% Daily Value: Vitamin A 10%; Vitamin C 0%; Calcium 4%; Iron 8%

Exchanges: 1 Starch, 3 Other Carbohydrate, 4 1/2 Fat

Carbohydrate Choices: 4

# GLAZED LEMON POUND CAKE

**16 servings**

~~~~~~~~~~~~~~~~~~~~~~

### CAKE

1 cup butter, softened
2 cups sugar
4 eggs
1 tablespoon grated lemon peel
3 cups all-purpose flour
1 teaspoon baking powder
1 teaspoon salt
1/2 teaspoon baking soda
1 cup milk

### GLAZE

1/3 cup sugar
1/4 cup lemon juice
2 tablespoons butter

**1.** Heat oven to 350°F. Generously grease 12-cup fluted tube cake pan with shortening.

**2.** In large bowl, beat 1 cup butter and 2 cups sugar with electric mixer on medium speed until light and fluffy, scraping bowl occasionally. Add eggs, one at a time, beating well and scraping bowl after each addition. Beat in lemon peel. On low speed, beat in flour, baking powder, salt, baking soda and milk until smooth, scraping bowl occasionally. Pour batter evenly into pan.

**3.** Bake 45 to 50 minutes or until toothpick inserted near center comes out clean. Cool upright in pan 15 minutes.

**4.** Meanwhile, in 1-quart non-aluminum saucepan, mix glaze ingredients. Heat over medium heat, stirring occasionally, until butter melts.

**5.** Place serving plate upside down over pan; turn plate and pan over. Remove pan. With long-tined fork or skewer, generously prick top and sides of cake. Brush warm glaze over cake, allowing glaze to soak into cake. Cool completely, about 1 hour 30 minutes.

**High Altitude (3500–6500 ft): Increase flour to 3 1/2 cups.**

**1 Serving:** Calories 350 (Calories from Fat 130); Total Fat 15g (Saturated Fat 7g; Trans Fat 1g); Cholesterol 90mg; Sodium 330mg; Total Carbohydrate 48g (Dietary Fiber 0g; Sugars 30g); Protein 5g

% Daily Value: Vitamin A 10%; Vitamin C 0%; Calcium 4%; Iron 8%

Exchanges: 1 Starch, 2 Other Carbohydrate, 3 Fat

Carbohydrate Choices: 3

# MAPLE-APPLE CAKE

**16 servings**

~~~~~~~~~~~~~~~~~~~~~

## CAKE
1 cup granulated sugar
1/2 cup packed brown sugar
3/4 cup butter or margarine,
   softened
3/4 cup maple-flavored syrup
4 eggs
3 cups all-purpose flour
2 teaspoons baking powder
1 teaspoon ground cinnamon
1/2 teaspoon salt
1/2 teaspoon ground nutmeg
1/4 teaspoon ground allspice
3 cups chopped peeled apples
   (3 medium)
1/2 cup chopped walnuts

## GLAZE
1/2 cup powdered sugar
3 tablespoons maple-flavored
   syrup
1 tablespoon butter or
   margarine, softened
Garnish
1 tablespoon chopped walnuts

**1.** Heat oven to 350°F. Grease 12-cup fluted tube cake pan with shortening; lightly flour.

**2.** In large bowl, beat granulated sugar, brown sugar and 3/4 cup butter with electric mixer on medium speed until smooth, scraping bowl occasionally. Beat in 3/4 cup syrup and eggs until blended, scraping bowl occasionally. On low speed, beat in flour, baking powder, cinnamon, salt, nutmeg and allspice until combined, scraping bowl occasionally. Stir in apples and 1/2 cup walnuts. Spread batter evenly in pan.

**3.** Bake 55 to 65 minutes or until toothpick inserted in center comes out clean. Cool upright in pan 15 minutes. Place serving plate upside down over pan; turn plate and pan over. Remove pan. Cool completely, about 1 hour.

**4.** In small bowl, mix glaze ingredients until smooth; spoon over top of cake. Sprinkle with 1 tablespoon walnuts.

**High Altitude (3500–6500 ft):** Heat oven to 375°F. Decrease sugar to 3/4 cup; increase flour to 3 1/2 cups. Bake 50 to 60 minutes.

**1 Serving:** Calories 380 (Calories from Fat 120); Total Fat 14g (Saturated Fat 5g; Trans Fat 0.5g); Cholesterol 80mg; Sodium 240mg; Total Carbohydrate 59g (Dietary Fiber 2g; Sugars 33g); Protein 5g
% Daily Value: Vitamin A 8%; Vitamin C 0%; Calcium 6%; Iron 10%
Exchanges: 2 Starch, 2 Other Carbohydrate, 2 1/2 Fat
Carbohydrate Choices: 4

# HAZELNUT CAKE

→ PREP TIME: 30 mins
START TO FINISH: 2 hrs

**16 servings**

~~~~~~~~~~~~~~~~~~

## CAKE
1/2 cup butter or margarine
2 packages (2 1/2 oz. each)
   hazelnuts (filberts) or pecans
3 eggs
1 1/2 cups sugar
1 teaspoon vanilla
2 cups all-purpose flour
2 1/4 teaspoons baking powder
1/4 teaspoon salt

## GLAZE
1/2 cup whipping (heavy) cream
1 cup semisweet chocolate chips
   (6 oz.)
1/2 teaspoon vanilla

**1.** Heat oven to 350°F. Lightly grease bottom only of 10-inch spring-form pan with shortening or cooking spray. In 1-quart saucepan, melt butter over low heat; set aside to cool.

**2.** Reserve 8 whole nuts for garnish. In food processor or blender, process remaining nuts until ground, making about 1 1/3 cups. Reserve 1 tablespoon for garnish.

**3.** In large bowl, beat eggs, sugar and 1 teaspoon vanilla with electric mixer on medium speed 2 to 3 minutes or until thick and lemon colored, scraping bowl occasionally. On low speed, beat in flour, baking powder, salt and ground nuts, scraping bowl occasionally. Continue beating, gradually adding cooled, melted butter until well blended, scraping bowl occasionally (mixture will be thick). Spread batter evenly in pan.

**4.** Bake 35 to 45 minutes or until toothpick inserted in center comes out clean. Cool in pan 15 minutes. Remove side of pan; run long knife under cake to loosen from pan bottom. Place heatproof serving plate upside down over cake; turn plate and cake over. Remove pan bottom. Cover cake with cloth towel; cool completely, about 30 minutes.

**5.** In 2-quart saucepan, heat whipping cream just to boiling; remove from heat. Stir in chocolate chips until melted and smooth. Stir in 1/2 teaspoon vanilla. Spread glaze over top of cake, allowing some to run down side of cake. Sprinkle reserved ground nuts around top edge of cake; arrange reserved whole nuts over ground nuts.

**High Altitude (3500–6500 ft): Heat oven to 375°F. Increase flour to 2 cups plus 2 tablespoons. Bake 30 to 40 minutes.**

**1 Serving:** Calories 340 (Calories from Fat 160); Total Fat 18g (Saturated Fat 7g; Trans Fat 0g); Cholesterol 65mg; Sodium 160mg; Total Carbohydrate 39g (Dietary Fiber 2g; Sugars 25g); Protein 5g
% Daily Value: Vitamin A 8%; Vitamin C 0%; Calcium 6%; Iron 10%
Exchanges: 1 Starch, 1 1/2 Other Carbohydrate, 3 1/2 Fat
Carbohydrate Choices: 2 1/2

**BAKING TIP:**
*No springform pan? Just use a 9-inch round cake pan. Line the pan with foil and generously grease the foil with shortening or cooking spray. Bake the cake for 45 to 55 minutes. After cooling for 15 minutes, use the foil to lift the cake out of the pan.*

# RASPBERRY-FUDGE CAKE

→ PREP TIME: 20 mins
START TO FINISH: 2 hrs 45 mins

**16 servings**

～～～～～～～～～～～

### CAKE

Unsweetened baking cocoa
1 cup all-purpose flour
3/4 teaspoon baking powder
1/4 teaspoon salt
3 oz. semisweet baking
    chocolate, cut into pieces
2 oz. unsweetened baking
    chocolate, cut into pieces
3/4 cup butter or margarine
3/4 cup sugar
3/4 cup seedless raspberry jam
1 tablespoon kirsch or
    maraschino cherry liquid
3 eggs

### TOPPING

1/4 cup seedless raspberry jam
1 oz. semisweet baking choco-
    late, cut into pieces
1 tablespoon butter or margarine
1 teaspoon light corn syrup

**1.** Heat oven to 350°F. Grease 9-inch springform pan with shortening or cooking spray; dust with cocoa. In small bowl, mix flour, baking powder and salt; set aside.

**2.** In 1-quart saucepan, melt 3 oz. semisweet chocolate, the unsweetened chocolate and 3/4 cup butter over low heat, stirring until smooth. Remove from heat; cool slightly.

**3.** In medium bowl, beat sugar, 3/4 cup jam, the kirsch and eggs with wire whisk until well blended. Stir in melted chocolate and flour mixture until well combined. Pour batter evenly into pan.

**4.** Bake 40 to 55 minutes or until toothpick inserted in center comes out clean. Remove side of pan; leave cake on pan bottom. Cool completely, about 1 hour 30 minutes.

**5.** Spread 1/4 cup jam over top of cooled cake. In 1-quart saucepan, melt remaining topping ingredients over low heat, stirring until smooth. Drizzle over top of cake.

**High Altitude (3500–6500 ft): Decrease sugar to 1/2 cup.**

**1 Serving:** Calories 280 (Calories from Fat 130); Total Fat 15g (Saturated Fat 7g; Trans Fat 0.5g); Cholesterol 65mg; Sodium 140mg; Total Carbohydrate 35g (Dietary Fiber 1g; Sugars 23g); Protein 3g

% Daily Value: Vitamin A 8%; Vitamin C 0%; Calcium 4%; Iron 6%

Exchanges: 1 Starch, 1 1/2 Other Carbohydrate, 2 1/2 Fat

Carbohydrate Choices: 2

# DOUBLE-CHOCOLATE CHUNK CUPCAKES

→ PREP TIME: 15 mins
START TO FINISH: 40 mins

**18 cupcakes**

2 cups all-purpose flour
1/2 cup packed brown sugar
1/4 cup unsweetened baking
   cocoa
1 teaspoon baking soda
1/4 teaspoon salt
1 cup buttermilk
1/2 cup butter or margarine,
   melted
1/2 teaspoon almond extract
1 egg
1/2 cup white vanilla baking
   chips or 3 oz. chopped white
   chocolate baking bar
1/2 cup milk chocolate chips
1/4 cup chopped slivered
   almonds

**1.** Heat oven to 375°F. Line 18 regular-size muffin cups with paper baking cups or grease cups with shortening or cooking spray. In large bowl, mix flour, brown sugar, cocoa, baking soda and salt. Beat in buttermilk, butter, almond extract and egg with electric mixer on medium speed just until dry ingredients are moistened, scraping bowl occasionally.

**2.** Gently stir in vanilla baking chips, milk chocolate chips and almonds. Divide batter evenly among muffin cups, filling each three-quarters full.

**3.** Bake 15 to 20 minutes or until toothpick inserted in center comes out clean. Cool 3 minutes; remove from muffin cups. Serve warm or cool.

**High Altitude (3500–6500 ft): No change.**

1 Cupcake: Calories 200 (Calories from Fat 90); Total Fat 10g (Saturated Fat 4.5g; Trans Fat 0g); Cholesterol 25mg; Sodium 170mg; Total Carbohydrate 24g (Dietary Fiber 1g; Sugars 12g); Protein 3g

% Daily Value: Vitamin A 4%; Vitamin C 0%; Calcium 6%; Iron 6%

Exchanges: 1 Starch, 1/2 Other Carbohydrate, 2 Fat

Carbohydrate Choices: 1 1/2

**BAKING TIP:**
*To substitute for buttermilk, use 1 tablespoon vinegar or lemon juice plus milk to make 1 cup.*

# BLACK-BOTTOM CUPCAKES

→ PREP TIME: 25 mins
START TO FINISH: 1 hr 40 mins

**18 cupcakes**

〰〰〰〰〰〰〰〰〰

## FILLING
2 packages (3 oz. each)
  cream cheese, softened
1/3 cup sugar
1 egg
1 cup semisweet chocolate chips
  (6 oz.)

## CUPCAKES
1 1/2 cups all-purpose flour
1 cup sugar
1/4 cup unsweetened baking
  cocoa
1 teaspoon baking soda
1/2 teaspoon salt
1 cup water
1/3 cup vegetable oil
1 tablespoon vinegar
1 teaspoon vanilla

## TOPPING
1/2 cup chopped almonds,
  if desired
2 tablespoons sugar, if desired

**1.** Heat oven to 350°F. Place paper baking cups in each of 18 regular-size muffin cups. In small bowl, mix all filling ingredients except chocolate chips until well blended. Stir in chocolate chips; set aside.

**2.** In large bowl, mix flour, 1 cup sugar, cocoa, baking soda and salt. Beat in remaining cupcake ingredients with electric mixer on medium speed 2 minutes, scraping bowl occasionally. Divide batter evenly among muffin cups, filling each half full.

**3.** Top batter in each cup with 1 rounded tablespoon filling. If desired, in small bowl, mix topping ingredients; sprinkle evenly over filling.

**4.** Bake 20 to 30 minutes or until filling is light golden brown. Cool 15 minutes; remove from muffin cups. Cool completely, about 30 minutes. Store in refrigerator.

**High Altitude (3500–6500 ft):** Heat oven to 375°F. Increase flour to 1 1/2 cups plus 2 tablespoons. Bake 25 to 35 minutes.

**1 Cupcake:** Calories 230 (Calories from Fat 100); Total Fat 11g (Saturated Fat 4.5g; Trans Fat 0g); Cholesterol 20mg; Sodium 170mg; Total Carbohydrate 30g (Dietary Fiber 1g; Sugars 20g); Protein 3g

% Daily Value: Vitamin A 4%; Vitamin C 0%; Calcium 0%; Iron 6%

Exchanges: 1 Starch, 1 Other Carbohydrate, 2 Fat

Carbohydrate Choices: 2

# APPLESAUCE CUPCAKES WITH BROWNED BUTTER FROSTING

→ PREP TIME: 35 mins
START TO FINISH: 1 hr 50 mins

**24 cupcakes**

~~~~~~~~~~~~~~~~~~~~~~~~

## CUPCAKES

1 1/4 cups granulated sugar
1 1/2 cups applesauce
1/2 cup butter, softened
2 eggs
2 1/2 cups all-purpose flour
1 teaspoon ground cinnamon
1 teaspoon baking powder
1/2 teaspoon baking soda
1/2 teaspoon salt
1/4 teaspoon ground nutmeg

## FROSTING

1/2 cup butter (do not use
   margarine)
4 cups powdered sugar
2 teaspoons vanilla
3 to 4 tablespoons milk

**1.** Heat oven to 350°F. Line 24 regular-size muffin cups with paper baking cups or grease cups with shortening or cooking spray. In large bowl, beat granulated sugar, applesauce, butter and eggs with electric mixer on medium speed until smooth and creamy, scraping bowl occasionally. On low speed, beat in flour, cinnamon, baking powder, baking soda, salt and nutmeg just until well blended, scraping bowl occasionally. Divide batter evenly among muffin cups.

**2.** Bake 25 to 35 minutes or until toothpick inserted in center comes out clean. Remove from muffin cups. Cool completely, about 30 minutes.

**3.** In 3-quart saucepan, melt butter over medium heat. Cook 3 to 5 minutes, stirring constantly and watching closely, until butter just begins to turn golden (butter will get foamy and bubble). Remove from heat. Cool 15 minutes.

**4.** With electric mixer on low speed, beat in powdered sugar, vanilla and enough milk until frosting is smooth and desired spreading consistency, adding 1 or 2 more teaspoons milk, if necessary. Spread frosting on cooled cupcakes (if frosting begins to harden, stir in an additional teaspoon milk).

**High Altitude (3500–6500 ft): Bake 20 to 25 minutes.**

**1 Cupcake:** Calories 260 (Calories from Fat 80); Total Fat 8g (Saturated Fat 4g; Trans Fat 0g); Cholesterol 40mg; Sodium 150mg; Total Carbohydrate 44g (Dietary Fiber 0g; Sugars 33g); Protein 2g

% Daily Value: Vitamin A 6%; Vitamin C 0%; Calcium 2%; Iron 4%

Exchanges: 1 Starch, 2 Other Carbohydrate, 1 1/2 Fat

Carbohydrate Choices: 3

# PEANUT BUTTER CUPS

→ PREP TIME: 20 mins
START TO FINISH: 1 hr

**24 cupcakes**

1 3/4 cups all-purpose flour
1 1/4 cups packed brown sugar
3 teaspoons baking powder
1 teaspoon salt
1 cup milk
1/3 cup shortening
1/3 cup peanut butter
1 teaspoon vanilla
2 eggs
24 miniature chocolate-covered
   peanut butter cup candies,
   unwrapped

**1.** Heat oven to 350°F. Place paper baking cups in each of 24 regular-size muffin cups. In large bowl, beat all ingredients except peanut butter cups with electric mixer on low speed until moistened, scraping bowl occasionally. Beat on medium speed 2 minutes, scraping bowl occasionally. Divide batter evenly among muffin cups, filling each two-thirds full.

**2.** Press 1 peanut butter cup into batter in each cup until top edge of candy is even with batter.

**3.** Bake 18 to 28 minutes or until tops spring back when touched lightly in center. Cool 5 minutes; remove from muffin cups. Serve warm or cool.

**High Altitude (3500–6500 ft): No change.**

1 Cupcake: Calories 170 (Calories from Fat 60); Total Fat 7g (Saturated Fat 2g; Trans Fat 0.5g); Cholesterol 20mg; Sodium 210mg; Total Carbohydrate 23g (Dietary Fiber 0g; Sugars 15g); Protein 3g
% Daily Value: Vitamin A 0%; Vitamin C 0%; Calcium 6%; Iron 6%
Exchanges: 1/2 Starch, 1 Other Carbohydrate, 1 1/2 Fat
Carbohydrate Choices: 1 1/2

> **BAKING TIP:**
> *You can decide if you want to use creamy or crunchy peanut butter in these treat-filled cupcakes—either one is peanutty scrumptious.*

*Everyone craves cookies—bake up a batch and become a kitchen magician—they'll vanish!*

# SOFT-AND-CHEWY CHOCOLATE CHIP COOKIES

→ PREP TIME: 1 hr 10 mins
START TO FINISH: 1 hr 10 mins

**6 dozen cookies**

~~~~~~~~~~~~~~~~~~~~~~~~

1 1/4 cups granulated sugar

1 1/4 cups packed brown sugar

1 1/2 cups butter or margarine, softened

2 teaspoons vanilla

3 eggs

4 1/4 cups all-purpose flour

2 teaspoons baking soda

1/2 teaspoon salt

1 to 2 bags (12 oz. each) chocolate chips (2 to 4 cups)

**1.** Heat oven to 375°F. In large bowl, beat granulated sugar, brown sugar and butter with electric mixer on medium speed until light and fluffy, scraping bowl occasionally. Beat in vanilla and eggs until well blended. On low speed, beat in flour, baking soda and salt until well combined, scraping bowl occasionally. Stir in chocolate chips.

**2.** Drop dough by rounded tablespoonfuls 2 inches apart onto ungreased cookie sheets.

**3.** Bake 8 to 10 minutes or until light golden brown. Cool 1 minute; remove from cookie sheets.

**High Altitude (3500–6500 ft): Bake 9 to 11 minutes.**

**1 Cookie:** Calories 120 (Calories from Fat 50); Total Fat 6g (Saturated Fat 3g; Trans Fat 0g); Cholesterol 20mg; Sodium 80mg; Total Carbohydrate 16g (Dietary Fiber 0g; Sugars 10g); Protein 1g

% Daily Value: Vitamin A 4%; Vitamin C 0%; Calcium 0%; Iron 4%

Exchanges: 1 Other Carbohydrate, 1 Fat

Carbohydrate Choices: 1

**VARIATIONS:**

**Chocolate Candy Cookies:** Substitute candy-coated chocolate pieces for the chocolate chips.

**Chocolate Chunk Cookies:** Substitute 1 to 2 bags (11. 5 to 12 oz. each) semisweet or white chocolate chunks for the chocolate chips.

# BROWN SUGAR–OATMEAL COOKIES

→ PREP TIME: 55 mins
START TO FINISH: 55 mins

**2 1/2 dozen cookies**

1 3/4 cups packed brown sugar
1/2 cup shortening
1/2 cup butter or margarine,
    softened
1 teaspoon vanilla
2 eggs
1 cup all-purpose flour
1 cup whole wheat flour
1 teaspoon baking powder
3 cups old-fashioned oats

**1.** Heat oven to 350°F. In large bowl, beat brown sugar, shortening and butter with electric mixer on medium speed until light and fluffy, scraping bowl occasionally. Beat in vanilla and eggs until well blended. On low speed, beat in all-purpose flour, whole wheat flour and baking powder until well combined, scraping bowl occasionally. Stir in oats.

**2.** Drop dough by heaping tablespoonfuls 2 inches apart onto ungreased cookie sheets.

**3.** Bake 10 to 14 minutes or until light golden brown. Cool 1 minute; remove from cookie sheets.

**High Altitude (3500–6500 ft): Heat oven to 375°F. Flatten cookies to about 1/2-inch thickness before baking.**

**1 Cookie:** Calories 170 (Calories from Fat 70); Total Fat 7g (Saturated Fat 2.5g; Trans Fat 1g); Cholesterol 20mg; Sodium 45mg; Total Carbohydrate 24g (Dietary Fiber 1g; Sugars 13g); Protein 3g

% Daily Value: Vitamin A 2%; Vitamin C 0%; Calcium 2%; Iron 6%

Exchanges: 1/2 Starch, 1 Other Carbohydrate, 1 1/2 Fat

Carbohydrate Choices: 1 1/2

> **BAKING TIP:**
> *Check your brown sugar often so you'll always be ready to go. If it's gotten hard, just seal it in a plastic bag with an apple wedge for a day or two to soften it, then throw away the apple. Soft, supple and ready to bake!*

# OATMEAL-RAISIN COOKIES

→ PREP TIME: 45 mins
START TO FINISH: 45 mins

**3 1/2 dozen cookies**

3/4 cup granulated sugar
1/4 cup packed brown sugar
1/2 cup butter or margarine,
    softened
1/2 teaspoon vanilla
1 egg
3/4 cup all-purpose flour
1/2 teaspoon baking soda
1/2 teaspoon ground cinnamon
1/4 teaspoon salt
1 1/2 cups quick-cooking oats
1/2 cup raisins
1/2 cup chopped nuts

**1.** Heat oven to 375°F. Grease cookie sheets with shortening or cooking spray. In large bowl, beat granulated sugar, brown sugar and butter with electric mixer on medium speed until light and fluffy, scraping bowl occasionally. Beat in vanilla and egg until well blended. On low speed, beat in flour, baking soda, cinnamon and salt until well combined, scraping bowl occasionally. Stir in oats, raisins and nuts.

**2.** Drop dough by rounded teaspoonfuls 2 inches apart onto cookie sheets.

**3.** Bake 7 to 10 minutes or until edges are light golden brown. Cool 1 minute; remove from cookie sheets.

**High Altitude (3500–6500 ft): Increase flour to 1 cup.**

**1 Cookie:** Calories 80 (Calories from Fat 30); Total Fat 3.5g (Saturated Fat 1.5g; Trans Fat 0g); Cholesterol 10mg; Sodium 45mg; Total Carbohydrate 10g (Dietary Fiber 0g; Sugars 6g); Protein 1g

% Daily Value: Vitamin A 0%; Vitamin C 0%; Calcium 0%; Iron 0%

Exchanges: 1/2 Other Carbohydrate, 1 Fat

Carbohydrate Choices: 1/2

> **BAKING TIP:**
> *Stop the raisin rut! Why not use another dried fruit? Try dried blueberries, cherries, cranberries, chopped dates, apricots or figs, or even dried mixed fruit.*

# FROSTED GINGER CUTOUTS

→ PREP TIME: 1 hr 20 mins
START TO FINISH: 3 hrs 20 mins

**3 dozen cookies**

〜〜〜〜〜〜〜〜〜〜〜〜

### COOKIES
1 cup shortening
1 cup molasses
3 cups all-purpose flour
1 1/2 teaspoons baking soda
1/2 teaspoon salt
1/2 teaspoon ground ginger
1/4 teaspoon ground nutmeg
1/4 teaspoon ground cloves

### FROSTING
1 package unflavored gelatin
3/4 cup water
3/4 cup granulated sugar
3/4 cup powdered sugar
3/4 teaspoon baking powder
1 teaspoon vanilla

**1.** In large bowl, beat shortening and molasses with electric mixer on medium speed until blended, scraping bowl occasionally. Stir in remaining cookie ingredients until well combined, scraping bowl occasionally. Cover dough with plastic wrap; refrigerate at least 2 hours for easier handling.

**2.** Heat oven to 350°F. On well-floured work surface, roll out dough with rolling pin to 1/4-inch thickness. Cut with floured 2 1/2-inch round cookie cutter; place 1 inch apart on ungreased cookie sheets.

**3.** Bake 6 to 9 minutes or until set. Cool 1 minute; remove from cookie sheets. Cool completely, about 10 minutes.

**4.** In 2-quart saucepan, pour gelatin over water; let stand 5 minutes. Stir in granulated sugar; heat over high heat until full rolling boil. Reduce heat to medium; simmer uncovered 10 minutes without stirring (temperature should read 220°F on candy thermometer). Remove from heat. With electric mixer on low speed, beat in powdered sugar until foamy. Add baking powder and vanilla; beat on low speed 5 minutes or until glossy and spreading consistency, scraping bowl occasionally.

**5.** Spread frosting on underside of each cookie to within 1/8 inch of edge. If desired, decorate cookies. Let stand until frosting is set before storing.

**High Altitude (3500–6500 ft): No change.**

**1 Cookie:** Calories 140 (Calories from Fat 50); Total Fat 6g (Saturated Fat 1.5g; Trans Fat 1g); Cholesterol 0mg; Sodium 100mg; Total Carbohydrate 22g (Dietary Fiber 0g; Sugars 12g); Protein 1g

% Daily Value: Vitamin A 0%; Vitamin C 0%; Calcium 2%; Iron 6%

Exchanges: 1 1/2 Other Carbohydrate, 1 Fat

Carbohydrate Choices: 1 1/2

> **BAKING TIP:**
> *This is an oldie but a goodie. When making the frosting, it's important to soak the gelatin in water for 5 minutes before heating it. This softens the gelatin so it'll dissolve completely when it's heated.*

# OLD-TIME SUGAR COOKIES

→ PREP TIME: 1 hr 15 mins
START TO FINISH: 1 hr 15 mins

**5 dozen cookies**

1 1/3 cups sugar
1/2 cup shortening
1/2 cup butter or margarine,
    softened
1/2 teaspoon vanilla
1/4 teaspoon almond extract
1 egg
2 cups all-purpose flour
1/2 teaspoon baking soda
1/2 teaspoon cream of tartar

**1.** Heat oven to 350°F. In large bowl, beat 1 cup of the sugar, the shortening and butter with electric mixer on medium speed until light and fluffy, scraping bowl occasionally. Beat in vanilla, almond extract and egg until well blended. On low speed, beat in flour, baking soda and cream of tartar until well combined, scraping bowl occasionally.

**2.** Shape dough into 1-inch balls. Roll balls in remaining 1/3 cup sugar; place 2 inches apart on ungreased cookie sheets. With bottom of glass dipped in sugar, flatten balls to 1/8-inch thickness.

**3.** Bake 7 to 12 minutes or until edges are light golden brown. Cool 1 minute; remove from cookie sheets.

**High Altitude (3500–6500 ft): Bake 8 to 13 minutes.**

**1 Cookie:** Calories 60 (Calories from Fat 30); Total Fat 3.5g (Saturated Fat 1g; Trans Fat 0g); Cholesterol 10mg; Sodium 20mg; Total Carbohydrate 8g (Dietary Fiber 0g; Sugars 4g); Protein 0g

% Daily Value: Vitamin A 0%; Vitamin C 0%; Calcium 0%; Iron 0%

Exchanges: 1/2 Other Carbohydrate, 1/2 Fat

Carbohydrate Choices: 1/2

# BASIC REFRIGERATOR COOKIES

→ **PREP TIME: 1 hr**
**START TO FINISH: 3 hrs**

**7 1/2 dozen cookies**

3/4 cup granulated sugar
3/4 cup packed brown sugar
1 cup butter or margarine,
    softened
1 1/2 teaspoons vanilla
2 eggs
3 cups all-purpose flour
1 1/2 teaspoons baking powder
3/4 teaspoon salt
1 cup finely chopped nuts

**1.** In large bowl, beat granulated sugar, brown sugar, butter, vanilla and eggs with electric mixer on medium speed until well blended, scraping bowl occasionally. On low speed, beat in flour, baking powder and salt until well combined, scraping bowl occasionally. Stir in nuts.

**2.** Divide dough into 3 equal parts; shape each into roll 1 1/2 inches in diameter. Wrap each roll in plastic wrap; refrigerate until firm, about 2 hours.

**3.** Heat oven to 425°F. Cut dough into 1/4-inch slices; place 1 inch apart on ungreased cookie sheets.

**4.** Bake 5 to 7 minutes or until light golden brown. Immediately remove from cookie sheets.

**High Altitude (3500–6500 ft): Add 3 tablespoons milk with sugar mixture.**

**1 Cookie:** Calories 60 (Calories from Fat 25); Total Fat 3g (Saturated Fat 1g; Trans Fat 0g); Cholesterol 10mg; Sodium 45mg; Total Carbohydrate 7g (Dietary Fiber 0g; Sugars 4g); Protein 0g

% Daily Value: Vitamin A 0%; Vitamin C 0%; Calcium 0%; Iron 0%

Exchanges: 1/2 Other Carbohydrate, 1/2 Fat

Carbohydrate Choices: 1/2

> **BAKING TIP:**
> *Make your own do-ahead dough. Cookie dough can be stored in the refrigerator for up to 2 weeks or in the freezer for up to 6 weeks. When you want, slice and bake the frozen dough as directed in the recipe.*

**VARIATIONS:**

**Coconut Refrigerator Cookies:** Add 1 cup coconut with nuts.

**Lemon or Orange Refrigerator Cookies:** Add 1 tablespoon grated lemon or orange peel with flour.

**Spice Refrigerator Cookies:** Add 1 teaspoon ground cinnamon, 1/2 teaspoon ground nutmeg and 1/4 to 1/2 teaspoon ground cloves with flour.

# PEANUT BUTTER COOKIES

→ PREP TIME: 50 mins
START TO FINISH: 50 mins

**4 dozen cookies**

~~~~~~~~~~~~~~~~~~~~~~~

1/2 cup granulated sugar
1/2 cup packed brown sugar
1/2 cup butter or margarine,
    softened
1/2 cup peanut butter
1 teaspoon vanilla
1 egg
1 1/4 cups all-purpose flour
1 teaspoon baking soda
1/2 teaspoon salt
4 teaspoons sugar

**1.** Heat oven to 375°F. In large bowl, beat 1/2 cup granulated sugar, the brown sugar and butter with electric mixer on medium speed until light and fluffy, scraping bowl occasionally. Beat in peanut butter, vanilla and egg until well blended. On low speed, beat in flour, baking soda and salt until well combined, scraping bowl occasionally.

**2.** Shape dough into 1-inch balls; place 2 inches apart on ungreased cookie sheets. With fork dipped in 4 teaspoons sugar, flatten balls in crisscross pattern.

**3.** Bake 6 to 9 minutes or until set and golden brown. Immediately remove from cookie sheets.

**High Altitude (3500–6500 ft): Increase flour to 1 1/3 cups.**

**1 Cookie:** Calories 70 (Calories from Fat 30); Total Fat 3.5g (Saturated Fat 1.5g; Trans Fat 0g); Cholesterol 10mg; Sodium 80mg; Total Carbohydrate 8g (Dietary Fiber 0g; Sugars 5g); Protein 1g

% Daily Value: Vitamin A 0%; Vitamin C 0%; Calcium 0%; Iron 0%

Exchanges: 1/2 Other Carbohydrate, 1/2 Fat

Carbohydrate Choices: 1/2

**VARIATIONS:**
**Chocolate Chip–Peanut Butter Cookies:** Stir 1 cup semisweet chocolate chips (6 oz.) into dough. 4 1/2 dozen cookies

**Nutty Peanut Butter Cookies:** Stir 1 cup chopped peanuts into dough. 4 1/2 dozen cookies

**Peanut Blossoms:** Increase 4 teaspoons sugar to 1/4 cup. Roll balls in sugar; place 1 inch apart on ungreased cookie sheets. Bake as directed in recipe. Immediately top each cookie with 1 milk chocolate candy drop or piece, pressing down firmly so cookie cracks around edge; remove from cookie sheets. 3 1/2 dozen cookies

**Peanut Butter and Jelly Thumbprints:** Increase 4 teaspoons sugar to 1/4 cup. Roll balls in sugar; place 1 inch apart on ungreased cookie sheets. With thumb or handle of wooden spoon, make deep indentation in center of each cookie. Bake as directed in recipe. Remove from cookie sheets; cool completely. Spoon 1/2 teaspoon jelly, jam or preserves into center of each cookie. 4 dozen cookies.

# SNICKERDOODLES

→ PREP TIME: 50 mins
START TO FINISH: 50 mins

**4 dozen cookies**

1 1/2 cups sugar
1/2 cup butter or margarine,
    softened
1 teaspoon vanilla
2 eggs
2 3/4 cups all-purpose flour
1 teaspoon cream of tartar
1/2 teaspoon baking soda
1/4 teaspoon salt
2 tablespoons sugar
2 teaspoons ground cinnamon

**1.** Heat oven to 400°F. In large bowl, beat 1 1/2 cups sugar and the butter with electric mixer on medium speed until light and fluffy, scraping bowl occasionally. Beat in vanilla and eggs until well blended. On low speed, beat in flour, cream of tartar, baking soda and salt until well combined, scraping bowl occasionally.

**2.** In small bowl, mix 2 tablespoons sugar and the cinnamon. Shape dough into 1-inch balls; roll in sugar-cinnamon mixture and place 2 inches apart on ungreased cookie sheets.

**3.** Bake 8 to 10 minutes or until set. Immediately remove from cookie sheets.

**High Altitude (3500–6500 ft): Bake 7 to 9 minutes.**

**1 Cookie:** Calories 70 (Calories from Fat 20); Total Fat 2g (Saturated Fat 1g; Trans Fat 0g); Cholesterol 15mg; Sodium 40mg; Total Carbohydrate 12g (Dietary Fiber 0g; Sugars 7g); Protein 1g

% Daily Value: Vitamin A 0%; Vitamin C 0%; Calcium 0%; Iron 2%

Exchanges: 1 Other Carbohydrate, 1/2 Fat

Carbohydrate Choices: 1

**VARIATIONS:**

**Chocolate Snickerdoodles:** Substitute 1/2 cup unsweetened baking cocoa for 1/2 cup of the flour. Bake 6 to 9 minutes.

**Whole Wheat Snickerdoodles:** Substitute 1 cup whole wheat flour for 1 cup of the all-purpose flour.

# SPICED CHOCOLATE CRINKLES

**5 dozen cookies**

~~~~~~~~~~~~~~~~~~~~~~~~~

1/4 cup butter or margarine
4 oz. unsweetened baking
    chocolate, cut into pieces
4 eggs
2 cups all-purpose flour
2 cups granulated sugar
1/2 cup chopped almonds
2 teaspoons baking powder
1/2 teaspoon salt
1/2 teaspoon ground ginger
1/2 teaspoon ground cinnamon
1/4 teaspoon ground cloves
Powdered sugar

**1.** In 3-quart saucepan, melt butter and chocolate over low heat, stirring constantly, until smooth. Remove from heat. Cool slightly, about 5 minutes.

**2.** With spoon, beat in eggs until well blended. Beat in remaining ingredients except powdered sugar until well combined. Cover dough with plastic wrap; refrigerate at least 1 hour for easier handling.

**3.** Heat oven to 300°F. Grease cookie sheets with shortening or cooking spray. Shape dough into 1-inch balls; roll in powdered sugar, coating heavily, and place 2 inches apart on cookie sheets.

**4.** Bake 13 to 18 minutes or until set. Immediately remove from cookie sheets.

**High Altitude (3500–6500 ft): No change.**

**1 Cookie:** Calories 80 (Calories from Fat 25); Total Fat 3g (Saturated Fat 1g; Trans Fat 0g); Cholesterol 15mg; Sodium 45mg; Total Carbohydrate 11g (Dietary Fiber 0g; Sugars 7g); Protein 1g

% Daily Value: Vitamin A 0%; Vitamin C 0%; Calcium 0%; Iron 2%

Exchanges: 1 Other Carbohydrate, 1/2 Fat

Carbohydrate Choices: 1

# GRANDMA'S DATE-FILLED COOKIES

→ **PREP TIME:** 1 hr
**START TO FINISH:** 3 hrs

**3 1/2 dozen cookies**

～～～～～～～～～～～～

## COOKIES
1 1/2 cups packed brown sugar
1 cup butter or margarine,
   softened
1 teaspoon vanilla
3 eggs
3 1/2 cups all-purpose flour
1 teaspoon baking soda

## FILLING
2 cups chopped dates
1 cup granulated sugar
1 cup water

**1.** In large bowl, beat brown sugar and butter with electric mixer on medium speed until light and fluffy, scraping bowl occasionally. Beat in vanilla and eggs until well blended. On low speed, beat in flour and baking soda until well combined, scraping bowl occasionally. Cover dough with plastic wrap; refrigerate at least 2 hours for easier handling.

**2.** Meanwhile, in 2-quart saucepan, mix filling ingredients; heat to boiling. Reduce heat to low; simmer uncovered 10 minutes, stirring frequently. Refrigerate until ready to use (mixture will thicken as it cools).

**3.** Heat oven to 375°F. Work with 1/3 of the dough at a time; keep remaining dough refrigerated. On well-floured work surface, roll out dough with rolling pin to 1/8-inch thickness. Cut with floured 2 1/2-inch round cookie cutter. In half of cookies, cut out and remove 1-inch round or desired shape of hole from center. Place whole cookies on ungreased cookie sheets.

**4.** Spoon 1 teaspoon cooled filling onto center of each whole cookie; top with dough ring. With fingertips or fork, press edges of dough to seal. Return dough centers to remaining dough for rerolling.

**5.** Bake 7 to 10 minutes or until light golden brown. Cool 1 minute; remove from cookie sheets.

**High Altitude (3500–6500 ft): No change.**

**1 Cookie:** Calories 160 (Calories from Fat 45); Total Fat 5g (Saturated Fat 2.5g; Trans Fat 0g); Cholesterol 25mg; Sodium 65mg; Total Carbohydrate 27g (Dietary Fiber 0g; Sugars 18g); Protein 2g

% Daily Value: Vitamin A 4%; Vitamin C 0%; Calcium 0%; Iron 4%

Exchanges: 2 Other Carbohydrate, 1 Fat

Carbohydrate Choices: 2

> **BAKING TIP:**
> *Just a few ingredients combine to create this soft, old-fashioned filled cookie. You can chop whole pitted dates or buy chopped dates.*

# MEXICAN WEDDING CAKES

→ PREP TIME: 1 hr 30 mins
START TO FINISH: 1 hr 30 mins

**4 1/2 dozen cookies**

4 1/2 dozen cookies
1 1/4 cups powdered sugar
1 cup butter or margarine,
   softened
2 teaspoons vanilla
2 cups all-purpose flour
1 cup finely chopped or ground
   almonds or pecans
1/4 teaspoon salt

**1.** Heat oven to 325°F. In large bowl, beat 1/2 cup of the powdered sugar, the butter and vanilla with electric mixer on medium speed until light and fluffy, scraping bowl occasionally. On low speed, beat in flour, almonds and salt until well combined, scraping bowl occasionally.

**2.** Shape dough into 1-inch balls; place 1 inch apart on ungreased cookie sheets.

**3.** Bake 13 to 17 minutes or until set but not brown. Immediately remove from cookie sheets; place on wire racks. Cool slightly, about 10 minutes.

**4.** Roll cookies in remaining 3/4 cup powdered sugar; return to wire racks. Cool completely, about 15 minutes. Reroll cookies in powdered sugar.

**High Altitude (3500–6500 ft): No change.**

**1 Cookie:** Calories 80 (Calories from Fat 40); Total Fat 4.5g (Saturated Fat 2g; Trans Fat 0g); Cholesterol 10mg; Sodium 35mg; Total Carbohydrate 9g (Dietary Fiber 0g; Sugars 5g); Protein 1g

% Daily Value: Vitamin A 2%; Vitamin C 0%; Calcium 0%; Iron 0%

Exchanges: 1/2 Other Carbohydrate, 1 Fat

Carbohydrate Choices: 1/2

> **BAKING TIP:**
> *Shape these buttery shortbread cookies into balls, crescents or small logs. For a fun variation, dip them into melted chocolate instead of the powdered sugar.*

PILLSBURY BAKING

●

**90**

# SUGAR-AND-SPICE SHORTBREAD STICKS

→ PREP TIME: 1 hr
START TO FINISH: 2 hrs

**4 dozen cookies**

~~~~~~~~~~~~~~~~~~~~~

### COOKIES
3/4 cup packed brown sugar
1 cup butter, softened
1 teaspoon vanilla
1 egg
2 3/4 cups all-purpose flour
3/4 teaspoon apple pie spice

### GLAZE
1 1/2 cups powdered sugar
1/2 teaspoon apple pie spice
1 to 2 tablespoons apple juice

**1.** In large bowl, beat brown sugar, butter, vanilla and egg with electric mixer on medium speed until light and fluffy, scraping bowl occasionally. On low speed, beat in flour and 3/4 teaspoon apple pie spice until well combined, scraping bowl occasionally.

**2.** Divide dough in half; shape each half into flattened disk. Wrap each in plastic wrap; refrigerate about 1 hour for easier handling.

**3.** Heat oven to 350°F. Work with half of dough at a time; keep remaining dough refrigerated. On lightly floured work surface, roll out dough with rolling pin into 12x6-inch rectangle. Cut dough rectangle lengthwise in half; cut each half into 1-inch-wide sticks. Place sticks 1/2 inch apart on ungreased cookie sheets.

**4.** Bake 12 to 15 minutes or until edges are light golden brown. Immediately remove from cookie sheets. Cool completely, about 10 minutes.

**5.** Meanwhile, in small bowl, mix glaze ingredients until smooth, adding enough apple juice for desired glaze consistency. Spread glaze on tops of cookies. Let stand until glaze is set before storing.

**High Altitude (3500–6500 ft): Bake 15 to 18 minutes.**

**1 Cookie:** Calories 90 (Calories from Fat 35); Total Fat 4g (Saturated Fat 2g; Trans Fat 0g); Cholesterol 15mg; Sodium 30mg; Total Carbohydrate 13g (Dietary Fiber 0g; Sugars 7g); Protein 0g
% Daily Value: Vitamin A 4%; Vitamin C 0%; Calcium 0%; Iron 2%
Exchanges: 1 Other Carbohydrate, 1 Fat
Carbohydrate Choices: 1

**BAKING TIP:**
*For well-shaped shortbread sticks, use the flat side of a clean ruler to straighten the sides of the dough into an even rectangle. Also use the ruler to cut the rectangle neatly in half and then into sticks.*

CHERISHED COOKIES ●

# CINNAMON TEA CAKES

→ PREP TIME: 1 hr 30 mins
START TO FINISH: 1 hr 30 mins

**4 1/2 dozen cookies**

~~~~~~~~~~~~~~~~~~~~~~

## COOKIES
1/2 cup powdered sugar
1 cup butter or margarine,
    softened
1 teaspoon vanilla
2 cups all-purpose flour
1 cup finely chopped or ground
    walnuts
1/2 teaspoon ground cinnamon
1/8 teaspoon salt

## COATING
1/4 cup granulated sugar
1 teaspoon ground cinnamon

**1.** Heat oven to 325°F. In large bowl, beat powdered sugar, butter and vanilla with electric mixer on medium speed until light and fluffy, scraping bowl occasionally. On low speed, beat remaining cookie ingredients until well combined, scraping bowl occasionally.

**2.** Shape dough into 1-inch balls; place 1 inch apart on ungreased cookie sheets.

**3.** Bake 14 to 16 minutes or until set but not brown. Meanwhile, in small bowl, mix coating ingredients; set aside. Immediately remove cookies from cookie sheets; place on wire racks. Cool slightly, about 3 minutes.

**4.** Roll warm cookies in coating; return to wire racks. Cool completely, about 15 minutes. Reroll cookies in coating.

**High Altitude (3500–6500 ft): Heat oven to 350°F.**

**1 Cookie:** Calories 70 (Calories from Fat 45); Total Fat 5g (Saturated Fat 2g; Trans Fat 0g); Cholesterol 10mg; Sodium 30mg; Total Carbohydrate 6g (Dietary Fiber 0g; Sugars 2g); Protein 0g

% Daily Value: Vitamin A 2%; Vitamin C 0%; Calcium 0%; Iron 0%

Exchanges: 1/2 Other Carbohydrate, 1 Fat

Carbohydrate Choices: 1/2

> **BAKING TIP:**
> *Use a small or mini food processor to grind the nuts. Process them with on-and-off motions into fine pieces, but not until they're ground into powder.*

# CHOCOLATE STAR GINGERSNAPS

→ PREP TIME: 1 hr 10 mins
START TO FINISH: 1 hr 10 mins

**4 dozen cookies**

〰〰〰〰〰〰〰〰〰〰

1 cup packed brown sugar
3/4 cup shortening
1/4 cup molasses
1 egg
2 3/4 cups all-purpose flour
1 teaspoon baking soda
1 teaspoon ground ginger
1 teaspoon ground cinnamon
1/4 teaspoon ground cloves
1/4 cup granulated sugar
48 chocolate star candies

**1.** Heat oven to 375°F. In large bowl, beat brown sugar, shortening and molasses with electric mixer on medium speed until smooth, scraping bowl occasionally. Beat in egg until well blended. On low speed, beat in flour, baking soda, ginger, cinnamon and cloves until well combined, scraping bowl occasionally.

**2.** Shape dough into 1-inch balls; roll in granulated sugar and place 2 inches apart on ungreased cookie sheets.

**3.** Bake 7 to 9 minutes or until tops are cracked and edges are set. Immediately press 1 candy in center of each cookie. Cool 1 minute; remove from cookie sheets.

**High Altitude (3500–6500 ft): Decrease brown sugar to 3/4 cup.**

**1 Cookie:** Calories 100 (Calories from Fat 40); Total Fat 4.5g (Saturated Fat 1.5g; Trans Fat 0.5g); Cholesterol 5mg; Sodium 35mg; Total Carbohydrate 15g (Dietary Fiber 0g; Sugars 9g); Protein 1g

% Daily Value: Vitamin A 0%; Vitamin C 0%; Calcium 0%; Iron 4%

Exchanges: 1 Other Carbohydrate, 1 Fat

Carbohydrate Choices: 1

# CHOCOLATE-HAZELNUT BISCOTTI

→ **PREP TIME:** 1 hr 15 mins
**START TO FINISH:** 1 hr 40 mins

**3 dozen biscotti**

1 cup sugar
1/2 cup butter or margarine,
    softened
2 teaspoons vanilla
3 eggs
2 2/3 cups all-purpose flour
1/4 cup unsweetened Dutch
    process baking cocoa
2 teaspoons baking powder
3/4 cup hazelnuts (filberts),
    toasted, chopped
1/2 cup miniature semisweet
    chocolate chips
2 oz. vanilla-flavored candy coat-
    ing or almond bark, chopped

**1.** Heat oven to 350°F. Lightly grease cookie sheet with shortening or cooking spray. In large bowl, beat sugar and butter with electric mixer on medium speed until light and fluffy, scraping bowl occasionally. Beat in vanilla and eggs until well blended. On low speed, beat in flour, cocoa and baking powder until well combined, scraping bowl occasionally. Stir in toasted hazelnuts and chocolate chips.

**2.** Divide dough in half; shape each into 10-inch log. Place logs 5 inches apart on cookie sheet; flatten each until 3 inches wide.

**3.** Bake 20 to 25 minutes or until firm when touched in center. Cool on cookie sheet 10 minutes. With serrated knife, cut diagonally into 1/2-inch-thick slices. Arrange slices, cut side down, on same cookie sheet.

**4.** Bake 10 minutes. Turn slices over; bake 5 to 10 minutes longer or until cut sides are lightly browned and crisp. Remove from cookie sheet; place on wire rack. Cool completely, about 10 minutes.

**5.** In small microwavable bowl, microwave candy coating on High 45 seconds, stirring once, until melted and smooth. If necessary, microwave 20 seconds longer. Drizzle over biscotti.

**High Altitude (3500–6500 ft): No change.**

**1 Biscotto:** Calories 130 (Calories from Fat 50); Total Fat 6g (Saturated Fat 2.5g; Trans Fat 0g); Cholesterol 25mg; Sodium 50mg; Total Carbohydrate 16g (Dietary Fiber 0g; Sugars 8g); Protein 2g

% Daily Value: Vitamin A 2%; Vitamin C 0%; Calcium 2%; Iron 4%

Exchanges: 1/2 Starch, 1/2 Other Carbohydrate, 1 Fat

Carbohydrate Choices: 1

> **BAKING TIP:**
> *To toast the chopped hazelnuts, spread them on cookie sheet. Bake in a 350°F oven for 8 to 10 minutes, stirring occasionally, until they're golden brown. To remove the skins, roll the warm nuts in a clean kitchen towel.*

# CRANBERRY-ORANGE PINWHEELS

➔ PREP TIME: 1 hr
START TO FINISH: 4 hrs

**3 dozen cookies**

~~~~~~~~~~~~~~~~~~~~

### COOKIES
3/4 cup packed brown sugar
1/2 cup butter or margarine,
　softened
1 egg
1 3/4 cups all-purpose flour
1 teaspoon baking powder
1 teaspoon grated orange peel
1/4 teaspoon salt
1/4 teaspoon ground allspice

### FILLING
3/4 cup whole berry cranberry
　sauce
1/4 cup orange marmalade
1 tablespoon cornstarch

**1.** In large bowl, beat brown sugar, butter and egg with electric mixer on medium speed until light and fluffy, scraping bowl occasionally. Beat in remaining cookie ingredients until well blended, scraping bowl occasionally. Cover dough with plastic wrap; refrigerate 1 hour for easier handling.

**2.** Meanwhile, in 1-quart saucepan, mix filling ingredients. Heat to boiling over medium heat, stirring constantly. Cover; refrigerate until thoroughly chilled.

**3.** On lightly floured work surface, roll dough with rolling pin into 16x8-inch rectangle. Spoon and spread cooled filling evenly over dough to within 1/2 inch of edges. Starting with one 16-inch side, roll up. Cut roll in half to form 2 (8-inch) rolls. Wrap each roll in plastic wrap; refrigerate at least 2 hours.

**4.** Heat oven to 375°F. Generously grease cookie sheets with shortening or cooking spray. With sharp knife, cut dough into 1/2-inch slices; place 2 inches apart on cookie sheets.

**5.** Bake 9 to 13 minutes or until light golden brown. Immediately remove from cookie sheets.

**High Altitude (3500–6500 ft): Increase flour to 2 cups.**

**1 Cookie:** Calories 80 (Calories from Fat 25); Total Fat 3g (Saturated Fat 1.5g; Trans Fat 0g); Cholesterol 15mg; Sodium 55mg; Total Carbohydrate 13g (Dietary Fiber 0g; Sugars 8g); Protein 0g

% Daily Value: Vitamin A 2%; Vitamin C 0%; Calcium 0%; Iron 2%

Exchanges: 1 Other Carbohydrate, 1/2 Fat

Carbohydrate Choices: 1

> **BAKING TIP:**
> *You can make the dough for these scrumptious cookies ahead of time. Refrigerate the roll of dough for a few days—when you're ready to bake the cookies, just slice and bake.*

# FAVORITE FUDGE BROWNIES

→ PREP TIME: 25 mins
START TO FINISH: 3 hrs

**24 bars**

~~~~~~~~~~~~~~~~~~~~~

## BROWNIES

3/4 cup butter or margarine,
   softened
5 oz. unsweetened baking chocolate, cut into pieces
1 tablespoon vanilla
2 1/4 cups granulated sugar
4 eggs
1 1/3 cups all-purpose flour
1 1/2 cups coarsely chopped nuts

## FROSTING

1 1/2 cups powdered sugar
2 tablespoons unsweetened baking cocoa
1/4 cup butter or margarine,
   softened
2 tablespoons milk
1/2 teaspoon vanilla

## GARNISH

Whole pecans or walnuts, if
   desired

**1.** Heat oven to 375°F. Grease 13x9-inch pan with shortening or cook-ing spray. In 1-quart saucepan, melt 3/4 cup butter and the chocolate over low heat, stirring constantly, until smooth. Remove from heat. Stir in 1 tablespoon vanilla; set aside.

**2.** In large bowl, beat granulated sugar and eggs with electric mixer on medium speed 3 to 4 minutes or until sugar is dissolved. Stir in flour, chocolate mixture and nuts just until well blended. Pour batter into pan.

**3.** Bake 25 to 35 minutes. DO NOT OVERBAKE. Cool completely, about 1 hour.

**4.** In small bowl, beat frosting ingredients with electric mixer on low speed until smooth; spread over cooled bars. Refrigerate 1 hour. Cut into 6 rows by 4 rows. If desired, garnish each bar with pecans.

**High Altitude (3500–6500 ft): No change.**

**1 Bar:** Calories 300 (Calories from Fat 150); Total Fat 17g (Saturated Fat 7g; Trans Fat 0g); Cholesterol 55mg; Sodium 65mg; Total Carbohydrate 35g (Dietary Fiber 2g; Sugars 26g); Protein 4g

% Daily Value: Vitamin A 6%; Vitamin C 0%; Calcium 2%; Iron 6%

Exchanges: 1 Starch, 1 1/2 Other Carbohydrate, 3 Fat

Carbohydrate Choices: 2

# FUDGY S'MORE BARS

→ PREP TIME: 20 mins
START TO FINISH: 1 hr 35 mins

**32 bars**

## CRUST
1 cup graham cracker crumbs
   (12 squares)
1/2 cup all-purpose flour
3/4 cup packed brown sugar
1/2 teaspoon baking soda
1/2 cup butter or margarine,
   softened

## TOPPING
4 cups miniature marshmallows
3/4 cup candy-coated chocolate
   pieces
1/4 cup hot fudge topping,
   heated

**1.** Heat oven to 350°F. Grease 13x9-inch pan with shortening or cooking spray. In large bowl, beat crust ingredients with electric mixer on low speed until coarse crumbs form, scraping bowl occasionally. Press mixture evenly in bottom of pan.

**2.** Bake 10 to 12 minutes or until golden brown. Sprinkle marshmallows evenly over crust; bake 1 to 2 minutes longer or until marshmallows begin to puff.

**3.** Sprinkle chocolate pieces evenly over marshmallows; drizzle warm topping over top. Cool completely, about 1 hour. Cut into 8 rows by 4 rows.

**High Altitude (3500–6500 ft): No change.**

**1 Bar:** Calories 120 (Calories from Fat 40); Total Fat 4.5g (Saturated Fat 2.5g; Trans Fat 0g); Cholesterol 10mg; Sodium 70mg; Total Carbohydrate 19g (Dietary Fiber 0g; Sugars 14g); Protein 0g

% Daily Value: Vitamin A 2%; Vitamin C 0%; Calcium 0%; Iron 0%

Exchanges: 1 Other Carbohydrate, 1 Fat

Carbohydrate Choices: 1

# CARAMEL-FUDGE BROWNIES

→ PREP TIME: 30 mins
START TO FINISH: 3 hrs

**24 brownies**

~~~~~~~~~~~~~~~~~~~~~~~~~~

## FILLING
1 bag (14 oz.) caramels,
   unwrapped
1/2 cup evaporated milk

## BROWNIES
1 cup butter
2 cups sugar
2 teaspoons vanilla
4 eggs, slightly beaten
1 1/4 cups all-purpose flour
3/4 cup unsweetened baking
   cocoa
1/4 teaspoon salt
1 bag (11.5 or 12 oz.) semisweet
   chocolate chunks (2 cups)
1 1/2 cups chopped pecans
1 teaspoon vegetable oil

**1.** Heat oven to 350°F. Grease 13x9-inch pan with shortening or cooking spray. In 1-quart saucepan, cook caramels and milk over low heat, stirring frequently, until caramels are melted and smooth.

**2.** In 2-quart saucepan, melt butter over low heat. Remove from heat. Stir in sugar, vanilla and eggs until well blended. Stir in flour, cocoa and salt until well combined. Stir in 1 1/2 cups of the chocolate chunks and 1 cup of the pecans. Spoon and spread batter evenly in pan.

**3.** Gently and evenly drizzle caramel filling over batter to prevent large pockets of caramel and to prevent caramel from reaching bottom of bars (caramel can cover entire surface of batter).

**4.** Bake 35 to 40 minutes or until set.

**5.** In 1-quart saucepan, melt remaining 1/2 cup chocolate chunks with oil over low heat, stirring frequently, until smooth. Drizzle over warm brownies. Sprinkle with remaining 1/2 cup pecans; press in lightly. Cool 20 minutes. Refrigerate until chocolate is set, about 1 hour 30 minutes. Cut into 6 rows by 4 rows. If refrigerated longer, let stand at room temperature 20 minutes before serving.

**High Altitude (3500–6500 ft): Increase flour to 1 1/2 cups.**

**1 Brownie:** Calories 380 (Calories from Fat 180); Total Fat 20g (Saturated Fat 9g; Trans Fat 0g); Cholesterol 60mg; Sodium 135mg; Total Carbohydrate 46g (Dietary Fiber 3g; Sugars 33g); Protein 5g

% Daily Value: Vitamin A 8%; Vitamin C 0%; Calcium 6%; Iron 8%

Exchanges: 1 Starch, 2 Other Carbohydrate, 4 Fat

Carbohydrate Choices: 3

> **BAKING TIP:**
> *You can use semisweet chocolate chips in place of the chunks in these incredibly indulgent brownies. For a colorful garnish, top each brownie with a fresh strawberry or raspberry.*

# PEANUT BRITTLE BARS

→ PREP TIME: 10 mins
START TO FINISH: 1 hr 45 mins

**48 bars**

~~~~~~~~~~~~~~~~~~~~~~~~~~~~~~

## CRUST
2 cups all-purpose flour
1 cup packed brown sugar
1 teaspoon baking soda
1/4 teaspoon salt
1 cup butter or margarine,
   cut into pieces

## TOPPING
2 cups salted peanuts
1 cup milk chocolate chips (6 oz.)
1 jar (12.5 oz.) caramel topping
3 tablespoons all-purpose flour

**1.** Heat oven to 350°F. Grease 15x10x1-inch pan with shortening or cooking spray. In large bowl, mix all crust ingredients except butter. With pastry blender or fork, cut in butter until crumbly. Press mixture evenly in bottom of pan.

**2.** Bake 8 to 14 minutes or until golden brown. Sprinkle peanuts and chocolate chips over warm base. In small bowl, mix caramel topping and 3 tablespoons flour until well blended; drizzle evenly over chocolate chips and peanuts.

**3.** Bake 12 to 18 minutes longer or until topping is set and golden brown. Cool completely, about 1 hour. Cut into 8 rows by 6 rows.

**High Altitude (3500–6500 ft): No change.**

**1 Bar:** Calories 150 (Calories from Fat 70); Total Fat 8g (Saturated Fat 3g; Trans Fat 0g); Cholesterol 10mg; Sodium 120mg; Total Carbohydrate 17g (Dietary Fiber 0g; Sugars 10g); Protein 3g

% Daily Value: Vitamin A 4%; Vitamin C 0%; Calcium 2%; Iron 2%

Exchanges: 1/2 Starch, 1/2 Other Carbohydrate, 1 1/2 Fat

Carbohydrate Choices: 1

# SALTED PEANUT CHEWS

→ PREP TIME: 35 mins
START TO FINISH: 1 hr 35 mins

**36 bars**

〜〜〜〜〜〜〜〜〜〜〜〜

## BASE
1 1/2 cups all-purpose flour
2/3 cup packed brown sugar
1/2 teaspoon baking powder
1/2 teaspoon salt
1/4 teaspoon baking soda
1/2 cup butter or margarine,
    softened
1 teaspoon vanilla
2 egg yolks
3 cups miniature marshmallows

## TOPPING
2/3 cup corn syrup
1/4 cup butter or margarine
2 teaspoons vanilla
1 bag (10 oz.) peanut butter chips
    (1 2/3 cups)
2 cups crisp rice cereal
2 cups salted peanuts

**1.** Heat oven to 350°F. In large bowl, beat base ingredients except marshmallows with electric mixer on low speed until crumbly. Press mixture firmly in bottom of ungreased 13x9-inch pan.

**2.** Bake 12 to 15 minutes or until light golden brown. Immediately sprinkle marshmallows evenly over base; bake 1 to 2 minutes longer or until marshmallows just begin to puff. Cool while preparing topping.

**3.** In 3-quart saucepan, mix topping ingredients except cereal and peanuts. Heat over low heat, stirring constantly, just until chips are melted and mixture is smooth. Remove from heat. Stir in cereal and peanuts. Immediately spoon warm topping over marshmallows; spread to cover. Refrigerate until firm, about 45 minutes. Cut into 6 rows by 6 rows.

**High Altitude (3500–6500 ft): Heat oven to 375°F.**

**1 Bar:** Calories 200 (Calories from Fat 90); Total Fat 11g (Saturated Fat 3g; Trans Fat 0g); Cholesterol 20mg; Sodium 160mg; Total Carbohydrate 23g (Dietary Fiber 1g; Sugars 13g); Protein 4g

% Daily Value: Vitamin A 4%; Vitamin C 0%; Calcium 0%; Iron 4%

Exchanges: 1 Starch, 1/2 Other Carbohydrate, 2 Fat

Carbohydrate Choices: 1 1/2

> **BAKING TIP:**
> *Sweet and salty, this bar is a crispy, crunchy treat.*

# CARAMEL APPLE BARS

→ PREP TIME: 30 mins
START TO FINISH: 1 hr 55 mins

**48 bars**

~~~~~~~~~~~~~~~~~~~~~~~~~~~~~~

### BASE AND TOPPING
2 cups all-purpose flour
2 cups quick-cooking oats
1 1/2 cups packed brown sugar
1 teaspoon baking soda
1 1/4 cups butter or margarine,
   melted

### FILLING
1 1/2 cups caramel topping
1/2 cup all-purpose flour
2 cups coarsely chopped peeled
   apples (2 medium)
1/2 cup chopped walnuts or
   pecans

**1.** Heat oven to 350°F. Grease 15x10x1-inch pan with shortening or cooking spray. In large bowl, beat base and topping ingredients with electric mixer on low speed until crumbly, scraping bowl occasionally. Press half of mixture (about 2 1/2 cups) evenly in bottom of pan; reserve remaining mixture for topping.

**2.** Bake 8 minutes. Meanwhile, in 1-quart saucepan, mix caramel topping and 1/2 cup flour until well blended. Heat to boiling over medium heat, stirring constantly. Boil 3 to 5 minutes, stirring constantly, until mixture thickens slightly.

**3.** Sprinkle apples and walnuts over warm base; pour caramel mixture evenly over top. Sprinkle with reserved topping mixture. Bake 20 to 25 minutes longer or until golden brown. Cool 30 minutes. Refrigerate until set, about 30 minutes. Cut into 8 rows by 6 rows.

**High Altitude (3500–6500 ft): Heat oven to 375°F.**

**1 Bar:** Calories 150 (Calories from Fat 50); Total Fat 6g (Saturated Fat 2.5g; Trans Fat 0g); Cholesterol 15mg; Sodium 95mg; Total Carbohydrate 22g (Dietary Fiber 0g; Sugars 12g); Protein 2g
% Daily Value: Vitamin A 4%; Vitamin C 0%; Calcium 0%; Iron 4%
Exchanges: 1 1/2 Other Carbohydrate, 1 Fat
Carbohydrate Choices: 1 1/2

### BAKING TIP:
*Use tart, firm-textured apples to complement the sweetness of the caramel. Choose Braeburn, Cortland, Granny Smith or Haralson.*

# ORANGE-SPICE PUMPKIN BARS WITH BROWNED BUTTER FROSTING

→ PREP TIME: 20 mins
START TO FINISH: 2 hrs 5 mins

**48 bars**

~~~~~~~~~~~~~~~~~~~~~~~~~~~~

## BARS
2 cups all-purpose flour
1 1/2 cups granulated sugar
2 teaspoons baking powder
1 teaspoon baking soda
2 teaspoons pumpkin pie spice
2 teaspoons grated orange peel
1/4 teaspoon salt
1/2 cup oil
1/2 cup orange juice
1 can (15 oz.) pumpkin (not pumpkin pie mix)
2 eggs

## FROSTING
1/3 cup butter (do not use margarine)
2 cups powdered sugar
1/2 teaspoon vanilla
2 to 4 tablespoons milk

**1.** Heat oven to 350°F. Grease 15x10x1-inch pan with shortening or cooking spray; lightly flour. In large bowl, beat bar ingredients with electric mixer on low speed until moistened, scraping bowl occasionally. Beat on medium speed 2 minutes, scraping bowl occasionally. Spread batter evenly in pan.

**2.** Bake 23 to 27 minutes or until toothpick inserted in center comes out clean. Cool completely, about 1 hour.

**3.** In 2-quart saucepan, heat butter over medium heat, stirring constantly, until light golden brown. Remove from heat. Stir in powdered sugar, vanilla and enough milk until smooth and desired spreading consistency. Immediately spread frosting over cooled bars. Refrigerate until set, about 15 minutes. Cut into 8 rows by 6 rows. If desired, garnish each bar with orange peel strip.

**High Altitude (3500–6500 ft): No change.**

**1 Bar:** Calories 100 (Calories from Fat 35); Total Fat 4g (Saturated Fat 1g; Trans Fat 0g); Cholesterol 10mg; Sodium 70mg; Total Carbohydrate 16g (Dietary Fiber 0g; Sugars 12g); Protein 0g

% Daily Value: Vitamin A 30%; Vitamin C 0%; Calcium 0%; Iron 2%

Exchanges: 1 Other Carbohydrate, 1 Fat

Carbohydrate Choices: 1

> **BAKING TIP:**
> *Pumpkin pie spice is a blend of spices to flavor pumpkin. If you want to make your own, mix 1 1/2 teaspoons cinnamon, 1/4 teaspoon ginger, 1/4 teaspoon nutmeg and 1/8 teaspoon cloves.*

# MINT TRUFFLE CUPS

→ PREP TIME: 35 mins
START TO FINISH: 2 hrs 40 mins

**2 dozen cookies**

~~~~~~~~~~~~~~~~~~~~~~~~~~~~

### CRUST
1/2 cup powdered sugar
1/2 cup butter or margarine,
  softened
1 egg
1 cup all-purpose flour
1/4 cup unsweetened baking
  cocoa

### FILLING
2/3 cup semisweet chocolate
  chips
1/2 cup whipping (heavy) cream
1/4 teaspoon peppermint extract

### TOPPING
12 thin rectangular creme de
  menthe chocolate candies,
  unwrapped, coarsely chopped

**1.** In medium bowl, beat powdered sugar and butter with electric mixer on medium speed until light and fluffy, scraping bowl occasionally. Beat in egg until well blended. On low speed, beat in flour and cocoa until well combined, scraping bowl occasionally. Cover dough with plastic wrap; refrigerate 1 to 2 hours for easier handling.

**2.** Heat oven to 325°F. Divide dough into 24 equal pieces. Place 1 piece in each of 24 ungreased mini muffin cups; press in bottom and up side of each cup, level with top of cup.

**3.** Bake 13 to 16 minutes or until set. Cool in pans on wire racks 20 minutes; remove from muffin cups.

**4.** Meanwhile, in 2-quart saucepan, heat filling ingredients over low heat, stirring constantly, until chocolate is melted and smooth. Remove from heat. Cool until filling thickens slightly, about 20 minutes.

**5.** Spoon about 2 teaspoons filling into each baked cup. Refrigerate until set, at least 30 minutes. Sprinkle chopped candies on top of each cookie; press in lightly. Store in refrigerator; let stand at room temperature about 30 minutes before serving.

**High Altitude (3500–6500 ft): Bake 15 to 18 minutes.**

**1 Cookie:** Calories 120 (Calories from Fat 70); Total Fat 8g (Saturated Fat 4.5g; Trans Fat 0g); Cholesterol 25mg; Sodium 35mg; Total Carbohydrate 11g (Dietary Fiber 0g; Sugars 6g); Protein 1g

% Daily Value: Vitamin A 4%; Vitamin C 0%; Calcium 0%; Iron 4%

Exchanges: 1 Other Carbohydrate, 1 1/2 Fat

Carbohydrate Choices: 1

**BAKING TIP:**
*Use peppermint extract, rather than mint, for this recipe, as peppermint blends better with the rest of the ingredients.*

# CHOCOLATE CHIP–PEANUT BUTTER BARS

PREP TIME: 15 mins
START TO FINISH: 2 hrs

**36 bars**

〜〜〜〜〜〜〜〜〜〜〜

### BASE AND TOPPING
2 1/4 cups quick-cooking oats
1 1/4 cups packed brown sugar
1 cup all-purpose flour
1/2 teaspoon baking soda
1 cup butter, softened

### FILLING
1 can (14 oz.) sweetened condensed milk (not evaporated)
1/4 cup peanut butter
1/2 teaspoon vanilla
1 cup semisweet chocolate chips (6 oz.)
1/2 cup coarsely chopped salted peanuts

**1.** Heat oven to 350°F. Grease 13x9-inch pan with shortening or cooking spray. In large bowl, beat base and topping ingredients with electric mixer on low speed until crumbly, scraping bowl occasionally. Reserve 2 cups crumb mixture for topping; press remaining mixture evenly in bottom of pan.

**2.** In small bowl, mix condensed milk, peanut butter and vanilla with spoon until well blended. Pour evenly over base. Sprinkle with chocolate chips and peanuts. Sprinkle reserved crumb mixture over top; press down gently.

**3.** Bake 25 to 30 minutes or until golden brown (center will not be set). Cool completely, about 1 hour 15 minutes. Cut into 6 rows by 6 rows.

**High Altitude (3500–6500 ft): Bake 30 to 35 minutes.**

**1 Bar:** Calories 190 (Calories from Fat 90); Total Fat 10g (Saturated Fat 4.5g; Trans Fat 0g); Cholesterol 15mg; Sodium 85mg; Total Carbohydrate 23g (Dietary Fiber 1g; Sugars 16g); Protein 3g

% Daily Value: Vitamin A 4%; Vitamin C 0%; Calcium 4%; Iron 4%

Exchanges: 1/2 Starch, 1 Other Carbohydrate, 2 Fat

Carbohydrate Choices: 1 1/2

# RASPBERRY-FILLED WHITE CHOCOLATE BARS

→ PREP TIME: 25 mins
START TO FINISH: 2 hrs 15 mins

**24 bars**

1/2 cup butter or margarine
1 bag (12 oz.) white vanilla
   baking chips (2 cups) or
   2 packages (6 oz. each)
   white chocolate baking bars,
   chopped
2 eggs
1/2 cup sugar
1 cup all-purpose flour
1/2 teaspoon salt
1 teaspoon amaretto or
   almond extract
1/2 cup raspberry spreadable
   fruit or jam
1/4 cup sliced almonds, toasted

**1.** Heat oven to 325°F. Grease 9-inch square pan or 8-inch square (2-quart) glass baking dish with shortening or cooking spray; lightly flour. In 1-quart saucepan, melt butter over low heat. Remove from heat. Add 1 cup of the vanilla baking chips (or 1 chopped white chocolate baking bar). LET STAND; DO NOT STIR.

**2.** In large bowl, beat eggs with electric mixer on medium speed until foamy. Gradually beat in sugar on high speed until lemon-colored, scraping bowl occasionally. On medium speed, beat in chip mixture until well blended. On low speed, beat in flour, salt and amaretto just until combined, scraping bowl occasionally. Spread half of batter (about 1 cup) evenly in pan; set remaining batter aside.

**3.** Bake 15 to 20 minutes or until light golden brown. Meanwhile, stir remaining 1 cup vanilla baking chips (or 1 chopped white chocolate baking bar) into remaining half of batter; set aside. In 1-quart saucepan, melt spreadable fruit over low heat, stirring occasionally.

**4.** Spread melted fruit evenly over warm base. Gently spoon teaspoonfuls of remaining batter over fruit (some fruit may show through batter). Sprinkle almonds evenly over top.

**5.** 25 to 35 minutes longer or until toothpick inserted in center comes out clean. Cool completely, about 1 hour. Cut into 6 rows by 4 rows.

**High Altitude (3500–6500 ft): No change.**

**1 Bar:** Calories 180 (Calories from Fat 80); Total Fat 9g (Saturated Fat 5g; Trans Fat 0g); Cholesterol 30mg; Sodium 95mg; Total Carbohydrate 21g (Dietary Fiber 0g; Sugars 16g); Protein 2g

% Daily Value: Vitamin A 4%; Vitamin C 0%; Calcium 4%; Iron 2%

Exchanges: 1 1/2 Other Carbohydrate, 2 Fat

Carbohydrate Choices: 1 1/2

> **BAKING TIP:**
> *To toast almonds, spread on ungreased cookie sheet; bake at 325°F 7 to 10 minutes, stirring occasionally, until golden brown.*

# ESPRESSO CHEESECAKE BARS

→ PREP TIME: 15 mins
START TO FINISH: 4 hrs 5 mins

**25 bars**

~~~~~~~~~~~~~~~~~~~~~~

1 1/2 cups chocolate cookie
   crumbs
1 teaspoon instant espresso
   coffee granules
1/4 cup butter or margarine,
   melted
1 package (8 oz.) cream cheese,
   softened
1/4 cup sugar
1/2 teaspoon vanilla
1 egg

**1.** Heat oven to 350°F. In small bowl, mix cookie crumbs, 1/2 teaspoon of the espresso coffee granules and the melted butter. Reserve 1/4 cup mixture for topping; press remaining mixture evenly in bottom of ungreased 8-inch square pan.

**2.** In medium bowl, beat cream cheese with electric mixer on medium speed until smooth and creamy. Beat in sugar, remaining 1/2 teaspoon espresso coffee granules, the vanilla and egg until well blended, scraping bowl occasionally. Pour over crust. Sprinkle with reserved crumb mixture.

**3.** Bake 15 to 20 minutes or just until center is set. Cool completely, about 30 minutes. Cover loosely; refrigerate until firm, 3 to 4 hours. With hot, wet knife, cut into 5 rows by 5 rows. Store in refrigerator.

**High Altitude (3500–6500 ft): Bake 20 to 25 minutes.**

**1 Bar:** Calories 90 (Calories from Fat 60); Total Fat 6g (Saturated Fat 3.5g; Trans Fat 0g); Cholesterol 25mg; Sodium 80mg; Total Carbohydrate 7g (Dietary Fiber 0g; Sugars 4g); Protein 1g

% Daily Value: Vitamin A 4%; Vitamin C 0%; Calcium 0%; Iron 2%

Exchanges: 1/2 Other Carbohydrate, 1 Fat

Carbohydrate Choices: 1/2

# SUNBURST LEMON BARS

→ PREP TIME: 15 mins
START TO FINISH: 2 hrs 5 mins

**36 bars**

~~~~~~~~~~~~~~~~~~~~~~~

## BASE
2 cups all-purpose flour
1/2 cup powdered sugar
1 cup butter or margarine,
   softened
Filling
4 eggs
2 cups granulated sugar
1/4 cup all-purpose flour
1 teaspoon baking powder
1/4 cup lemon juice

## GLAZE
1 cup powdered sugar
2 to 3 tablespoons lemon juice

**1.** Heat oven to 350°F. In large bowl, beat base ingredients with electric mixer on low speed until crumbly, scraping bowl occasionally. Press mixture evenly in bottom of ungreased 13x9-inch pan.

**2.** Bake 20 to 30 minutes or until light golden brown. Meanwhile, in large bowl, lightly beat eggs with wire whisk. Beat in remaining filling ingredients except lemon juice. Beat in 1/4 cup lemon juice until well blended.

**3.** Pour filling evenly over warm base; bake 25 to 30 minutes longer or until top is light golden brown. Cool completely, about 1 hour.

**4.** In small bowl, mix glaze ingredients until smooth, adding enough lemon juice for desired spreading consistency. Spread glaze over cooled bars. Cut into 6 rows by 6 rows.

### High Altitude (3500–6500 ft): No change.

**1 Bar:** Calories 150 (Calories from Fat 50); Total Fat 6g (Saturated Fat 3g; Trans Fat 0g); Cholesterol 35mg; Sodium 55mg; Total Carbohydrate 22g (Dietary Fiber 0g; Sugars 16g); Protein 2g

% Daily Value: Vitamin A 4%; Vitamin C 0%; Calcium 0%; Iron 2%

Exchanges: 1 1/2 Other Carbohydrate, 1 Fat

Carbohydrate Choices: 1 1/2

**BAKING TIP:**
*One lemon yields about 3 tablespoons of juice, so buy 2 lemons to squeeze for this recipe.*

*Choose simple or sensational desserts— whatever you wish is right here!*

# FROSTED IRISH CREAM BROWNIES

➜ PREP TIME: 15 mins
START TO FINISH: 2 hrs

**48 brownies**

### BROWNIES
1 box (1 lb 3.8 oz.) fudge brownie
   mix
1/2 cup vegetable oil
1/4 cup Irish cream liqueur
2 eggs

### FROSTING
1/2 cup butter or margarine,
   softened
2 cups powdered sugar
2 tablespoons Irish cream
   liqueur
1/2 teaspoon vanilla
2 to 3 teaspoons milk

### GLAZE
1 oz. semisweet baking
   chocolate, chopped
1 teaspoon butter or margarine

**1.** Heat oven to 350°F. Grease bottom only of 13x9-inch pan with shortening. In medium bowl, stir brownie mix, oil, 1/4 cup liqueur and the eggs with spoon until well blended. Spread batter in pan.

**2.** Bake 28 to 30 minutes or until brownies are set and begin to pull away from sides of pan. DO NOT OVERBAKE. Cool completely, about 45 minutes.

**3.** In small bowl, beat 1/2 cup butter until light and fluffy. Beat in all remaining frosting ingredients, adding enough milk for desired spreading consistency. Spread over cooled brownies.

**4.** In small microwavable bowl, microwave glaze ingredients on High 30 seconds; stir until melted and smooth. Drizzle over frosted brownies. Refrigerate until firm, about 30 minutes. For brownies, cut into 8 rows by 6 rows.

**High Altitude (3500–6500 ft): Add 3 tablespoons all-purpose flour to dry brownie mix; decrease oil to 1/4 cup.**

1 **Brownie:** Calories 120 (Calories from Fat 50); Total Fat 5g (Saturated Fat 2g, Trans Fat 0g); Cholesterol 15mg; Sodium 60mg; Total Carbohydrate 16g (Dietary Fiber 0g, Sugars 13g); Protein 0g
% Daily Value: Vitamin A 0%; Vitamin C 0%; Calcium 0%; Iron 0%
Exchanges: 1/2 Starch, 1/2 Other Carbohydrate, 1 Fat
Carbohydrate Choices: 1

**BAKING TIP:**
*Irish cream liqueur contains Irish whiskey, sugar and cream. Depending on the brand, the liqueur may have a spicy toffee or honey-chocolate flavor.*

# CRANBERRY-APPLE PIE SQUARES

→ PREP TIME: 40 mins
START TO FINISH: 2 hrs 40 mins

**12 servings**

CRUST

1 1/2 cups all-purpose flour
1 tablespoon granulated sugar
1/4 teaspoon salt
1/2 cup butter or margarine
1 egg yolk
1/4 cup milk

FILLING

8 1/2 cups thinly sliced, peeled
   baking apples (3 lb.; about
   9 medium)
1 cup granulated sugar
1/4 cup all-purpose flour
2 teaspoons ground cinnamon
1/2 teaspoon salt
1 cup chopped fresh or frozen
   (thawed) cranberries

TOPPING

1 cup all-purpose flour
1/2 cup packed brown sugar
1/2 cup butter or margarine,
   softened
1 cup caramel topping, heated
Vanilla or cinnamon ice cream,
   if desired

**1.** Heat oven to 375°F. In large bowl, mix 1 1/2 cups flour, 1 tablespoon granulated sugar and 1/4 teaspoon salt. With pastry blender or fork, cut in 1/2 cup butter until mixture resembles coarse crumbs. In small bowl, beat egg yolk and milk with fork until well blended. Add to flour mixture; stir just until dry ingredients are moistened.

**2.** On lightly floured work surface, roll dough with rolling pin into 15x11-inch rectangle; place in ungreased 13x9-inch pan. Press in bottom and 1 inch up sides of pan.

**3.** In large microwavable bowl, microwave apples on High 6 to 8 minutes, stirring every 2 minutes, until apples are fork-tender. Stir in remaining filling ingredients except cranberries until well mixed. Spoon apple mixture over crust. Sprinkle with cranberries.

**4.** In medium bowl, mix 1 cup flour, the brown sugar and 1/2 cup butter until crumbly; sprinkle over fruit.

**5.** Bake 45 to 60 minutes or until topping is deep golden brown, apples are tender and filling is bubbly. Cool 1 hour before serving. Serve topped with caramel topping and, if desired, ice cream.

**High Altitude (3500–6500 ft): Heat oven to 400°F. Increase flour in filling to 1/2 cup. Microwave apples on High 8 to 10 minutes.**

**1 Serving:** Calories 500 (Calories from Fat 150); Total Fat 17g (Saturated Fat 8g; Trans Fat 1g); Cholesterol 60mg; Sodium 350mg; Total Carbohydrate 83g (Dietary Fiber 4g; Sugars 52g); Protein 4g

% Daily Value: Vitamin A 15%; Vitamin C 4%; Calcium 4%; Iron 10%

Exchanges: 1 Starch, 4 1/2 Other Carbohydrate, 3 Fat

Carbohydrate Choices: 5 1/2

# CHOCOLATE CHIP GINGERBREAD WITH ORANGE HARD SAUCE

**9 servings**

~~~~~~~~~~~~~~~~~~~~~~~~

### GINGERBREAD

3 eggs
1/2 cup molasses
1/4 cup granulated sugar
3/4 cup buttermilk
1/2 cup butter, melted
2 cups all-purpose flour
1 teaspoon baking soda
1 teaspoon ground ginger
1 teaspoon ground cinnamon
1/2 teaspoon salt
1/2 teaspoon ground cloves
1/2 cup miniature semisweet
  chocolate chips

### SAUCE

2/3 cup powdered sugar
1/3 cup butter, softened
1 teaspoon grated orange peel
1 tablespoon orange juice

**1.** Heat oven to 350°F. Grease bottom only of 8- or 9-inch square pan with shortening or cooking spray. In large bowl, beat eggs with electric mixer on medium speed 2 to 3 minutes or until slightly thickened. Gradually beat in molasses and granulated sugar until well blended, scraping bowl occasionally. Beat in buttermilk and melted butter.

**2.** On low speed, beat in remaining gingerbread ingredients except chocolate chips until smooth, scraping bowl occasionally. Stir in chocolate chips. Pour batter into pan.

**3.** Bake 8-inch pan 43 to 53 minutes (9-inch pan 30 to 40 minutes) or until toothpick inserted in center comes out clean. Cool 20 minutes.

**4.** In small bowl, beat powdered sugar and 1/3 cup butter with electric mixer on low speed until smooth and creamy, scraping bowl occasionally. Beat in orange peel and orange juice until well blended. Top individual servings with 1 tablespoon sauce.

**High Altitude (3500–6500 ft):** For gingerbread, decrease sugar to 2 tablespoons; decrease butter to 1/3 cup. Bake 8-inch pan 42 to 47 minutes (9-inch pan 40 to 45 minutes).

**1 Serving:** Calories 450 (Calories from Fat 200); Total Fat 22g (Saturated Fat 11g; Trans Fat 1g); Cholesterol 115mg; Sodium 440mg; Total Carbohydrate 57g (Dietary Fiber 2g; Sugars 31g); Protein 6g

% Daily Value: Vitamin A 15%; Vitamin C 0%; Calcium 8%; Iron 15%

Exchanges: 2 Starch, 2 Other Carbohydrate, 4 Fat

Carbohydrate Choices: 4

**BAKING TIP:**
*To substitute for buttermilk, use 2 1/4 teaspoons vinegar or lemon juice plus milk to make 3/4 cup.*

# PUMPKIN PIE SQUARES

**12 servings**

~~~~~~~~~~~~~~~~~~~~~~~~~~~~

## CRUST
3/4 cup all-purpose flour
3/4 cup oats
1/2 to 1 cup chopped nuts
1/2 cup butter or margarine,
 softened
1 box (4-serving size) butterscotch pudding and pie filling
 mix (not instant)

## FILLING
2 eggs
1 cup coconut, if desired
1 1/2 teaspoons pumpkin pie
 spice
1 can (15 oz.) pumpkin
 (not pumpkin pie mix)
1 can (14 oz.) sweetened
 condensed milk (not
 evaporated)

**1.** Heat oven to 350°F. In large bowl, mix crust ingredients until well combined. Press mixture evenly in bottom of ungreased 13x9-inch pan.

**2.** In same bowl, beat eggs with wire whisk. Stir in remaining filling ingredients until blended. Pour over crust.

**3.** Bake 35 to 45 minutes or until knife inserted in center comes out clean. Cool completely, about 1 hour. If desired, serve topped with whipped cream or ice cream. Store in refrigerator.

**High Altitude (3500–6500 ft): Heat oven to 375°F. Bake crust about 8 minutes. Pour filling over crust; bake 38 to 48 minutes.**

**1 Serving:** Calories 310 (Calories from Fat 140); Total Fat 15g (Saturated Fat 6g; Trans Fat 0.5g); Cholesterol 65mg; Sodium 150mg; Total Carbohydrate 38g (Dietary Fiber 2g; Sugars 25g); Protein 7g

% Daily Value: Vitamin A 120%; Vitamin C 2%; Calcium 10%; Iron 8%

Exchanges: 2 Starch, 1/2 Other Carbohydrate, 3 Fat

Carbohydrate Choices: 2 1/2

# MOCHA MACAROON TORTE

→ **PREP TIME: 35 mins**
**START TO FINISH: 4 hrs 35 mins**

**12 servings**

~~~~~~~~~~~~~~~~~~~~~~~~~

1 roll (18 oz.) refrigerated chocolate chunk or chocolate chip
cookies
1 package (8 oz.) cream cheese,
softened
1 egg
1/2 cup sugar
1/2 cup coconut
2 tablespoons brewed coffee
1 teaspoon vanilla
1 cup semisweet chocolate chips
(6 oz.)
1/4 cup chopped pecans

**1.** Heat oven to 350°F. In ungreased 10- or 9-inch springform pan, break up cookie dough; press evenly in bottom of pan.

**2.** Bake 12 to 18 minutes or until light golden brown. Cool on wire rack 10 minutes.

**3.** Meanwhile, in medium bowl, beat cream cheese with electric mixer on medium speed until light and fluffy. Beat in egg until smooth. Beat in 1/4 cup of the sugar, the coconut, coffee and vanilla until well blended, scraping bowl occasionally. Stir in 1/3 cup of the chocolate chips.

**4.** Spoon and carefully spread cream cheese mixture over crust. Sprinkle with remaining 1/4 cup sugar, the pecans and remaining 2/3 cup chocolate chips.

**5.** Bake 30 to 45 minutes longer or until filling is set and edges are golden brown. Cool 10 minutes. Run knife around side of pan to loosen. Carefully remove side of pan; leave torte on pan bottom. Cool 1 hour. Refrigerate 1 to 2 hours or until chilled before serving. Store in refrigerator.

**High Altitude (3500–6500 ft): Bake crust 16 to 20 minutes. After topping crust, bake 35 to 50 minutes.**

**1 Serving:** Calories 420 (Calories from Fat 220); Total Fat 25g (Saturated Fat 11g; Trans Fat 0g); Cholesterol 45mg; Sodium 200mg; Total Carbohydrate 45g (Dietary Fiber 2g; Sugars 32g); Protein 4g

% Daily Value: Vitamin A 6%; Vitamin C 0%; Calcium 2%; Iron 10%

Exchanges: 1 Starch, 2 Other Carbohydrate, 5 Fat

Carbohydrate Choices: 3

# BAKED APPLE DESSERT

→ PREP TIME: 25 mins
START TO FINISH: 55 mins

**10 servings**

~~~~~~~~~~~~~~~~~~~~

8 tablespoons butter or
    margarine
1 package (10 oz.) shortbread or
    oatmeal cookies, crushed
1/2 cup sugar
2 teaspoons ground cinnamon
8 cups sliced peeled apples (2
    2/3 lb.; 8 medium)
1 tablespoon sugar
1 tablespoon lemon juice
1/3 cup chopped almonds, if
    desired
Whipped cream, if desired

**1.** In 10-inch skillet, melt 6 tablespoons of the butter over medium heat. Stir in cookie crumbs, 1/2 cup sugar and the cinnamon. Cook 3 minutes, stirring frequently. Place crumbs in bowl; set aside.

**2.** In same skillet, mix remaining 2 tablespoons butter, the sliced apples, 1 tablespoon sugar and the lemon juice. Cover; cook over medium heat about 10 minutes, stirring frequently, until apples are tender.

**3.** Heat oven to 375°F. In ungreased 2-quart casserole, layer half of apples and half of crumbs. Repeat layers. If desired, sprinkle with almonds.

**4.** Bake 25 to 30 minutes or until golden brown. If desired, serve warm with whipped cream.

**High Altitude (3500–6500 ft): No change.**

**1 Serving:** Calories 340 (Calories from Fat 150); Total Fat 16g (Saturated Fat 6g; Trans Fat 2g); Cholesterol 30mg; Sodium 190mg; Total Carbohydrate 45g (Dietary Fiber 3g; Sugars 31g); Protein 2g

% Daily Value: Vitamin A 8%; Vitamin C 4%; Calcium 2%; Iron 6%

Exchanges: 1 Starch, 2 Other Carbohydrate, 3 Fat

Carbohydrate Choices: 3

●

# GINGERED APPLE-BERRY CRISP

→ PREP TIME: 15 mins
START TO FINISH: 55 mins

**6 servings (1/2 cup each)**

### TOPPING

3/4 cup quick-cooking oats
3/4 cup crushed gingersnaps
1/2 cup all-purpose flour
1/4 cup packed brown sugar
1/2 cup butter or margarine, cut
   into pieces

### FRUIT MIXTURE

1 cup frozen unsweetened blueberries
1 cup frozen unsweetened raspberries
1/2 teaspoon ground ginger
1 can (21 oz.) apple pie filling

**1.** Heat oven to 350°F. Grease 12x8-inch (2-quart) glass baking dish with shortening or cooking spray. In large bowl, mix all topping ingredients except butter. With pastry blender or fork, cut in butter until crumbly.

**2.** In large bowl, mix fruit mixture ingredients; pour into baking dish. Sprinkle topping evenly over fruit.

**3.** Bake 35 to 40 minutes or until fruit mixture is bubbly and topping is golden brown, covering with foil during last 15 to 20 minutes of baking if necessary to prevent excessive browning.

**High Altitude (3500–6500 ft): Heat oven to 375°F.**

**1 Serving:** Calories 460 (Calories from Fat 160); Total Fat 18g (Saturated Fat 8g; Trans Fat 1.5g); Cholesterol 40mg; Sodium 200mg; Total Carbohydrate 70g (Dietary Fiber 7g; Sugars 43g); Protein 4g

% Daily Value: Vitamin A 15%; Vitamin C 15%; Calcium 4%; Iron 10%

Exchanges: 1 Starch, 3 1/2 Other Carbohydrate, 3 1/2 Fat

Carbohydrate Choices: 4 1/2

**BAKING TIP:**

*To crush the cookies easily, place them in a plastic bag and roll them with a rolling pin until they crumble. Or, use a food processor with 10 to 15 quick on-and-off motions.*

# RASPBERRY-PEACH COBBLER

→ **PREP TIME: 15 mins**
**START TO FINISH: 1 hr**

**9 servings**

~~~~~~~~~~~~~~~~~~~~~~

## BISCUITS
1 cup all-purpose flour
1/2 cup sugar
1 teaspoon baking powder
1/4 teaspoon salt
3/4 cup sour cream
2 tablespoons butter or margarine, melted
1 egg
1 tablespoon sugar

## FRUIT MIXTURE
3/4 cup sugar
3 tablespoons cornstarch
1 package (10 oz.) frozen raspberries in syrup, thawed, drained and reserving liquid
1 bag (16 oz.) frozen sliced peaches, thawed, drained

**1.** Heat oven to 375°F. In medium bowl, mix flour, 1/2 cup sugar, the baking powder and salt. Stir in sour cream, butter and egg until well blended; set aside.

**2.** In 2-quart saucepan, mix 3/4 cup sugar, the cornstarch and reserved raspberry liquid. Cook over medium heat, stirring occasionally, until mixture boils. Boil 1 minute, stirring constantly. Stir in raspberries and peaches. Cook 1 minute, stirring constantly. Pour into ungreased 2-quart casserole.

**3.** Spoon biscuit mixture over hot fruit mixture, forming 9 biscuits around edge of casserole. Sprinkle biscuits with 1 tablespoon sugar.

**4.** Bake 35 to 45 minutes or until biscuits are golden brown. Serve warm.

**High Altitude (3500–6500 ft): Decrease sour cream to 1/2 cup.**

**1 Serving:** Calories 330 (Calories from Fat 60); Total Fat 7g (Saturated Fat 4g; Trans Fat 0g); Cholesterol 45mg; Sodium 160mg; Total Carbohydrate 63g (Dietary Fiber 3g; Sugars 48g); Protein 3g

% Daily Value: Vitamin A 8%; Vitamin C 45%; Calcium 6%; Iron 6%

Exchanges: 1 Starch, 3 Other Carbohydrate, 1 1/2 Fat

Carbohydrate Choices: 4

# BLUEBERRY SQUARES

→ PREP TIME: 25 mins
START TO FINISH: 3 hrs 15 mins

**12 servings**

～～～～～～～～～～

### PASTRY

1 cup butter or margarine,
  softened
1/2 cup granulated sugar
2 3/4 cups all-purpose flour
1/4 teaspoon salt
1/2 teaspoon vanilla
1 egg

### FILLING

3 cups fresh or frozen
  blueberries
1 cup sugar
3 tablespoons cornstarch
1 teaspoon powdered sugar
Ice cream or whipped cream, if
  desired

**1.** In large bowl, beat butter and 1/2 cup granulated sugar with electric mixer on medium speed until well blended, scraping bowl occasionally. On low speed, beat in flour, salt, vanilla and egg, scraping bowl occasionally, until a dough forms. Cover; refrigerate until firm, about 2 hours.

**2.** Meanwhile, in 2-quart saucepan, mix blueberries, 1 cup sugar and the cornstarch. Cook over medium heat, stirring constantly, until mixture boils. Boil 3 minutes, stirring constantly, until thickened. Remove from heat; cool.

**3.** Heat oven to 375°F. Pat two-thirds of chilled pastry dough in bottom and 1/2 inch up sides of ungreased 13x9-inch pan. Spread blueberry mixture evenly over dough. Roll out remaining one-third of dough to 1/4-inch thickness. With fluted wheel, cut dough into 1/2-inch-wide strips. Arrange strips in lattice design over filling (strips may break apart but will bake together). Trim and seal edges.

**4.** Bake 30 to 40 minutes or until top is golden brown. Cool slightly, about 15 minutes. Sprinkle with powdered sugar; cut into squares. If desired, serve with ice cream or whipped cream.

**High Altitude (3500–6500 ft): No change.**

**1 Serving:** Calories 380 (Calories from Fat 150); Total Fat 16g (Saturated Fat 8g; Trans Fat 1g); Cholesterol 60mg; Sodium 160mg; Total Carbohydrate 54g (Dietary Fiber 2g; Sugars 28g); Protein 4g

% Daily Value: Vitamin A 10%; Vitamin C 4%; Calcium 0%; Iron 8%

Exchanges: 1 1/2 Starch, 2 Other Carbohydrate, 3 Fat

Carbohydrate Choices: 3 1/2

# CHOCOLATE MALTED MILK CHEESECAKE

→ PREP TIME: 25 mins
START TO FINISH: 5 hrs 20 mins

**18 servings**

~~~~~~~~~~~~~~~~~~~~~~~~

5 packages (8 oz. each) cream
  cheese, softened

1 1/2 cups sugar

1 cup malted milk powder

1/2 cup unsweetened baking
  cocoa

1 container (8 oz.) sour cream
  (about 1 cup)

2 teaspoons vanilla

1/4 teaspoon salt

5 eggs

1 cup whipping (heavy) cream,
  whipped

1/2 cup chopped chocolate-
  covered malted milk balls

**1.** Heat oven to 350°F. Line bottom only of 13x9-inch pan with foil; grease foil with shortening or cooking spray. In large bowl, beat cream cheese with electric mixer on medium speed until light and fluffy.

**2.** In medium bowl, mix sugar, malted milk powder and cocoa; add to cream cheese. Beat on low speed until combined; beat on medium speed until smooth, scraping bowl occasionally. Beat in sour cream, vanilla and salt until well blended, scraping bowl occasionally. Beat in eggs, one at a time, just until blended. Pour batter into pan.

**3.** Place pan in larger shallow pan; place in oven. Add hot water to shallow pan until half full. Bake 50 to 55 minutes or until set. Remove cheesecake from water bath; place on wire rack. Cool in pan until luke-warm, about 1 hour.

**4.** Place cookie sheet upside down over pan; carefully turn cookie sheet and pan over. Remove pan. Refrigerate cheesecake at least 3 hours or overnight. Top individual servings with whipped cream and chopped malted milk balls. Store in refrigerator.

**High Altitude (3500–6500 ft): No change.**

**1 Serving:** Calories 420 (Calories from Fat 280); Total Fat 31g (Saturated Fat 19g; Trans Fat 1g); Cholesterol 150mg; Sodium 260mg; Total Carbohydrate 27g (Dietary Fiber 0g; Sugars 23g); Protein 8g

% Daily Value: Vitamin A 35%; Vitamin C 6%; Calcium 10%; Iron 10%

Exchanges: 2 Other Carbohydrate, 1 High-Fat Meat, 4 1/2 Fat

Carbohydrate Choices: 2

**BAKING TIP:**
*For a real holiday bash, cut this rectangular cheesecake into bite-size squares and serve them as part of a holiday dessert buffet. For extra pizzazz, place each piece in a small foil cup.*

# ORANGE CHEESECAKE WITH RASPBERRY SAUCE

**16 servings**

〜〜〜〜〜〜〜〜〜〜〜〜

### CRUST
1 package (9 oz.) chocolate wafer
  cookies, crushed
6 tablespoons butter or
  margarine, melted

### FILLING
4 packages (8 oz. each) cream
  cheese, softened
1 1/3 cups sugar
4 eggs
2 tablespoons orange-flavored
  liqueur or orange juice
1 teaspoon grated orange peel

### SAUCE
1 package (10 oz.) frozen raspberries in syrup, thawed
3 tablespoons sugar
1 teaspoon cornstarch

**1.** Heat oven to 325°F. In medium bowl, mix crust ingredients; press in bottom and 2 inches up side of ungreased 9-inch springform pan.

**2.** In large bowl, beat cream cheese with electric mixer on medium speed until smooth and creamy. Gradually beat in 1 1/3 cups sugar until smooth, scraping bowl occasionally. On low speed, beat in eggs, one at a time, just until blended. Add liqueur and orange peel; beat on medium speed 2 minutes, scraping bowl occasionally. Pour filling into crust.

**3.** Bake 55 to 65 minutes or until almost set. Cool completely, about 2 hours 30 minutes. Refrigerate at least 4 hours or overnight before serving.

**4.** In food processor or blender, process raspberries with syrup until smooth. If desired, strain to remove seeds. In 1-quart saucepan, mix 3 tablespoons sugar and the cornstarch. Stir in raspberry puree. Cook over medium heat, stirring constantly, until mixture boils and thickens. Cool to room temperature.

**5.** Carefully remove side of pan; leave cheesecake on pan bottom. Serve cheesecake with sauce. Store in refrigerator.

**High Altitude (3500–6500 ft):** Place pan with 1 to 1 1/2 inches of water on rack below cheesecake during baking. After baking, cool cheese-cake 10 minutes; run knife around edge to loosen but do not remove side of pan.

**1 Serving:** Calories 430 (Calories from Fat 250); Total Fat 28g (Saturated Fat 16g; Trans Fat 1.5g); Cholesterol 125mg; Sodium 300mg; Total Carbohydrate 38g (Dietary Fiber 1g; Sugars 29g); Protein 7g

% Daily Value: Vitamin A 20%; Vitamin C 2%; Calcium 6%; Iron 8%

Exchanges: 2 Starch, 1/2 Other Carbohydrate, 5 1/2 Fat

Carbohydrate Choices: 2 1/2

> **BAKING TIP:**
> *Use a knife dipped in water to make the smoothest cuts in the cheese-cake. And for easier cutting, make the cheesecake 24 to 36 hours ahead of serving and keep it refrigerated.*

# CHOCOLATE-COVERED CHEESECAKE BITES

→ **PREP TIME: 1 hr 20 mins**
**START TO FINISH: 5 hrs 55 mins**

**48 cheesecake bites**

~~~~~~~~~~~~~~~~~~~~~~~~~~~~

## CRUST
1 cup graham cracker crumbs
1/4 cup chopped pecans
1/4 cup butter or margarine,
　melted

## FILLING
2 packages (8 oz. each) cream
　cheese, softened
1/2 cup sugar
1 teaspoon grated orange peel
1/4 cup sour cream
1/2 teaspoon vanilla
2 eggs

## COATING
24 oz. semisweet baking
　chocolate, cut into pieces
3 tablespoons shortening

**1.** Heat oven to 300°F. Line 8-inch square pan with heavy-duty foil so foil extends over sides of pan. Grease foil with shortening or cooking spray. In small bowl, mix crust ingredients; press evenly in bottom of pan.

**2.** In large bowl, beat cream cheese with electric mixer on medium speed until smooth. Beat in remaining filling ingredients until smooth, scraping bowl occasionally. Pour over crust.

**3.** Bake 40 to 45 minutes or until edges are set (center will be soft but will be set when cool). Refrigerate cheesecake until chilled, about 1 hour 30 minutes. Freeze until firm, about 2 hours.

**4.** Remove cheesecake from pan by lifting foil. Cut into 8 rows by 6 rows, making 48 pieces. Remove pieces from foil; place on sheet of waxed paper.

**5.** In 1-quart saucepan, melt coating ingredients over low heat, stirring frequently, until smooth. Cool slightly, 2 to 3 minutes. Pour into 2-cup measuring cup. Spear each cheesecake bite with fork; dip into melted coating to cover bottom and sides, letting excess drip off. Place on waxed paper.

**6.** Spoon about 1 teaspoon melted coating over each bite, smoothing top with back of spoon. Let stand until firm before serving, about 20 minutes. Store in refrigerator.

**High Altitude (3500–6500 ft): Heat oven to 325°F.**

**1 Cheesecake Bite:** Calories 150 (Calories from Fat 90); Total Fat 10g (Saturated Fat 6g; Trans Fat 0g); Cholesterol 25mg; Sodium 50mg; Total Carbohydrate 13g (Dietary Fiber 0g; Sugars 11g); Protein 2g

% Daily Value: Vitamin A 4%; Vitamin C 0%; Calcium 0%; Iron 4%

Exchanges: 1 Other Carbohydrate, 2 Fat

Carbohydrate Choices: 1

# APPLE CRÈME CARAMEL

→ PREP TIME: 25 mins
START TO FINISH: 3 hrs 5 mins

**6 servings**

~~~~~~~~~~~~~~~~~~~~~~~~~

**CARAMEL**
1 medium apple
3/4 cup sugar
1 tablespoon water

**CUSTARD**
2 eggs
2 egg yolks
1/2 cup sugar
1 teaspoon vanilla
1 pint (2 cups) whipping (heavy)
    cream

**1.** Heat oven to 350°F. Peel and core apple. Cut into thin slices; cut each slice in half crosswise. Arrange in bottoms of 6 (6-oz.) ungreased custard cups.

**2.** In heavy 2-quart saucepan, mix 3/4 cup sugar and the water. With pastry brush dipped in water, wash any sugar off inside of pan. Without stirring, cook over medium-high heat 5 to 6 minutes or until mixture begins to turn amber in color. Gently swirl pan as mixture darkens to golden brown (watch carefully, as mixture can burn in seconds). Immediately remove from heat. Carefully pour over apples in custard cups. Place custard cups in 13x9-inch pan.

**3.** In medium bowl, beat eggs, egg yolks, 1/2 cup sugar and the vanilla with electric mixer on medium speed until well combined. Gradually beat in whipping cream until blended. Carefully pour over caramel mixture in cups.

**4.** Place pan with cups in oven; pour hot water into pan until about halfway up sides of custard cups. Bake 50 to 60 minutes or until knife inserted in center comes out clean (apples may float to top). Remove cups from water; place on wire rack. Cool 30 minutes. Refrigerate until completely chilled, about 1 hour.

**5.** To unmold, run thin knife around inside edge of each cup. Place bottom of cup in hot water for 30 to 60 seconds to loosen caramel. Unmold onto individual dessert plates. Store in refrigerator.

**High Altitude (3500–6500 ft): Bake 1 hour to 1 hour 10 minutes.**

**1 Serving:** Calories 460 (Calories from Fat 250); Total Fat 28g (Saturated Fat 16g; Trans Fat 0.5g); Cholesterol 230mg; Sodium 50mg; Total Carbohydrate 48g (Dietary Fiber 0g; Sugars 47g); Protein 5g

% Daily Value: Vitamin A 20%; Vitamin C 0%; Calcium 8%; Iron 2%

Exchanges: 3 Other Carbohydrate, 1/2 Medium-Fat Meat, 5 Fat

Carbohydrate Choices: 3

# AMARETTO CRÈME BRÛLÉE

→ PREP TIME: 15 mins
START TO FINISH: 5 hrs 45 mins

**6 servings**

〜〜〜〜〜〜〜〜〜〜〜〜

6 egg yolks
1/2 cup sugar
1 pint (2 cups) whipping (heavy)
  cream
1/4 cup amaretto
1 teaspoon vanilla
1/8 teaspoon salt
2 tablespoons sugar
1/4 cup sliced almonds, toasted

**1.** Heat oven to 350°F. Place 6 (6-oz.) oval or round ceramic ramekins in 13x9-inch pan. In medium bowl, beat egg yolks and 1/2 cup sugar with wire whisk until light and fluffy. Beat in whipping cream, amaretto, vanilla and salt until well blended.

**2.** Place strainer over 4-cup measuring cup or another medium bowl. Pour egg yolk mixture into strainer to remove any lumps; discard lumps. Pour about 1/2 cup mixture into each ramekin.

**3.** Pour hot water into pan until halfway up sides of ramekins; cover pan loosely with foil. Bake 40 to 50 minutes or until edges are set but center still jiggles slightly when gently shaken. Remove ramekins from water bath; place on wire racks. Cool 30 minutes. Pour water from pan.

**4.** Transfer ramekins to same pan. Cover; refrigerate at least 3 hours or up to 24 hours before serving.

**5.** Set oven control to broil. Sprinkle top of each custard with 1 teaspoon sugar. Watching constantly, broil custards 4 to 6 inches from heat 1 to 4 minutes or until sugar bubbles and is caramelized. Refrigerate at least 1 hour or up to 3 hours to harden topping.

**6.** Just before serving, sprinkle toasted almonds over chilled crème brûlée. Store in refrigerator.

**High Altitude (3500–6500 ft): Bake 55 to 60 minutes.**

**1 Serving:** Calories 420 (Calories from Fat 290); Total Fat 32g (Saturated Fat 17g; Trans Fat 0.5g); Cholesterol 300mg; Sodium 85mg; Total Carbohydrate 28g (Dietary Fiber 0g; Sugars 26g); Protein 5g

% Daily Value: Vitamin A 25%; Vitamin C 0%; Calcium 8%; Iron 4%

Exchanges: 1 Starch, 1 Other Carbohydrate, 6 Fat

Carbohydrate Choices: 2

> **BAKING TIP:**
>
> *Use ceramic ramekins, not glass custard cups, when preparing this yummy dessert. Then, instead of using the broiler to melt the sugar, you can use a small torch, sold in cookware stores. To toast the almonds, see page 110.*

# IRISH CRÈME BRÛLÉE

→ **PREP TIME:** 30 mins
**START TO FINISH:** 9 hrs 30 mins

**8 servings**

~~~~~~~~~~~~~~~~~~~~~~~~~~~~~~~~~~~

1 pint (2 cups) whipping (heavy) cream
3/4 cup Irish cream liqueur
3 eggs
3 egg yolks
1/4 cup granulated sugar
1/4 cup packed brown sugar

**1.** Heat oven to 325°F. Place ungreased 1 1/2-quart ceramic casserole in 13x9-inch pan. In 2-quart saucepan, heat whipping cream and liqueur over medium-low heat just until hot; DO NOT BOIL. Set aside.

**2.** In medium bowl, stir eggs, egg yolks and granulated sugar with spoon until well blended. Gradually add hot cream mixture to egg mixture, stirring constantly. Strain mixture through fine strainer into casserole.

**3.** Place pan with casserole in oven; pour hot water into pan until halfway up side of casserole. Bake 25 to 30 minutes or until mixture is set when casserole is jiggled. Remove from oven. Remove casserole from pan of water; place on wire rack. Cool 30 minutes.

**4.** Cover casserole with lid or plastic wrap, not allowing wrap to touch surface of custard; refrigerate at least 8 hours or overnight.

**5.** Set oven control to broil. With paper towel, carefully blot any surface liquid from top of custard. Spoon brown sugar into fine strainer. With fingers or back of spoon, press brown sugar through strainer evenly over top of custard. Broil 6 to 8 inches from heat 30 to 60 seconds, rotating or moving dish if sugar is melting unevenly, until brown sugar is melted and bubbly (watch carefully, as topping burns easily). Cool 2 minutes to harden sugar. Serve immediately.

**High Altitude (3500–6500 ft):** Heat oven to 350°F. Bake 30 to 35 minutes.

**1 Serving:** Calories 330 (Calories from Fat 220); Total Fat 24g (Saturated Fat 14g; Trans Fat 0.5g); Cholesterol 250mg; Sodium 70mg; Total Carbohydrate 22g (Dietary Fiber 0g; Sugars 22g); Protein 6g

**% Daily Value:** Vitamin A 20%; Vitamin C 0%; Calcium 10%; Iron 4%

**Exchanges:** 1 1/2 Other Carbohydrate, 1 Medium-Fat Meat, 4 Fat

**Carbohydrate Choices:** 1 1/2

**BAKING TIP:**
*Be sure to use a ceramic casserole, not a glass one, when preparing this restaurant-inspired dessert. Broil the sugar topping just before serving the crème brûlée so the moisture from the custard does not soften the crisp topping.*

# RICE PUDDING BAKE

→ PREP TIME: 35 mins
START TO FINISH: 1 hr 45 mins

**9 servings**

~~~~~~~~~~~~~~~~~~~~~~

### RICE MIXTURE

1/2 cup uncooked regular long-
  grain white rice
2 tablespoons sugar
2 cups milk
1 tablespoon butter or margarine

### PUDDING

6 eggs
1 cup sugar
1/2 teaspoon ground cinnamon
1/4 teaspoon salt
1/4 teaspoon ground nutmeg
1/2 cup raisins
2 cups milk
Whipped cream, if desired

**1.** In 2-quart saucepan, mix rice mixture ingredients. Heat to boiling. Reduce heat to low; cook uncovered 20 to 25 minutes, stirring occasionally, until creamy. Remove from heat; cool 10 minutes.

**2.** Heat oven to 350°F. Lightly grease 8-inch square (2-quart) glass baking dish with shortening or cooking spray. In large bowl, beat eggs with wire whisk until blended. Stir in remaining pudding ingredients and the rice mixture. Pour into baking dish.

**3.** Bake 55 to 60 minutes or until set. Serve warm or cold. If desired, serve with whipped cream. Store in refrigerator.

**High Altitude (3500–6500 ft): In step 1, remove rice mixture from heat. Stir in raisins; cool 10 minutes.**

**1 Serving:** Calories 280 (Calories from Fat 60); Total Fat 7g (Saturated Fat 3g; Trans Fat 0g); Cholesterol 155mg; Sodium 170mg; Total Carbohydrate 46g (Dietary Fiber 0g; Sugars 36g); Protein 9g

% Daily Value: Vitamin A 8%; Vitamin C 0%; Calcium 15%; Iron 6%

Exchanges: 1 Starch, 2 Other Carbohydrate, 1 Medium-Fat Meat

Carbohydrate Choices: 3

# FROZEN PISTACHIO CREAM DESSERT WITH RUBY RASPBERRY SAUCE

→ PREP TIME: 30 mins
START TO FINISH: 5 hrs 30 mins

**9 servings**

## CRUST

1 cup vanilla wafer cookie
  crumbs (about 30 cookies)
1/2 cup finely chopped pistachio
  nuts
3 tablespoons butter or
  margarine, melted

## FILLING

1 package (8 oz.) fat-free cream
  cheese, softened
1 box (4-serving size) pistachio
  instant pudding and pie
  filling mix
1 1/4 cups skim milk
1 container (8 oz.) frozen fat-free
  whipped topping, thawed

## SAUCE

1 package (10 oz.) frozen
  raspberries in syrup,
  partially thawed
2 tablespoons sugar
2 tablespoons orange-flavored
  liqueur or orange juice

## GARNISH

Reserved 1 cup fat-free whipped
  topping
1 to 2 tablespoons chopped
  pistachio nuts

**1.** In medium bowl, mix crust ingredients; press firmly in bottom of ungreased 8-inch square pan or 9-inch springform pan.

**2.** In medium bowl, beat cream cheese with electric mixer on medium speed until light and fluffy. On low speed, beat in pudding mix and milk until combined; beat on medium speed until smooth, scraping bowl occasionally. Reserve 1 cup of the whipped topping for garnish; cover and refrigerate. With rubber spatula, fold remaining whipped topping into cream cheese mixture until well blended. Spoon over crust. Freeze until firm, at least 4 hours.

**3.** Meanwhile, in blender or food processor, blend raspberries, sugar and liqueur until smooth. Place strainer over small bowl; pour raspberry mixture into strainer. Press with back of spoon through strainer to remove seeds; discard seeds.

**4.** Let dessert thaw in refrigerator about 1 hour before serving. Carefully run knife around sides of pan. If using springform pan, remove side of pan; leave dessert on pan bottom. Top each serving with reserved whipped topping, the raspberry sauce and about 1/2 teaspoon chopped pistachios.

**High Altitude (3500–6500 ft): No change.**

**1 Serving:** Calories 290 (Calories from Fat 90); Total Fat 10g (Saturated Fat 3.5g; Trans Fat 0.5g); Cholesterol 15mg; Sodium 430mg; Total Carbohydrate 42g (Dietary Fiber 2g; Sugars 29g); Protein 7g
% Daily Value: Vitamin A 10%; Vitamin C 10%; Calcium 10%; Iron 4%
Exchanges: 2 Starch, 1 Other Carbohydrate, 1 1/2 Fat
Carbohydrate Choices: 3

> **BAKING TIP:**
> *Bake yourself a gift—a wonderful lower-calorie and -fat dessert perfect to serve during the holidays. If you prefer to use regular cream cheese and whipped topping, that also works well.*

# RASPBERRY-GLAZED DOUBLE-CHOCOLATE DESSERT

START TO FINISH: 4 hrs 15 mins

**16 servings**

~~~~~~~~~~~~~~~~~~~~~~~~~

### CAKE
16 oz. semisweet baking
   chocolate, cut into pieces
1 cup unsalted butter
6 eggs

### WHITE CHOCOLATE GANACHE
8 oz. white chocolate baking bar,
   cut into pieces
1/2 cup whipping (heavy) cream
1 tablespoon unsalted butter

### RASPBERRY GLAZE
1 package (10 oz.) frozen
   raspberries in syrup, thawed
1 tablespoon cornstarch

### TOPPING
1 cup whipping (heavy) cream,
   whipped
1 cup fresh raspberries

**1.** Heat oven to 400°F. Grease 9-inch springform pan with shortening or cooking spray. In 2-quart saucepan, melt semisweet baking chocolate and 1 cup butter over medium-low heat, stirring constantly, until smooth. Cool completely, about 35 minutes.

**2.** In small bowl, beat eggs with electric mixer on high speed 5 minutes or until light and lemon colored. With rubber spatula, fold cooled chocolate into eggs until well blended. Pour into pan.

**3.** Bake 15 minutes (dessert will be soft in center). Cool completely in pan on wire rack 1 hour 30 minutes. Refrigerate until firm, about 1 hour 30 minutes.

**4.** Meanwhile, in small bowl, place white chocolate baking bar. In 1-quart saucepan, heat 1/2 cup whipping cream and 1 tablespoon butter just to boiling. Pour over chocolate; stir until melted and smooth. Cool completely, about 5 minutes. Refrigerate until chilled, about 1 hour.

**5.** Place strainer over another 1-quart saucepan; pour raspberries into strainer. Press mixture with back of spoon through strainer to remove seeds; discard seeds. Stir in cornstarch. Cook over medium heat, stirring constantly, until mixture boils and thickens. Cool completely, about 30 minutes.

**6.** Spread white chocolate ganache on top of cooled dessert. Spread raspberry glaze over ganache. Refrigerate at least 30 minutes to allow ganache and glaze to set up before serving. Serve or continue to refrigerate until serving time.

**7.** If dessert has been refrigerated longer than 8 hours, let stand at room temperature 1 hour. Remove side of pan; leave dessert on pan bottom. Spoon whipped cream into pastry bag with large star tip; pipe cream onto edge of dessert. Garnish with fresh raspberries.

**High Altitude (3500–6500 ft):** Use 10-inch springform pan. Bake 20 minutes.

**1 Serving:** Calories 460 (Calories from Fat 310); Total Fat 34g (Saturated Fat 20g; Trans Fat 1g); Cholesterol 135mg; Sodium 50mg; Total Carbohydrate 33g (Dietary Fiber 3g; Sugars 29g); Protein 5g

% Daily Value: Vitamin A 15%; Vitamin C 4%; Calcium 8%; Iron 8%

Exchanges: 1 Starch, 1 Other Carbohydrate, 7 Fat

Carbohydrate Choices: 2

# LEMON CREAM MERINGUE

→ PREP TIME: 25 mins
START TO FINISH: 7 hrs 40 mins

**12 servings**

~~~~~~~~~~~~~~~~~~~~~~

## MERINGUE SHELL
4 egg whites
1 teaspoon lemon juice
3/4 cup sugar

## FILLING
1/2 cup butter or margarine
1 cup sugar
1/3 cup lemon juice
4 egg yolks
2 teaspoons grated lemon peel
1 cup whipping (heavy) cream,
   whipped

## TOPPING
2 kiwifruit, peeled, sliced
1 orange, peeled, sectioned
Whipped cream
Grated lemon peel

**1.** Heat oven to 275°F. Line cookie sheet with cooking parchment paper. In large bowl, beat egg whites and 1 teaspoon lemon juice with electric mixer on medium speed until soft peaks form. On high speed, gradually beat in 3/4 cup sugar, 1 tablespoon at a time, until stiff glossy peaks form and sugar is almost dissolved. Spread two-thirds of meringue into 10-inch round on cookie sheet. Using remaining one-third of meringue, spoon or pipe dollops around edge of round to form shell.

**2.** Bake 30 minutes. DO NOT OPEN OVEN. Turn oven off; let meringue shell stand in oven with door closed 1 hour. Remove meringue shell from oven; cool completely, about 30 minutes.

**3.** Meanwhile, in 2-quart saucepan, melt butter over medium heat. Stir in 1 cup sugar, 1/3 cup lemon juice and the egg yolks. Heat to boiling. Boil 2 minutes, stirring constantly. Stir in 2 teaspoons lemon peel. Cool 15 minutes. Cover top surface with waxed paper; refrigerate until thoroughly chilled, about 1 hour.

**4.** With rubber spatula, fold whipped cream into cooled lemon mixture. Carefully remove meringue shell from paper; place on serving plate. Spoon filling evenly into meringue shell. Refrigerate until set, 4 to 6 hours. Before serving, garnish with kiwifruit, orange sections and additional whipped cream; sprinkle with additional lemon peel.

**High Altitude (3500–6500 ft): No change.**

**1 Serving:** Calories 320 (Calories from Fat 170); Total Fat 18g (Saturated Fat 10g; Trans Fat 0.5g); Cholesterol 125mg; Sodium 85mg; Total Carbohydrate 35g (Dietary Fiber 0g; Sugars 34g); Protein 3g

% Daily Value: Vitamin A 15%; Vitamin C 15%; Calcium 4%; Iron 0%

Exchanges: 1/2 Starch, 2 Other Carbohydrate, 3 1/2 Fat

Carbohydrate Choices: 2

> **BAKING TIP:**
> *To section the oranges easily, peel down to the membrane. With a sharp knife, cut and remove the sections; discard the membrane.*

# STRAWBERRY-RHUBARB MERINGUE CLOUDS

→ PREP TIME: 35 mins
START TO FINISH: 2 hrs 35 mins

**8 servings**

〜〜〜〜〜〜〜〜〜〜〜〜〜〜〜〜

## MERINGUE SHELLS
3 egg whites
1/4 teaspoon cream of tartar
1/2 cup sugar

## FILLING
2 cups sliced fresh or frozen
   rhubarb
2/3 cup sugar
2 tablespoons cornstarch
1/2 cup water
1 cup halved fresh strawberries

**1.** Heat oven to 225°F. Grease 2 cookie sheets with shortening or cooking spray. In large bowl, beat egg whites and cream of tartar with electric mixer on medium speed until soft peaks form. On high speed, gradually beat in 1/2 cup sugar until stiff glossy peaks form and sugar is almost dissolved. Spoon meringue into 8 (4- to 5-inch) rounds on cookie sheets, hollowing center slightly with back of spoon to form shells.

**2.** Bake 1 hour. DO NOT OPEN OVEN. Turn oven off; let meringue shells stand in oven with door closed 1 hour.

**3.** Meanwhile, in 2-quart saucepan, mix all filling ingredients except strawberries. Cook over medium-low heat 15 to 20 minutes, stirring frequently, until filling is slightly thickened and rhubarb is soft. Stir in strawberries. Cool completely, about 1 hour.

**4.** Spoon about 1/4 cup filling into each meringue shell. Store filling in refrigerator.

**High Altitude (3500–6500 ft): No change.**

**1 Serving:** Calories 140 (Calories from Fat 0); Total Fat 0g (Saturated Fat 0g; Trans Fat 0g); Cholesterol 0mg; Sodium 20mg; Total Carbohydrate 33g (Dietary Fiber 0g; Sugars 31g); Protein 2g

% Daily Value: Vitamin A 0%; Vitamin C 10%; Calcium 6%; Iron 0%

Exchanges: 1/2 Starch, 1 1/2 Other Carbohydrate

Carbohydrate Choices: 2

***B**ring home your own blue ribbon with these delectable pies! And yes, they are "easy as pie."*

# PASTRY FOR PIES AND TARTS

→ PREP TIME: 20 mins
START TO FINISH: 20 mins

## ONE-CRUST PIE OR TART

1 cup all-purpose flour
1/2 teaspoon salt
1/3 cup shortening
2 to 4 tablespoons ice water

## TWO-CRUST PIE OR TART

2 cups all-purpose flour
1 teaspoon salt
2/3 cup shortening
5 to 7 tablespoons ice water

**1.** In medium bowl, mix flour and salt. With pastry blender or fork, cut in shortening until mixture resembles coarse crumbs. Sprinkle with water, 1 tablespoon at a time, while tossing and mixing lightly with fork; add water until dough is just moist enough to form a ball when lightly pressed together. (Too much water causes dough to become sticky and tough; too little water causes edges to crack and pastry to tear easily while rolling.)

**2.** For ONE-CRUST PIE or TART: Shape dough into 1 ball; flatten ball to 1/2-inch thickness, rounding and smoothing edges. On lightly floured work surface, roll dough lightly from center to edge with floured rolling pin into 11-inch round. Fold pastry in half; place in 9-inch glass pie plate, or 9- or 10-inch tart pan. Unfold pastry; gently press in bottom and up side of plate or pan (do not stretch pastry). If using pie plate, fold edge under to form a standing rim; flute edges. If using tart pan, trim pastry edges if necessary.

- For BAKED SHELL (UNFILLED): Generously prick bottom and side of pastry with fork. Bake at 450°F 9 to 12 minutes or until lightly browned. Cool completely on wire rack. Continue as directed in recipe.
- For FILLED PIE or TART: Fill and bake as directed in recipe.

**3.** For TWO-CRUST PIE or TART: Shape dough into 2 balls; flatten 1 ball to 1/2-inch thickness, rounding and smoothing edges. On lightly floured work surface, roll dough lightly from center to edge with floured rolling pin into 11-inch round. Fold pastry in half; place in 9-inch glass pie plate, or 9- or 10-inch tart pan. Unfold pastry; gently press in bottom and up side of plate or pan (do not stretch pastry). Trim pastry even with pie plate or tart pan edge. Roll out remaining pastry; set aside. Continue as directed in recipe.

High Altitude (3500–6500 ft): No change.

VARIATIONS:
**Cheese Pastry:** For One-Crust pastry, add 1/4 to 1/2 cup shredded Cheddar or American cheese to flour. Omit salt. (For Two-Crust pastry, use 1/2 to 1 cup.)

**Whole Wheat Pastry:** For One-Crust pastry, substitute up to 1/2 cup whole wheat flour for all-purpose flour. Additional water may be necessary. (For Two-Crust pastry, use up to 1 cup whole wheat flour.)

# RASPBERRY-CHERRY PIE

→ **PREP TIME:** 35 mins
**START TO FINISH:** 3 hrs 20 mins

**8 servings**

~~~~~~~~~~~~~~~~~~

### CRUST
Pastry for Two-Crust Pie (page 142)
or 1 box (15 oz.) refrigerated pie crusts, softened as directed on box

### FILLING
2 cups fresh or frozen whole raspberries (do not thaw)
1/4 to 1/2 cup sugar
1 tablespoon all-purpose flour
1 can (21 oz.) cherry pie filling

**1.** Heat oven to 400°F. Using 9-inch glass pie plate, make pastry as directed in recipe or place pie crust in pie plate as directed on box for Two-Crust Pie.

**2.** In large bowl, gently mix filling ingredients; spoon into pastry-lined pie plate. Top with second pastry; seal edge and flute. Cut slits or shapes in several places in top of pie. Cover edge with 2- to 3-inch-wide strips of foil to prevent excessive browning; remove foil during last 15 minutes of baking.

**3.** Place foil or cookie sheet on oven rack below pie to catch any spills; bake pie 40 to 45 minutes or until crust is golden brown and filling is bubbly. Cool on wire rack at least 2 hours before serving.

**High Altitude (3500–6500 ft):** Heat oven to 425°F. Bake 45 to 55 minutes.

**1 Serving:** Calories 390 (Calories from Fat 160); Total Fat 18g (Saturated Fat 4.5g; Trans Fat 3g); Cholesterol 0mg; Sodium 300mg; Total Carbohydrate 53g (Dietary Fiber 4g; Sugars 26g); Protein 4g

% Daily Value: Vitamin A 0%; Vitamin C 10%; Calcium 2%; Iron 10%

Exchanges: 1 1/2 Starch, 2 Other Carbohydrate, 3 1/2 Fat

Carbohydrate Choices: 3 1/2

# CHERRY-BLUEBERRY PIE

→ PREP TIME: 30 mins
START TO FINISH: 3 hrs 25 mins

**8 servings**

~~~~~~~~~~~~~~~~~~~~~~~~~~~

### CRUST
Pastry for Two-Crust Pie (page 142)
or 1 box (15 oz.) refrigerated pie crusts, softened as directed on box

### FILLING
1/2 cup sugar
2 tablespoons cornstarch
1/4 teaspoon ground cinnamon
1 can (21 oz.) cherry pie filling
1 1/2 cups frozen blueberries

### CRUST GLAZE
1 egg white
1 teaspoon water
2 teaspoons sugar

**1.** Heat oven to 425°F. Using 9-inch glass pie plate, make pastry as directed in recipe or place 1 pie crust in pie plate as directed on box for Two-Crust Pie.

**2.** In large bowl, mix 1/2 cup sugar, the cornstarch and cinnamon. Stir in pie filling and blueberries; spoon into pastry-lined pie plate. Top with second pastry; seal edge and flute. Cut slits or shapes in several places in top of pie.

**3.** In small bowl, beat egg white and water with fork until blended; brush over top of pie (discard any remaining egg white mixture). Sprinkle with 2 teaspoons sugar. Cover edge with 2- to 3-inch-wide strips of foil to prevent excessive browning; remove foil during last 15 minutes of baking.

**4.** Bake 45 to 55 minutes or until crust is golden brown. Cool on wire rack at least 2 hours before serving.

**High Altitude (3500–6500 ft): No change.**

**1 Serving:** Calories 440 (Calories from Fat 160); Total Fat 18g (Saturated Fat 4.5g; Trans Fat 3g); Cholesterol 0mg; Sodium 310mg; Total Carbohydrate 64g (Dietary Fiber 3g; Sugars 34g); Protein 5g

% Daily Value: Vitamin A 0%; Vitamin C 8%; Calcium 0%; Iron 10%

Exchanges: 2 Starch, 2 Other Carbohydrate, 3 1/2 Fat

Carbohydrate Choices: 4

# GINGER-LEMON-BLUEBERRY PIE

→ PREP TIME: 35 mins
START TO FINISH: 3 hrs 20 mins

**8 servings**

~~~~~~~~~~~~~~~~~~~~~~~~~

## CRUST

Pastry for Two-Crust Pie (page 142)
or 1 box (15 oz.) refrigerated pie crusts, softened as directed on box
6 teaspoons sugar
1 teaspoon half-and-half

## FILLING

5 cups fresh blueberries
1/2 cup sugar
2 tablespoons chopped crystallized ginger
2 tablespoons quick-cooking tapioca
1 teaspoon grated lemon peel
1 tablespoon fresh lemon juice

**1.** Heat oven to 400°F. Before placing 1 pastry or pie crust in 9-inch glass pie plate, sprinkle with 1 1/2 teaspoons of the sugar. With rolling pin, roll lightly to coat pastry with sugar. Place, sugared side up, in pie plate and continue as directed for Two-Crust Pie.

**2.** In large bowl, mix filling ingredients; spoon into pastry-lined pie plate. Top with second pastry; seal edge and flute. Cut slits or shapes in several places in top of pie.

**3.** Brush top of pie with half-and-half; sprinkle with remaining 4 1/2 teaspoons sugar. Cover edge with 2- to 3-inch-wide strips of foil to prevent excessive browning; remove foil during last 15 minutes of baking.

**4.** Place foil or cookie sheet on oven rack below pie to catch any spills; bake pie 35 to 45 minutes or until crust is golden brown and filling is bubbly. Cool on wire rack at least 2 hours before serving.

**High Altitude (3500–6500 ft): Heat oven to 425°F. Bake 45 to 55 minutes.**

**1 Serving:** Calories 400 (Calories from Fat 160); Total Fat 18g (Saturated Fat 4.5g; Trans Fat 3g); Cholesterol 0mg; Sodium 300mg; Total Carbohydrate 57g (Dietary Fiber 3g; Sugars 24g); Protein 4g

% Daily Value: Vitamin A 0%; Vitamin C 10%; Calcium 0%; Iron 10%

Exchanges: 1 Starch, 3 Other Carbohydrate, 3 1/2 Fat

Carbohydrate Choices: 4

# PERFECT APPLE PIE

**8 servings**

~~~~~~~~~~~~~~~~~~~~~~~~~

## CRUST

Pastry for Two-Crust Pie (page 142)
or 1 box (15 oz.) refrigerated pie crusts, softened as directed on box

## FILLING

6 cups thinly sliced, peeled apples (6 medium)
3/4 cup sugar
2 tablespoons all-purpose flour
3/4 teaspoon ground cinnamon
1/4 teaspoon salt
1/8 teaspoon ground nutmeg
1 tablespoon lemon juice

**1.** Heat oven to 425°F. Using 9-inch glass pie plate, make pastry as directed in recipe or place 1 pie crust in pie plate as directed on box for Two-Crust Pie.

**2.** In large bowl, gently mix filling ingredients; spoon into pastry-lined pie plate. Top with second pastry; seal edge and flute. Cut slits or shapes in several places in top of pie. Cover edge with 2- to 3-inch-wide strips of foil to prevent excessive browning; remove foil during last 15 minutes of baking.

**3.** Bake 40 to 45 minutes or until apples are tender and crust is golden brown. Cool on wire rack at least 2 hours before serving.

**High Altitude (3500–6500 ft): No change.**

**1 Serving:** Calories 400 (Calories from Fat 160); Total Fat 18g (Saturated Fat 4.5g; Trans Fat 3g); Cholesterol 0mg; Sodium 370mg; Total Carbohydrate 57g (Dietary Fiber 3g; Sugars 28g); Protein 4g

% Daily Value: Vitamin A 0%; Vitamin C 4%; Calcium 0%; Iron 10%

Exchanges: 1 Starch, 3 Other Carbohydrate, 3 1/2 Fat

Carbohydrate Choices: 4

**BAKING TIP:**

*Tart apples, such as Granny Smith, McIntosh or Pippin, make the most flavorful pies. Or you can substitute two 21-ounce cans of apple pie filling for the fresh apple filling.*

**VARIATION:**

**Caramel Pecan Apple Pie:** Immediately after removing pie from oven, drizzle with 1/3 cup caramel topping; sprinkle with 2 to 4 tablespoons chopped pecans.

# FRESH STRAWBERRY PIE

**8 servings**

~~~~~~~~~~~~~~~~~~~~~~~~~~~~~~~

## CRUST
Pastry for One-Crust Pie (page 142)
or 1 refrigerated pie crust (from 15-oz. box), softened as directed on box

## FILLING
3 pints (6 cups) fresh strawberries
1 cup sugar
3 tablespoons cornstarch
1/2 cup water
4 to 5 drops red food color, if desired

## TOPPING
1/2 cup whipping (heavy) cream, whipped, sweetened

**1.** Heat oven to 450°F. Using 9-inch glass pie plate, make pastry as directed in recipe or place pie crust as directed on box for One-Crust Baked Shell. Bake 9 to 11 minutes or until lightly browned. Cool completely.

**2.** Meanwhile, in small bowl, crush enough strawberries to make 1 cup. In 2-quart saucepan, mix sugar and cornstarch; stir in crushed strawberries and water. Cook, stirring constantly, until mixture boils and thickens. If desired, stir in food color. Cool completely, about 30 minutes.

**3.** Place remaining strawberries, whole or sliced, in cooled baked shell. Pour cooked strawberry mixture evenly over berries. Refrigerate until set, about 3 hours, before serving.

**4.** Just before serving, top pie with sweetened whipped cream. Store in refrigerator.

**High Altitude (3500–6500 ft): No change.**

**1 Serving:** Calories 340 (Calories from Fat 120); Total Fat 14g (Saturated Fat 5g; Trans Fat 1.5g); Cholesterol 15mg; Sodium 150mg; Total Carbohydrate 51g (Dietary Fiber 3g; Sugars 35g); Protein 3g
% Daily Value: Vitamin A 4%; Vitamin C 50%; Calcium 2%; Iron 6%
Exchanges: 1 Starch, 2 1/2 Other Carbohydrate, 2 1/2 Fat
Carbohydrate Choices: 3 1/2

## VARIATIONS:
**Fresh Peach Pie:** Substitute sliced fresh peaches for strawberries. Omit red food color.

**Fresh Raspberry Pie:** Substitute fresh raspberries for strawberries.

# STRAWBERRY FUDGE PIE

→ PREP TIME: 30 mins
START TO FINISH: 3 hrs 20 mins

**8 servings**

~~~~~~~~~~~~~~~~~~~~

**CRUST**
Pastry for One-Crust Pie (page
   142)
or 1 refrigerated pie crust (from
   15-oz. box), softened as
   directed on box

**BROWNIE LAYER**
1 pouch (10.25 oz.) fudge
   brownie mix
1/4 cup vegetable oil
2 tablespoons water
1 egg

**CHEESECAKE LAYER**
1 package (8 oz.) cream cheese,
   softened
1/4 cup sugar
1 teaspoon vanilla
1 egg

**TOPPING**
2 cups fresh strawberries, halved
2 tablespoons hot fudge topping

**1.** Heat oven to 350°F. Using 9-inch glass pie plate, make pastry as directed in recipe or place pie crust in pie plate as directed on box for One-Crust Filled Pie.

**2.** In large bowl, beat brownie layer ingredients 50 strokes with spoon. Spread in bottom of pastry-lined pie plate. Cover edge with 2- to 3-inch-wide strips of foil to prevent excessive browning. Bake 15 minutes. Remove foil; bake 15 to 20 minutes longer or until top of brownie layer is shiny and center is set.

**3.** Meanwhile, in small bowl, beat cheesecake layer ingredients with electric mixer on medium speed until smooth.

**4.** Working quickly, drop cream cheese mixture by small spoonfuls over partially baked brownie layer; carefully spread to cover. Bake 18 to 20 minutes or until cream cheese is set. Cool on wire rack at least 1 hour.

**5.** Arrange strawberry halves, cut side down, over top of cream cheese layer. Refrigerate at least 1 hour before serving.

**6.** Just before serving, in small microwavable dish, microwave fudge topping on Medium (50%) 30 seconds. Spoon into small resealable food-storage plastic bag; seal bag (topping will be very hot). Cut small hole in one bottom corner of bag; squeeze bag to drizzle topping over pie. Store in refrigerator.

**High Altitude (3500–6500 ft): For brownie layer, see pouch for high altitude directions.**

**1 Serving:** Calories 510 (Calories from Fat 260); Total Fat 29g (Saturated Fat 11g; Trans Fat 2.5g); Cholesterol 85mg; Sodium 390mg; Total Carbohydrate 55g (Dietary Fiber 3g; Sugars 32g); Protein 7g

% Daily Value: Vitamin A 10%; Vitamin C 15%; Calcium 6%; Iron 15%

Exchanges: 2 Starch, 1 1/2 Other Carbohydrate, 5 1/2 Fat

Carbohydrate Choices: 3 1/2

# BLACK BOTTOM STRAWBERRY CREAM PIE

→ PREP TIME: 25 mins
START TO FINISH: 2 hrs 50 mins

**8 servings**

~~~~~~~~~~~~~~~~~~~~~~~~~

## CRUST
Pastry for One-Crust Pie (page
   142)
or 1 refrigerated pie crust (from
   15-oz. box), softened as
   directed on box

## FILLING
2/3 cup hot fudge topping
1 package (8 oz.) cream cheese,
   softened
1 cup powdered sugar
1 pint (2 cups) fresh strawberries, quartered
1/2 cup strawberry pie glaze

## TOPPING
1/2 cup whipping (heavy) cream,
   whipped, if desired

**1.** Heat oven to 450°F. Using 9-inch glass pie plate, make pastry as directed in recipe or place pie crust in pie plate as directed on box for One-Crust Baked Shell. Bake 9 to 11 minutes or until lightly browned. Cool completely, about 15 minutes.

**2.** Spread hot fudge topping in bottom of cooled baked shell. Refrigerate 1 hour.

**3.** In small bowl, beat cream cheese and powdered sugar with electric mixer on medium speed until smooth. Carefully spread over chocolate layer in cooled baked shell.

**4.** In medium bowl, gently mix strawberries and pie glaze; spoon evenly over cream cheese layer. Refrigerate until firm, about 1 hour, before serving.

**5.** If desired, just before serving, pipe or spoon whipped cream around edge of pie. Store in refrigerator.

**High Altitude (3500–6500 ft): No change.**

**1 Serving:** Calories 450 (Calories from Fat 190); Total Fat 21g (Saturated Fat 9g; Trans Fat 2g); Cholesterol 30mg; Sodium 330mg; Total Carbohydrate 60g (Dietary Fiber 2g; Sugars 39g); Protein 5g

% Daily Value: Vitamin A 8%; Vitamin C 20%; Calcium 6%; Iron 10%

Exchanges: 2 Starch, 2 Other Carbohydrate, 4 Fat

Carbohydrate Choices: 4

> **BAKING TIP:**
> *Hot fudge topping is much thicker than chocolate-flavored syrup, so resist the urge to substitute. Its thickness helps form the "black bottom" of this layered pie. Chocolate-flavored topping does not work in this recipe.*

# BANANA CREAM PUDDING PIE

**8 servings**

〰〰〰〰〰〰〰〰〰〰〰

## CRUST

Pastry for One-Crust Pie (page 142)
or 1 refrigerated pie crust (from 15-oz. box), softened as directed on box

## FILLING

3/4 cup sugar
1/4 cup cornstarch
1/4 teaspoon salt
3 cups milk
3 egg yolks, slightly beaten
2 tablespoons butter or margarine
2 teaspoons vanilla
2 to 3 medium bananas, sliced

## TOPPING

Sweetened whipped cream or whipped topping, if desired

**1.** Heat oven to 450°F. Using 9-inch glass pie plate, make pastry as directed in recipe or place pie crust as directed on box for One-Crust Baked Shell. Bake 9 to 11 minutes or until lightly browned. Cool completely, about 30 minutes.

**2.** Meanwhile, in 1 1/2- to 2-quart saucepan, mix sugar, cornstarch and salt. Stir in milk until smooth. Cook over medium heat, stirring constantly, until mixture boils and thickens; boil and stir 2 minutes. Remove from heat.

**3.** In small bowl, beat egg yolks with wire whisk. Stir about 1/4 cup hot mixture into egg yolks. Gradually stir yolk mixture into hot mixture. Cook, stirring constantly, just until mixture begins to bubble. Remove from heat; stir in butter and vanilla. Cool until lukewarm, about 20 minutes.

**4.** Arrange banana slices in cooled baked shell. Pour cooled pudding over bananas. Refrigerate until set, about 3 hours, before serving.

**5.** If desired, just before serving, top pie with whipped cream. Store in refrigerator.

**High Altitude (3500–6500 ft): In step 2, cook over medium-high heat. In step 3, cook over medium-high heat 2 minutes, stirring constantly, until mixture begins to bubble and is thickened.**

**1 Serving:** Calories 350 (Calories from Fat 140); Total Fat 15g (Saturated Fat 5g; Trans Fat 1.5g); Cholesterol 95mg; Sodium 290mg; Total Carbohydrate 46g (Dietary Fiber 1g; Sugars 27g); Protein 6g

% Daily Value: Vitamin A 8%; Vitamin C 2%; Calcium 10%; Iron 6%

Exchanges: 2 Starch, 1 Other Carbohydrate, 3 Fat

Carbohydrate Choices: 3

> **BAKING TIP:**
> *For sweetened whipped cream, whip 1 cup whipping cream until soft peaks form, then beat in 2 tablespoons powdered sugar.*

# VANILLA CREAM PIE

→ **PREP TIME: 1 hr**
**START TO FINISH: 4 hrs**

**8 servings**

~~~~~~~~~~~~~~~~~~~~~

## CRUST

1 refrigerated pie crust (from
15-oz. pkg.) or Pastry for
One-Crust Pie (page 142)

## FILLING

3/4 cup sugar
1/4 cup cornstarch
1/4 teaspoon salt
3 cups milk
3 egg yolks, slightly beaten
2 tablespoons butter or
margarine
2 teaspoons vanilla

**1.** Heat oven to 450°F. Prepare pie crust for one-crust baked shell using 9-inch pie pan. Bake at 450°F for 9 to 11 minutes or until light golden brown. Cool 30 minutes or until completely cooled.

**2.** In medium saucepan, combine sugar, cornstarch and salt; mix well. Stir in milk until smooth. Cook over medium heat until mixture boils and thickens, stirring constantly. Boil 2 minutes. Remove from heat.

**3.** Stir about 1/4 cup hot mixture into egg yolks. Gradually stir yolk mixture into hot mixture. Cook just until mixture begins to bubble, stirring constantly.

**4.** Remove from heat; stir in butter and vanilla. Pour into cooled baked shell. Refrigerate 3 hours or until set. If desired, top with whipped cream. Store in refrigerator.

**1 Serving:** Calories 300 (Calories from Fat 120); Total Fat 13g (Saturated Fat 5g; Trans Fat 0); Cholesterol 95mg; Sodium 250mg; Total Carbohydrate 40g (Dietary Fiber 0g; Sugars 24g); Protein 5g

% Daily Value: Vitamin A 8%; Vitamin C 0%; Calcium 15%; Iron 2%

Exchanges: 1 1/2 Starch, 1 Fruit, 2 1/2 Other Carbohydrate, 2 1/2 Fat

Carbohydrate Choices: 2 1/2

## VARIATIONS:

**Banana Cream Pie:** Cool filling in saucepan to lukewarm. Slice 2 or 3 bananas into cooled baked shell. Pour filling over bananas.

**Butterscotch Cream Pie:** Substitute firmly packed brown sugar for sugar.

**Chocolate Cream Pie:** Increase sugar to 1 cup and add 2 oz. unsweetened chocolate to filling mixture before cooking.

**Coconut Cream Pie:** Stir 1 cup coconut into cooked filling with margarine and vanilla.

# SOUTHERN PEACH PIE WITH BERRY SAUCE

→ **PREP TIME:** 45 mins
**START TO FINISH:** 3 hrs 15 mins

**8 servings**

〜〜〜〜〜〜〜〜〜〜〜〜

### CRUST
Pastry for Two-Crust Pie (page 142)
or 1 box (15 oz.) refrigerated pie crusts, softened as directed on box

### FILLING
5 1/2 to 6 cups sliced peeled peaches (8 to 9 medium)
1 tablespoon lemon juice
1 cup sugar
1/4 cup cornstarch
1/4 teaspoon salt
1/4 teaspoon ground nutmeg

### SAUCE
1/4 cup sugar
1 tablespoon cornstarch
1 bag (12 oz.) frozen whole raspberries or blackberries, thawed, drained and liquid reserved
1/2 teaspoon almond extract

**1.** Heat oven to 400°F. Using 9-inch glass pie plate, make pastry as directed in recipe or place pie crust in pie plate as directed on box for Two-Crust Pie.

**2.** In large bowl, gently mix peaches and lemon juice to coat. Gently stir in remaining filling ingredients. Spoon into pastry-lined pie plate. Top with second pastry; seal edge and flute. Cut slits or shapes in several places in top of pie. Cover edge with 2- to 3-inch-wide strips of foil to prevent excessive browning; remove foil during last 15 minutes of baking.

**3.** Bake 35 to 45 minutes or until golden brown. Cool on wire rack at least 1 hour before serving.

**4.** Meanwhile, in 2-quart saucepan, mix 1/4 cup sugar and 1 tablespoon cornstarch. If necessary, add water to reserved raspberry liquid to measure 1/2 cup. Gradually stir liquid into sugar mixture, cooking and stirring over medium heat until thickened. Stir in almond extract; gently fold in raspberries. Cool completely, about 1 hour.

**5.** Serve sauce over individual servings of pie.

**High Altitude (3500–6500 ft): Bake 45 to 55 minutes.**

**1 Serving:** Calories 490 (Calories from Fat 160); Total Fat 18g (Saturated Fat 4.5g; Trans Fat 3g); Cholesterol 0mg; Sodium 370mg; Total Carbohydrate 78g (Dietary Fiber 7g; Sugars 46g); Protein 4g

% Daily Value: Vitamin A 4%; Vitamin C 15%; Calcium 2%; Iron 10%

Exchanges: 1 Starch, 4 Other Carbohydrate, 3 1/2 Fat

Carbohydrate Choices: 5

> **BAKING TIP:**
> *For easier peeling, submerge peaches in boiling water for about 30 seconds; remove them with a slotted spoon and transfer to ice water— the skins will slide right off.*

PRIZED PIES

●

# FLUFFY KEY LIME PIE

→ PREP TIME: 40 mins
START TO FINISH: 3 hrs 25 mins

**8 servings**

~~~~~~~~~~~~~~~~~~~~~~~~~~~~~

## CRUST
Pastry for One-Crust Pie (page 142)
or 1 refrigerated pie crust (from 15-oz. box), softened as directed on box

## FILLING
1 envelope unflavored gelatin
1 cup sugar
1/2 cup fresh Key lime or regular lime juice
1/4 cup water
4 pasteurized eggs, separated
1 teaspoon grated lime peel
2 drops green food color
1 cup whipping (heavy) cream

## TOPPING
Sweetened whipped cream, if desired

**1.** Heat oven to 450°F. Using 9-inch glass pie plate, make pastry as directed in recipe or place pie crust in pie plate as directed on box for One-Crust Baked Shell. Bake 9 to 11 minutes or until lightly browned. Cool completely, about 30 minutes.

**2.** Meanwhile, in 1-quart saucepan, mix gelatin, 1/2 cup of the sugar, the lime juice, water and egg yolks. Cook over medium heat 6 to 7 minutes, stirring constantly, until mixture boils and thickens slightly. Remove from heat; stir in lime peel and food color. Pour mixture into large bowl. Refrigerate until mixture mounds slightly, about 45 minutes.

**3.** In another large bowl, beat egg whites with electric mixer on high speed until soft peaks form. Gradually add remaining 1/2 cup sugar, beating until stiff peaks form. In small bowl, beat whipping cream until stiff peaks form.

**4.** Fold egg whites and whipped cream into cooled lime mixture; spoon into cooled baked shell. Refrigerate until firm, about 2 hours, before serving.

**5.** If desired, just before serving, top pie with sweetened whipped cream. Store in refrigerator.

**High Altitude (3500–6500 ft): No change.**

**1 Serving:** Calories 370 (Calories from Fat 190); Total Fat 21g (Saturated Fat 9g; Trans Fat 1.5g); Cholesterol 140mg; Sodium 190mg; Total Carbohydrate 39g (Dietary Fiber 0g; Sugars 27g); Protein 6g

% Daily Value: Vitamin A 10%; Vitamin C 4%; Calcium 4%; Iron 6%

Exchanges: 1 1/2 Starch, 1 Other Carbohydrate, 4 Fat

Carbohydrate Choices: 2 1/2

> **BAKING TIP:**
> *Pasteurized eggs are uncooked eggs that have been heat-treated. Since the egg whites in this recipe are not cooked, be sure to use pasteurized eggs—you can find them in the dairy case at large supermarkets.*

# LEMON MERINGUE PIE

→ PREP TIME: 55 mins
START TO FINISH: 5 hrs 40 mins

**8 servings**

## CRUST

Pastry for One-Crust Pie (page
  142)
or 1 refrigerated pie crust (from
  15-oz. box), softened as
  directed on box

## FILLING

1 1/4 cups sugar
1/3 cup cornstarch
1/2 teaspoon salt
1 1/2 cups cold water
3 egg yolks
2 tablespoons butter or
  margarine
1 tablespoon grated lemon peel
1/2 cup fresh lemon juice

## MERINGUE

3 egg whites
1/4 teaspoon cream of tartar
1/2 teaspoon vanilla
1/4 cup sugar

**1.** Heat oven to 450°F. Using 9-inch glass pie plate, make pastry as directed in recipe or place pie crust in pie plate as directed on box for One-Crust Baked Shell. Bake 9 to 11 minutes or until lightly browned. Cool completely, about 30 minutes.

**2.** Meanwhile, in 2-quart saucepan, mix 1 1/4 cups sugar, the cornstarch and salt. Gradually stir in cold water until smooth. Cook over medium heat, stirring constantly, until mixture boils; boil 1 minute, stirring constantly. Remove from heat.

**3.** In small bowl, beat egg yolks with wire whisk. Stir about 1/4 cup of hot mixture into egg yolks. Gradually stir yolk mixture into hot mixture. Cook over low heat, stirring constantly, until mixture boils; boil 1 minute, stirring constantly. Remove from heat. Stir in butter, lemon peel and lemon juice. Cool slightly, about 15 minutes.

**4.** Reduce oven temperature to 350°F. Pour filling into cooled baked shell. In small deep bowl, beat egg whites, cream of tartar and vanilla with electric mixer on medium speed about 1 minute or until soft peaks form. On high speed, beat in 1/4 cup sugar, 1 tablespoon at a time, until stiff glossy peaks form and sugar is dissolved. Spoon meringue onto hot filling, spreading to edge of crust to seal well and prevent shrinkage.

**5.** Bake 12 to 15 minutes or until meringue is light golden brown. Cool completely on wire rack, about 1 hour. Refrigerate until filling is set, about 3 hours, before serving. Store in refrigerator.

**High Altitude (3500–6500 ft): In step 5, bake about 20 minutes or until meringue is light golden brown.**

**1 Serving:** Calories 360 (Calories from Fat 120); Total Fat 14g (Saturated Fat 4g; Trans Fat 1.5g); Cholesterol 85mg; Sodium 340mg; Total Carbohydrate 56g (Dietary Fiber 0g; Sugars 38g); Protein 4g

% Daily Value: Vitamin A 4%; Vitamin C 4%; Calcium 0%; Iron 6%

Exchanges: 1 1/2 Starch, 2 Other Carbohydrate, 2 1/2 Fat

Carbohydrate Choices: 4

# GOLDEN PECAN PIE

→ PREP TIME: 40 mins
START TO FINISH: 3 hrs 30 mins

**8 servings**

~~~~~~~~~~~~~~~~~~~~~~~~~~~~

## CRUST

Pastry for One-Crust Pie (page 142)
or 1 refrigerated pie crust (from 15-oz. box), softened as directed on box

## FILLING

1/3 cup packed brown sugar
1 1/2 teaspoons all-purpose flour
1 1/4 cups light corn syrup
1 1/4 teaspoons vanilla
3 eggs
1 1/2 cups pecan halves or broken pecans
2 tablespoons butter or margarine, melted

**1.** Heat oven to 375°F. Using 9-inch glass pie plate, make pastry as directed in recipe or place pie crust in pie plate as directed on box for One-Crust Filled Pie.

**2.** In large bowl, beat brown sugar, flour, corn syrup, vanilla and eggs with wire whisk until well blended. Stir in pecans and butter. Pour into pastry-lined pie plate. Cover edge with 2- to 3-inch-wide strips of foil to prevent excessive browning; remove foil during last 15 minutes of baking.

**3.** Bake 40 to 50 minutes or until filling is puffed and pie is golden brown. Cool on wire rack at least 2 hours before serving. Store in refrigerator.

**High Altitude (3500–6500 ft): No change.**

1 **Serving:** Calories 520 (Calories from Fat 240); Total Fat 27g (Saturated Fat 5g; Trans Fat 1.5g); Cholesterol 85mg; Sodium 260mg; Total Carbohydrate 63g (Dietary Fiber 2g; Sugars 29g); Protein 6g

% Daily Value: Vitamin A 4%; Vitamin C 0%; Calcium 4%; Iron 10%

Exchanges: 2 Starch, 2 Other Carbohydrate, 5 Fat

Carbohydrate Choices: 4

## VARIATIONS:

**Orange Pecan Pie:** Add 1/2 teaspoon grated orange peel to filling. If desired, garnish with candied orange peel.

# VIENNA CHOCOLATE PIE

→ **PREP TIME:** 25 mins
**START TO FINISH:** 1 hr 55 mins

**8 servings**

## CRUST
Pastry for One-Crust Pie (page 142)
or 1 refrigerated pie crust (from 15-oz. box), softened as directed on box

## FILLING
1 1/2 cups sugar
3 tablespoons all-purpose flour
3/4 teaspoon instant coffee granules or crystals
1/4 teaspoon ground cinnamon
Dash salt
4 eggs
1/2 cup butter or margarine, softened
2 oz. unsweetened baking chocolate, melted
1/2 cup buttermilk
1 1/2 teaspoons vanilla
1/4 cup slivered almonds

**1.** Heat oven to 400°F. Using 9-inch glass pie plate, make pastry as directed in recipe or place pie crust in pie plate as directed on box for One-Crust Filled Pie.

**2.** In medium bowl, mix sugar, flour, instant coffee, cinnamon and salt. In large bowl, beat eggs with electric mixer on high speed until light in color. Beat in sugar mixture until blended. Beat in remaining filling ingredients except almonds until well combined (filling may look curdled). Pour into pastry-lined pie plate. Sprinkle with almonds. Cover edge with 2- to 3-inch-wide strips of foil to prevent excessive browning; remove foil during last 15 minutes of baking.

**3.** Bake 25 to 30 minutes or until center is set and crust is deep golden brown. Cool completely on wire rack, about 1 hour, before serving. Store in refrigerator.

**High Altitude (3500–6500 ft): Bake 30 to 35 minutes.**

**1 Serving:** Calories 510 (Calories from Fat 260); Total Fat 29g (Saturated Fat 11g; Trans Fat 2g); Cholesterol 135mg; Sodium 290mg; Total Carbohydrate 56g (Dietary Fiber 2g; Sugars 39g); Protein 7g

% Daily Value: Vitamin A 10%; Vitamin C 0%; Calcium 6%; Iron 10%

Exchanges: 2 Starch, 2 Other Carbohydrate, 5 1/2 Fat

Carbohydrate Choices: 4

> **BAKING TIP:**
> *To substitute for buttermilk, use 1 1/2 teaspoons vinegar or lemon juice plus milk to make 1/2 cup.*

# RASPBERRY CREAM HEART

→ **PREP TIME:** 35 mins
**START TO FINISH:** 50 mins

**8 servings**

~~~~~~~~~~~~~~~~~~~~~~~~~~~~~

1 box (15 oz.) refrigerated pie
  crusts, softened as directed
  on box
1 package (8 oz.) cream cheese,
  softened
1/4 cup powdered sugar
1 jar (14 oz.) strawberry pie glaze
2 1/2 cups fresh raspberries
1 teaspoon powdered sugar

**1.** Heat oven to 450°F. Cut out paper pattern for 11x10-inch heart. Remove 1 pie crust from pouch; unroll on ungreased cookie sheet. With paper pattern as a guide, cut crust into heart shape. Generously prick crust with fork.

**2.** Bake 8 to 10 minutes or until light golden brown. Cool 15 minutes. Repeat with remaining pie crust to make second heart.

**3.** In small bowl, beat cream cheese and 1/4 cup powdered sugar with electric mixer on medium speed until smooth. Place 1 cooled baked crust on serving plate; spread with cream cheese mixture.

**4.** Reserve 1/2 cup of the pie glaze; spread remaining glaze over cream cheese mixture. Top with second crust. Spread reserved 1/2 cup glaze over top crust. Arrange raspberries, stem side down, over top. Sprinkle with 1 teaspoon powdered sugar. Store in refrigerator.

**High Altitude (3500–6500 ft): Heat oven to 425°F.**

**1 Serving:** Calories 510 (Calories from Fat 220); Total Fat 24g (Saturated Fat 11g; Trans Fat 0.5g); Cholesterol 40mg; Sodium 320mg; Total Carbohydrate 69g (Dietary Fiber 4g; Sugars 34g); Protein 4g

% Daily Value: Vitamin A 8%; Vitamin C 25%; Calcium 4%; Iron 4%

Exchanges: 1 1/2 Starch, 3 Other Carbohydrate, 4 1/2 Fat

Carbohydrate Choices: 4 1/2

**BAKING TIP:**

*Frozen raspberries can be used in place of the fresh berries. No need to thaw them—just arrange them on the tart 20 minutes before serving.*

# CHOCOLATE-PECAN PIE

**10 servings**

## CRUST

Pastry for One-Crust Pie (page 142)
or 1 refrigerated pie crust (from 15-oz. box), softened as directed on box

## FILLING

1 cup light corn syrup
1/2 cup sugar
1/4 cup butter or margarine, melted
1 teaspoon vanilla
3 eggs
1 cup semisweet chocolate chips (6 oz.)
1 1/2 cups pecan halves

## TOPPING

10 pecan halves
1/2 cup whipping (heavy) cream, whipped

**1.** Heat oven to 325°F. Using 9-inch glass pie plate, make pastry as directed in recipe or place pie crust in pie plate as directed on box for One-Crust Filled Pie.

**2.** In large bowl, beat corn syrup, sugar, butter, vanilla and eggs with wire whisk until well blended. Reserve 2 tablespoons chocolate chips for topping; stir remaining chocolate chips and the 1 1/2 cups pecans into corn syrup mixture. Pour into pastry-lined pie plate, spreading evenly. Cover edge with 2- to 3-inch-wide strips of foil to prevent excessive browning; remove foil during last 15 minutes of baking.

**3.** Bake 55 to 65 minutes or until deep golden brown and filling is set. Cool completely, about 1 hour.

**4.** Meanwhile, line cookie sheet with waxed paper. In small microwavable bowl, microwave reserved 2 tablespoons chocolate chips on Medium (50%) 1 minute to 1 minute 30 seconds or until melted; stir. Dip each of 10 pecan halves into chocolate; place on cookie sheet. Refrigerate until chocolate is set, 15 to 20 minutes, before serving.

**5.** Just before serving, top pie with whipped cream and chocolate-dipped pecans. Store in refrigerator.

**High Altitude (3500–6500 ft):** Heat oven to 350°F. Bake 50 to 55 minutes.

**1 Serving:** Calories 560 (Calories from Fat 300); Total Fat 34g (Saturated Fat 11g; Trans Fat 1.5g); Cholesterol 90mg; Sodium 210mg; Total Carbohydrate 58g (Dietary Fiber 3g; Sugars 33g); Protein 6g

% Daily Value: Vitamin A 8%; Vitamin C 0%; Calcium 4%; Iron 10%

Exchanges: 2 Starch, 2 Other Carbohydrate, 6 1/2 Fat

Carbohydrate Choices: 4

> **BAKING TIP:**
> *Whipping cream whips more quickly and gives more volume if both the cream and the equipment are cold. Place the bowl and beaters in the freezer 15 minutes before using and leave the whipping cream in the refrigerator until ready to whip.*

# FRENCH SILK CHOCOLATE PIE

→ PREP TIME: 1 hr
START TO FINISH: 3 hrs

**10 servings**

~~~~~~~~~~~~~~~~~~~~~~~~~

**CRUST**
Pastry for One-Crust Pie (page 142)
or 1 refrigerated pie crust (from 15-oz. box), softened as directed on box

**FILLING**
3 oz. unsweetened baking chocolate, cut into pieces
1 cup butter, softened (do not use margarine)
1 cup sugar
1/2 teaspoon vanilla
4 pasteurized eggs or 1 cup fat-free egg product

**TOPPING**
1/2 cup sweetened whipped cream
Chocolate curls, if desired

**1.** Heat oven to 450°F. Using 9-inch glass pie plate, make pastry as directed in recipe or place pie crust in pie plate as directed on box for One-Crust Baked Shell. Bake 9 to 11 minutes or until lightly browned. Cool completely, about 30 minutes.

**2.** Meanwhile, in 1-quart saucepan, melt chocolate over low heat; cool. In small bowl, beat butter with electric mixer on medium speed until fluffy. Gradually beat in sugar until light and fluffy. Beat in cooled chocolate and vanilla until blended. Add 1 egg (or 1/4 cup egg product) at a time, beating on high speed 2 minutes after each addition; beat until mixture is smooth and fluffy.

**3.** Pour filling into cooled baked shell. Refrigerate at least 2 hours before serving.

**4.** Just before serving, top pie with whipped cream and, if desired, chocolate curls. Store in refrigerator.

**High Altitude (3500–6500 ft): No change.**

**1 Serving:** Calories 460 (Calories from Fat 300); Total Fat 34g (Saturated Fat 15g; Trans Fat 2.5g); Cholesterol 140mg; Sodium 270mg; Total Carbohydrate 33g (Dietary Fiber 2g; Sugars 21g); Protein 5g
% Daily Value: Vitamin A 15%; Vitamin C 0%; Calcium 2%; Iron 8%
Exchanges: 1 Starch, 1 Other Carbohydrate, 7 Fat
Carbohydrate Choices: 2

**BAKING TIP:**
*Pasteurized eggs are uncooked eggs that have been heat-treated. Be sure to use pasteurized eggs or egg product in this recipe since they're not cooked. Pasteurized eggs can be found in the dairy case at large supermarkets.*

# STREUSEL-TOPPED PUMPKIN PIE

→ **PREP TIME:** 30 mins
**START TO FINISH:** 2 hrs

**8 servings**

~~~~~~~~~~~~~~~~~~~~~~~~~~

## CRUST
Pastry for One-Crust Pie
   (page 142)
or 1 refrigerated pie crust (from
   15-oz. box), softened as
   directed on box

## FILLING
1 can (15 oz.) pumpkin (not
   pumpkin pie mix)
1 can (12 oz.) evaporated milk
   (1 1/2 cups)
1/2 cup granulated sugar
2 eggs, slightly beaten
1 1/2 teaspoons pumpkin pie
   spice
1/4 teaspoon salt

## STREUSEL
1/4 cup packed brown sugar
2 tablespoons all-purpose flour
2 tablespoons butter or
   margarine, softened
1/2 cup chopped pecans

## TOPPING
1 teaspoon grated orange peel
1 container (8 oz.) frozen
   whipped topping, thawed
   (3 cups)

**1.** Heat oven to 425°F. Using 9-inch glass pie plate, make pastry as directed in recipe or place pie crust in pie plate as directed on box for One-Crust Filled Pie.

**2.** In large bowl, mix filling ingredients until well blended; pour into pastry-lined pie plate. Cover edge with 2- to 3-inch-wide strips of foil to prevent excessive browning.

**3.** Bake 15 minutes. Reduce oven temperature to 350°F; bake 15 minutes longer. Meanwhile, in small bowl, mix streusel ingredients.

**4.** Remove foil; sprinkle streusel over filling. Bake 15 to 20 minutes or until knife inserted in center comes out clean. Cool completely on wire rack, about 1 hour, before serving.

**5.** Just before serving, gently fold orange peel into whipped topping; garnish pie with topping. Store in refrigerator.

**High Altitude (3500–6500 ft):** In step 4, bake 20 to 30 minutes.

**1 Serving:** Calories 470 (Calories from Fat 240); Total Fat 26g (Saturated Fat 11g; Trans Fat 1.5g); Cholesterol 75mg; Sodium 310mg; Total Carbohydrate 50g (Dietary Fiber 3g; Sugars 30g); Protein 8g

% Daily Value: Vitamin A 170%; Vitamin C 2%; Calcium 15%; Iron 10%

Exchanges: 2 Starch, 1 1/2 Other Carbohydrate, 5 Fat

Carbohydrate Choices: 3

> **BAKING TIP:**
> *The streusel topping adds a new twist to traditional pumpkin pie.*
> *Walnuts can be used in place of the pecans.*

# SWEET POTATO PIE

→ PREP TIME: 30 mins
START TO FINISH: 2 hrs 10 mins

**8 servings**

~~~~~~~~~~~~~~~~~~~~~~~~

## CRUST
Pastry for One-Crust Pie (page 142)
or 1 refrigerated pie crust (from 15-oz. box), softened as directed on box

## FILLING
1 1/2 cups mashed canned sweet potatoes
2/3 cup packed brown sugar
1 teaspoon ground cinnamon
1/2 teaspoon ground allspice
1 cup half-and-half
1 tablespoon dry sherry or lemon juice
2 eggs, beaten

## TOPPING
Sweetened whipped cream or whipped topping

**1.** Heat oven to 425°F. Using 9-inch glass pie plate, make pastry as directed in recipe or place pie crust in pie plate as directed on box for One-Crust Filled Pie.

**2.** In blender or food processor, process filling ingredients until well blended; pour into pastry-lined pie plate. Cover edge with 2- to 3-inch-wide strips of foil to prevent excessive browning; remove foil during last 15 minutes of baking.

**3.** Bake 15 minutes. Reduce oven temperature to 350°F; bake 30 to 40 minutes longer or until center is set. Cool completely on wire rack, about 45 minutes, before serving. Top pie with sweetened whipped cream. Store in refrigerator.

**High Altitude (3500–6500 ft): No change.**

**1 Serving:** Calories 360 (Calories from Fat 160); Total Fat 18g (Saturated Fat 7g; Trans Fat 1.5g); Cholesterol 80mg; Sodium 210mg; Total Carbohydrate 46g (Dietary Fiber 2g; Sugars 30g); Protein 5g
% Daily Value: Vitamin A 140%; Vitamin C 4%; Calcium 8%; Iron 10%
Exchanges: 1 Starch, 2 Other Carbohydrate, 3 1/2 Fat
Carbohydrate Choices: 3

> **BAKING TIP:**
> *See page 151 for Sweetened Whipped Cream. For an elegant touch, pipe the sweetened whipped cream onto the pie using a large open-star tip.*

# RHUBARB-STRAWBERRY TART

→ PREP TIME: 30 mins
START TO FINISH: 3 hrs 30 mins

**12 servings**

~~~~~~~~~~~~~~~~~~~~~~

## CRUST
Pastry for One-Crust Tart
  (page 142)
or 1 refrigerated pie crust
  (from 15-oz. box), softened
  as directed on box

## FILLING
2 eggs
3/4 cup granulated sugar
3 tablespoons all-purpose flour
1/4 teaspoon almond extract
3 cups coarsely sliced fresh
  rhubarb
2 cups sliced fresh strawberries

## TOPPING
1/2 cup packed brown sugar
1/4 cup all-purpose flour
1/4 teaspoon ground nutmeg
2 tablespoons butter or
  margarine, cut into pieces

**1.** Heat oven to 375°F. Using 10-inch tart pan with removable bottom, make pastry as directed in recipe or place pie crust in pan as directed on box for One-Crust Filled Tart. Trim edge if necessary.

**2.** In large bowl, beat eggs with wire whisk. Beat in granulated sugar, 3 tablespoons flour and the almond extract until well blended. Alternately layer rhubarb and strawberries in pastry-lined pan. Pour egg mixture over fruit.

**3.** In small bowl, mix brown sugar, 1/4 cup flour and the nutmeg. With pastry blender or fork, cut in butter until mixture resembles coarse crumbs. Sprinkle over top. Cover edge with 2- to 3-inch-wide strips of foil to prevent excessive browning; remove foil during last 15 minutes of baking.

**4.** Bake 50 to 60 minutes or until crust is golden brown and filling is set in center. Cool completely on wire rack, about 2 hours, before serving. Remove side of pan; cut tart into wedges. Store in refrigerator.

**High Altitude (3500–6500 ft): Bake 53 to 57 minutes.**

**1 Serving:** Calories 230 (Calories from Fat 80); Total Fat 9g (Saturated Fat 2.5g; Trans Fat 1g); Cholesterol 40mg; Sodium 125mg; Total Carbohydrate 36g (Dietary Fiber 2g; Sugars 23g); Protein 3g

% Daily Value: Vitamin A 4%; Vitamin C 15%; Calcium 8%; Iron 6%

Exchanges: 1 Starch, 1 1/2 Other Carbohydrate, 1 1/2 Fat

Carbohydrate Choices: 2 1/2

> **BAKING TIP:**
> *A 1-pound bag of frozen unsweetened rhubarb can be used in place of the fresh rhubarb in this tart. Increase the baking time to 55 to 65 minutes.*

# STRAWBERRY-KIWI TART

→ PREP TIME: 30 mins
START TO FINISH: 2 hrs

**8 servings**

〜〜〜〜〜〜〜〜〜〜〜〜

## CRUST

Pastry for One-Crust Tart
  (page 142)
or 1 refrigerated pie crust
  (from 15-oz. box), softened
  as directed on box

## FILLING

1 1/2 cups vanilla low-fat yogurt
1 container (8 oz.) reduced-fat
  sour cream (1 cup)
1 box (4-serving size) vanilla
  instant pudding and pie filling
  mix
2 tablespoons orange
  marmalade

## TOPPING

1 cup halved fresh strawberries
2 kiwifruit, peeled, thinly sliced
2 tablespoons orange
  marmalade

**1.** Heat oven to 450°F. Using 9-inch tart pan with removable bottom or 9-inch glass pie plate, make pastry as directed in recipe or place pie crust in pan as directed on box for One-Crust Baked Shell. Bake 9 to 11 minutes or until lightly browned. Cool completely, about 30 minutes.

**2.** In medium bowl, mix filling ingredients with wire whisk until well blended; pour into cooled baked shell. Arrange strawberries on filling around outer edge of pie; arrange kiwifruit in center.

**3.** In small microwavable bowl, microwave marmalade on High 5 to 10 seconds or until melted; brush over fruit. Refrigerate until set, about 1 hour, before serving. Store in refrigerator.

**High Altitude (3500–6500 ft): No change.**

**1 Serving:** Calories 310 (Calories from Fat 120); Total Fat 13g (Saturated Fat 4.5g; Trans Fat 1.5g); Cholesterol 15mg; Sodium 370mg; Total Carbohydrate 44g (Dietary Fiber 2g; Sugars 26g); Protein 5g

% Daily Value: Vitamin A 4%; Vitamin C 50%; Calcium 10%; Iron 6%

Exchanges: 1 Starch, 2 Other Carbohydrate, 2 1/2 Fat

Carbohydrate Choices: 3

# BANANA SPLIT TART

→ PREP TIME: 20 mins
START TO FINISH: 1 hr 15 mins

**16 servings**

## CRUST
1 box (15 oz.) refrigerated pie
 crusts, softened as directed
 on box

## FILLING
1/2 cup semisweet chocolate
 chips, melted
2 containers (6 oz. each) banana
 crème low-fat yogurt
2 small bananas, sliced
1 can (21 oz.) strawberry pie
 filling with more fruit
1 cup fresh strawberries, sliced

**1.** Heat oven to 375°F. Remove pie crusts from pouches; unroll 1 crust in center of ungreased large cookie sheet. Unroll second crust and place over first crust, matching edges and pressing to seal. With rolling pin, roll out into 14-inch round. Fold 1/2 inch of crust edge under, forming border; press to seal seam. If desired, flute edge. Prick crust generously with fork.

**2.** Bake 20 to 25 minutes or until golden brown. Cool completely, about 30 minutes.

**3.** Spread half of the melted chocolate chips evenly over cooled baked crust. Spread yogurt over chocolate. Arrange banana slices on top of yogurt. Spread pie filling evenly over bananas. Arrange strawberries over pie filling. Drizzle remaining melted chocolate chips over top. Cut into wedges to serve. Store in refrigerator.

**High Altitude (3500–6500 ft): Bake 17 to 22 minutes.**

**1 Serving:** Calories 220 (Calories from Fat 80); Total Fat 9g (Saturated Fat 3.5g; Trans Fat 0g); Cholesterol 0mg; Sodium 125mg; Total Carbohydrate 33g (Dietary Fiber 1g; Sugars 17g); Protein 2g

% Daily Value: Vitamin A 0%; Vitamin C 6%; Calcium 4%; Iron 0%

Exchanges: 2 Other Carbohydrate, 2 Fat

Carbohydrate Choices: 2

> **BAKING TIP:**
> *To melt the chips, place them in a microwavable bowl. Microwave on High for 45 seconds, then stir until smooth. If needed, microwave another 10 to 15 seconds.*

# COUNTRY APPLE-PEAR TART

→ PREP TIME: 30 mins
START TO FINISH: 1 hr 30 mins

**6 servings**

~~~~~~~~~~~~~~~~~~~

## CRUST

1 refrigerated pie crust (from 15-oz. box), softened as directed on box

## FILLING

2 cups thinly sliced, peeled apples (2 medium)

2 cups thinly sliced, peeled pears (3 medium)

3/4 cup fresh cranberries

1/3 cup granulated sugar

2 tablespoons all-purpose flour

1/4 teaspoon ground nutmeg

## TOPPING

1/4 cup all-purpose flour

1/4 cup packed brown sugar

2 tablespoons butter or margarine, cut into pieces

1 teaspoon milk

1 tablespoon granulated sugar

2 tablespoons sliced almonds

**1.** Heat oven to 425°F. Line cookie sheet with cooking parchment paper. Remove pie crust from pouch; unroll on cookie sheet.

**2.** In large bowl, gently mix filling ingredients to coat. Spoon filling evenly onto pastry, spreading to within 2 inches of edge.

**3.** In small bowl, mix 1/4 cup flour, the brown sugar and butter until crumbly; sprinkle over filling. Fold edge of pie crust up over filling, pleating to fit and leaving about 5 to 6 inches in center uncovered. Brush pie crust with milk; sprinkle with 1 tablespoon granulated sugar.

**4.** Bake 10 minutes. Reduce oven temperature to 350°F; sprinkle almonds over filling. Bake 20 to 30 minutes longer or until edge is deep golden brown and fruit is tender. Immediately loosen tart by running pancake turner under bottom; place on wire rack. Cool at least 30 minutes before serving.

**High Altitude (3500–6500 ft): In step 4, increase second bake time to 25 to 35 minutes.**

**1 Serving:** Calories 390 (Calories from Fat 130); Total Fat 15g (Saturated Fat 5g; Trans Fat 0g); Cholesterol 15mg; Sodium 180mg; Total Carbohydrate 61g (Dietary Fiber 4g; Sugars 34g); Protein 3g

% Daily Value: Vitamin A 4%; Vitamin C 4%; Calcium 2%; Iron 4%

Exchanges: 1 Starch, 3 Other Carbohydrate, 3 Fat

Carbohydrate Choices: 4

*K*ids are cool—let them be creative! Maybe the pretzels don't look like the photo or the cookies are lopsided—no harm, it's all just fun!

# MINI SOFT PRETZELS AND DIP

→ **PREP TIME:** 25 mins
**START TO FINISH:** 30 mins

**24 servings**

〜〜〜〜〜〜〜〜〜〜〜〜〜

1 can (11 oz.) refrigerated
    breadsticks (12 breadsticks)
1 egg, beaten
Coarse salt, if desired
1 jar (5 oz.) sharp process
    cheese spread with bacon
2 tablespoons milk

**1.** Heat oven to 375°F. Unroll dough; separate into 12 breadsticks. Cut each in half lengthwise. Roll each breadstick lightly into 10-inch-long rope.

**2.** To shape each pretzel, shape rope into a circle, overlapping dough about 2 inches from each end, leaving ends free. Take 1 end in each hand; twist once at point where dough overlaps. Lift ends over opposite side of circle. Place pretzels 1 inch apart on ungreased cookie sheet.

**3.** Brush each pretzel with beaten egg; sprinkle with salt if desired.

**4.** Bake 13 to 15 minutes or until golden brown. Immediately remove from cookie sheet.

**5.** Meanwhile, in small microwavable bowl, microwave cheese spread and milk on High 1 minute, stirring once halfway through cooking, until melted and hot.

**6.** Serve warm pretzels with warm cheese dip.

**High Altitude (3500–6500 ft): No change.**

**1 Serving:** Calories 60 (Calories from Fat 20); Total Fat 2.5g (Saturated Fat 1g; Trans Fat 0g); Cholesterol 15mg; Sodium 180mg; Total Carbohydrate 7g (Dietary Fiber 0g; Sugars 1g); Protein 2g
% Daily Value: Vitamin A 0%; Vitamin C 0%; Calcium 4%; Iron 2%
Exchanges: 1/2 Starch, 1/2 Fat
Carbohydrate Choices: 1/2

# CHEESY BREADSTICK DUNKERS

→ PREP TIME: 10 mins
START TO FINISH: 25 mins

**12 servings**

~~~~~~~~~~~~~~~~~~~~~~~

1 can (11 oz.) refrigerated
    breadsticks (12 breadsticks)
1/3 cup finely shredded sharp
    Cheddar cheese (1 1/3 oz.)
1/4 cup real bacon bits
2 tablespoons Parmesan dry
    bread crumbs

**1.** Heat oven to 375°F. Unroll dough on ungreased cookie sheet; do not separate. Top dough evenly with cheese, bacon bits and bread crumbs.

**2.** Bake 13 to 15 minutes or until golden brown. Cut into 12 long strips. Serve warm.

**High Altitude (3500–6500 ft): No change.**

**1 Serving:** Calories 100 (Calories from Fat 25); Total Fat 3g (Saturated Fat 1g; Trans Fat 0g); Cholesterol 5mg; Sodium 310mg; Total Carbohydrate 13g (Dietary Fiber 0g; Sugars 2g); Protein 4g

% Daily Value: Vitamin A 0%; Vitamin C 0%; Calcium 0%; Iron 4%

Exchanges: 1 Starch, 1/2 Fat

Carbohydrate Choices: 1

> **BAKING TIP:**
> *A warm bowl of soup becomes so much more exciting when the kids add these inside-out bacon cheese sandwiches made just for dunking.*

# TWISTY DIPPERS

→ PREP TIME: 10 mins
START TO FINISH: 25 mins

**6 servings (4 dippers each)**

~~~~~~~~~~~~~~~~~~~~

1 can (8 oz.) refrigerated crescent
  dinner rolls
1 tablespoon butter or
  margarine, melted
2 teaspoons cinnamon-sugar
  blend

**1.** Heat oven to 375°F. Grease cookie sheet with shortening or cooking spray. Unroll dough into 1 large rectangle; firmly press perforations to seal. Press dough into 12x7-inch rectangle.

**2.** Brush dough with melted butter; sprinkle with cinnamon-sugar blend. Cut dough crosswise into 12 (7x1-inch) strips; cut strips in half crosswise. Twist each strip; place on cookie sheet.

**3.** Bake 9 to 13 minutes or until deep golden brown. Serve warm or cool with yogurt or pudding for dipping.

**High Altitude (3500–6500 ft): No change.**

**1 Serving:** Calories 160 (Calories from Fat 90); Total Fat 10g (Saturated Fat 3.5g; Trans Fat 2g); Cholesterol 5mg; Sodium 310mg; Total Carbohydrate 16g (Dietary Fiber 0g; Sugars 3g); Protein 3g

% Daily Value: Vitamin A 0%; Vitamin C 0%; Calcium 0%; Iron 4%

Exchanges: 1 Starch, 2 Fat

Carbohydrate Choices: 1

> **BAKING TIP:**
> *It's a snap to make your own cinnamon sugar—just combine*
> *2 tablespoons of sugar with 1 teaspoon cinnamon, and you're done.*

# STUFFED CRUST PIZZA SNACKS

→ PREP TIME: 30 mins
START TO FINISH: 55 mins

**24 servings (2 snacks and**

**1 tablespoon sauce each)**

~~~~~~~~~~~~~~~~~~~~~~~

2 cans (13.8 oz. each)
  refrigerated pizza crust
8 oz. mozzarella cheese, cut into
  48 cubes
48 slices pepperoni (3 oz.)
1/4 cup olive or vegetable oil
1 1/2 teaspoons Italian seasoning
2 tablespoons grated Parmesan
  cheese
1 jar (14 oz.) pizza sauce, heated

**1.** Heat oven to 400°F. Grease 1 (13x9-inch) pan or 2 (9-inch) metal pie pans with shortening or cooking spray. Remove dough from both cans. Unroll dough; starting at center, press out dough into 2 (12x8-inch) rectangles. Cut each into 24 squares.

**2.** Top each square with cheese cube and pepperoni slice. Wrap dough around filling to completely cover, firmly pressing edges to seal. Place seam side down with sides touching in pan.

**3.** In small bowl, mix oil and Italian seasoning; drizzle over filled dough in pan. Sprinkle with Parmesan cheese.

**4.** Bake 16 to 22 minutes or until golden brown. Serve warm with warm pizza sauce for dipping.

**High Altitude (3500–6500 ft): Bake 18 to 24 minutes.**

**1 Serving:** Calories 160 (Calories from Fat 70); Total Fat 7g (Saturated Fat 2.5g; Trans Fat 0g); Cholesterol 10mg; Sodium 440mg; Total Carbohydrate 17g (Dietary Fiber 0g; Sugars 3g); Protein 6g

% Daily Value: Vitamin A 2%; Vitamin C 2%; Calcium 8%; Iron 6%

Exchanges: 1 Starch, 1/2 Medium-Fat Meat, 1 Fat

Carbohydrate Choices: 1

# NUTTY CHEDDAR CRACKERS

→ PREP TIME: 50 mins
START TO FINISH: 1 hr

**4 dozen crackers**

~~~~~~~~~~~~~~~~~~~

1 1/2 cups all-purpose flour
1/4 cup butter or margarine
1 cup shredded Cheddar cheese
   (4 oz.)
1/2 cup sunflower nuts
1/4 teaspoon Worcestershire
   sauce
6 to 8 tablespoons cold water

**1.** Heat oven to 375°F. Lightly grease cookie sheets with shortening or cooking spray. Place flour in medium bowl. With pastry blender or fork, cut in butter until mixture resembles coarse crumbs.

**2.** Stir in cheese, sunflower nuts and Worcestershire sauce. Sprinkle with water, 1 tablespoon at a time, while tossing and mixing lightly with fork until dough is just moist enough to form a ball when lightly pressed together.

**3.** On lightly floured work surface, roll dough with rolling pin to 1/8-inch thickness. With lightly floured 2-inch Christmas cookie cutters, cut dough into desired shapes; place 1 inch apart on cookie sheets.

**4.** Bake 8 to 10 minutes or until golden brown. Immediately remove from cookie sheets. Serve warm or cool.

**High Altitude (3500–6500 ft): Bake 9 to 11 minutes.**

1 Cracker: Calories 40 (Calories from Fat 25); Total Fat 2.5g (Saturated Fat 1g; Trans Fat 0g); Cholesterol 5mg; Sodium 20mg; Total Carbohydrate 3g (Dietary Fiber 0g; Sugars 0g); Protein 1g

% Daily Value: Vitamin A 0%; Vitamin C 0%; Calcium 0%; Iron 0%

Exchanges: 1/2 Fat

Carbohydrate Choices: 0

> **BAKING TIP:**
> *It's fun to make your own better-tasting crackers. Use other kinds of chopped nuts or let the kids sprinkle the tops with chili powder for a spicier version.*

# MONSTER COOKIES

→ **PREP TIME:** 1 hr
**START TO FINISH:** 1 hr 15 mins

**4 dozen cookies**

1 cup granulated sugar
1 cup packed brown sugar
1 cup peanut butter
1/2 cup butter or margarine,
   softened
3 eggs
4 1/2 cups quick-cooking oats
2 teaspoons baking soda
1 cup semisweet chocolate chips
   (6 oz.)
1 cup candy-coated chocolate
   candies
1 cup chopped peanuts
1/2 cup raisins

**1.** Heat oven to 350°F. In large bowl, beat granulated sugar, brown sugar, peanut butter and butter with electric mixer on medium speed until light and fluffy, scraping bowl occasionally. Beat in eggs, one at a time, until well blended. On low speed, beat in oats and baking soda until well mixed, scraping bowl occasionally. Stir in chocolate chips, chocolate candies, peanuts and raisins.

**2.** Drop dough by heaping tablespoonfuls 2 1/2 inches apart onto ungreased cookie sheets.

**3.** Bake 11 to 14 minutes or until light golden brown. Cool 2 minutes; remove from cookie sheets.

**High Altitude (3500–6500 ft): Add 1/4 cup water with eggs; add 1/4 cup all-purpose flour with oats. Bake 13 to 16 minutes.**

**1 Cookie:** Calories 180 (Calories from Fat 80); Total Fat 9g (Saturated Fat 3g; Trans Fat 0g); Cholesterol 20mg; Sodium 110mg; Total Carbohydrate 22g (Dietary Fiber 2g; Sugars 15g); Protein 4g

% Daily Value: Vitamin A 0%; Vitamin C 0%; Calcium 2%; Iron 4%

Exchanges: 1 Starch, 1/2 Other Carbohydrate, 1 1/2 Fat

Carbohydrate Choices: 1 1/2

# HAPPY FACE COOKIE POPS

→ PREP TIME: 45 mins
START TO FINISH: 1 hr 45 mins

**24 cookie pops**

〜〜〜〜〜〜〜〜〜〜〜〜〜〜〜

1 roll (18 oz.) refrigerated
   sugar cookies
24 flat wooden sticks with round
   ends
1 can (1 lb.) vanilla creamy ready-
   to-spread frosting
Food color
Assorted small candies

**1.** Heat oven to 350°F. Cut cookie dough into 24 equal pieces. Roll each piece into ball; flatten each slightly in hand. Insert wooden stick into side of each; place 2 inches apart on ungreased cookie sheets, overlapping wooden sticks as necessary.

**2.** Bake 10 to 12 minutes or until edges are light golden brown. Cool on cookie sheets 5 minutes. Remove from cookie sheets; place on wire racks. Cool completely, about 1 hour (do not pick up cookie pops using sticks until completely cooled).

**3.** Divide frosting into small bowls or cups; add food color as desired. Frost cookies; decorate with candies to make faces.

**High Altitude (3500–6500 ft): Bake 12 to 14 minutes.**

**1 Cookie Pop:** Calories 230 (Calories from Fat 60); Total Fat 7g (Saturated Fat 3.5g; Trans Fat 1g); Cholesterol 5mg; Sodium 60mg; Total Carbohydrate 40g (Dietary Fiber 0g; Sugars 33g); Protein 0g

% Daily Value: Vitamin A 0%; Vitamin C 0%; Calcium 0%; Iron 2%

Exchanges: 2 1/2 Other Carbohydrate, 1 1/2 Fat

Carbohydrate Choices: 2 1/2

# OOEY GOOEY CANDY AND CHOCOLATE BARS

→ **PREP TIME: 15 mins**
**START TO FINISH: 1 hr 30 mins**

**24 bars**

~~~~~~~~~~~~~~~~~~~~~~~~~~~

1 roll (18 oz.) refrigerated
   chocolate chip cookies
1 cup quick-cooking oats
10 vanilla caramels, unwrapped
1 tablespoon milk
1 cup miniature marshmallows
1/3 cup candy-coated chocolate
   candies

**1.** Heat oven to 350°F. Grease 8-inch square pan with shortening or cooking spray. In medium bowl, break up cookie dough. Stir or knead in oats. Press dough evenly in bottom of pan.

**2.** Bake 15 to 20 minutes or until golden brown.

**3.** Meanwhile, in 1-quart saucepan, heat caramels and milk over low heat, stirring frequently, until caramels are melted and smooth. Remove from heat.

**4.** Sprinkle marshmallows evenly over partially baked crust; bake 1 to 2 minutes longer or until marshmallows are puffy.

**5.** Drizzle melted caramels evenly over warm bars; sprinkle chocolate candies over top. Cool completely, about 1 hour. With hot, wet knife, cut into 6 rows by 4 rows.

**High Altitude (3500–6500 ft): In step 2, bake 19 to 24 minutes.**

**1 Bar:** Calories 150 (Calories from Fat 60); Total Fat 6g (Saturated Fat 2g; Trans Fat 1g); Cholesterol 0mg; Sodium 80mg; Total Carbohydrate 22g (Dietary Fiber 0g; Sugars 12g); Protein 2g

% Daily Value: Vitamin A 0%; Vitamin C 0%; Calcium 0%; Iron 4%

Exchanges: 1 1/2 Other Carbohydrate, 1 Fat

Carbohydrate Choices: 1 1/2

**BAKING TIP:**
*Want to buy just the 10 caramels you need for this recipe? Go to a large market that has a bulk candy section.*

# CHOCOLATE-DIPPED PEANUT BUTTER FINGERS

→ **PREP TIME: 35 mins**
**START TO FINISH: 1 hr**

**32 cookies**

~~~~~~~~~~~~~~~~~~~~

1 roll (18 oz.) refrigerated peanut
    butter cookies
1/3 cup all-purpose flour
8 oz. sweet baking chocolate,
    broken into squares
1 tablespoon vegetable oil
Finely chopped peanuts and/or
    multicolored candy sprinkles

**1.** Heat oven to 375°F. In large bowl, break up cookie dough. Stir or knead in flour until well blended.

**2.** Divide dough into 32 equal pieces. Shape each into 2 1/2-inch-long log; place 2 inches apart on ungreased cookie sheets. With knife, make 3 shallow (about 1/4-inch-deep) cuts lengthwise in each log.

**3.** Bake 6 to 8 minutes or until golden brown. Immediately remove from cookie sheets; place on wire racks. Cool completely, about 15 minutes.

**4.** In microwavable measuring cup, microwave chocolate and oil on High 30 to 60 seconds, stirring every 15 seconds, until smooth. Dip 1/3 of each cookie into chocolate, allowing excess to drip off. Dip into peanuts; return to wire racks. Let stand until chocolate is set before storing.

**High Altitude (3500–6500 ft): Increase flour to 1/2 cup. Bake 7 to 9 minutes.**

**1 Cookie:** Calories 130 (Calories from Fat 60); Total Fat 7g (Saturated Fat 2.5g; Trans Fat 0g); Cholesterol 0mg; Sodium 80mg; Total Carbohydrate 15g (Dietary Fiber 0g; Sugars 9g); Protein 2g

% Daily Value: Vitamin A 0%; Vitamin C 0%; Calcium 0%; Iron 2%

Exchanges: 1 Other Carbohydrate, 1 1/2 Fat

Carbohydrate Choices: 1

> **BAKING TIP:**
> *If you'd prefer semisweet or milk chocolate, use that instead of the sweet baking chocolate.*

# SPIRAL SNOWMEN COOKIES

→ PREP TIME: 1 hr
START TO FINISH: 1 hr 15 mins

**20 large cookies**

~~~~~~~~~~~~~~~~~~~~

1 roll (18 oz.) refrigerated sugar
  cookies
2 tablespoons all-purpose flour
Large gumdrops
Miniature candy-coated
  chocolate baking bits
Miniature semisweet
  chocolate chips
Coarse sugar

**1.** Heat oven to 350°F. In large bowl, break up cookie dough. Stir or knead in flour until well blended. Divide dough in half; wrap each half in plastic wrap. Freeze 10 minutes.

**2.** Shape half of dough into 1 1/2-inch balls. With fingers, roll each ball into 10-inch rope, about 1/4 inch wide; carefully place on ungreased cookie sheet. Use 1 rope for each cookie; starting at top, make small spiral with rope for head, continuing to make larger spiral for body (see photo).

**3.** Cut hat shapes from gumdrops; place on heads. Add baking bits for buttons; add miniature chocolate chips for eyes and noses. Cut small pieces from red gumdrop for mouths. Sprinkle cookies with coarse sugar. Repeat with remaining half of dough.

**4.** Bake 9 to 13 minutes or until edges are light golden brown. Cool 1 minute; remove from cookie sheet.

**High Altitude (3500–6500 ft): Bake 14 to 18 minutes.**

**1 Large Cookie:** Calories 140 (Calories from Fat 45); Total Fat 5g (Saturated Fat 1.5g; Trans Fat 1g); Cholesterol 10mg; Sodium 70mg; Total Carbohydrate 24g (Dietary Fiber 0g; Sugars 14g); Protein 0g

% Daily Value: Vitamin A 0%; Vitamin C 0%; Calcium 0%; Iron 4%

Exchanges: 1 1/2 Other Carbohydrate, 1 Fat

Carbohydrate Choices: 1 1/2

> **BAKING TIP:**
> *To make Spiral Snowmen on a Stick, insert a flat wooden stick with round ends into the bottom spiral of each cookie before baking.*

# GINGERBREAD TEDDIES

→ PREP TIME: 1 hr
START TO FINISH: 1 hr

**2 dozen cookies**

〜〜〜〜〜〜〜〜〜〜〜〜

1 roll (18 oz.) refrigerated gingerbread cookies
Decorating icing (in tubes)

**1.** Heat oven to 350°F. Cut cookie dough into 4 equal pieces. Work with 1 piece of dough at a time; refrigerate remaining dough until ready to use.

**2.** Cut piece of dough into 6 equal pieces. Use 1 piece for each cookie; shape dough into 1-inch ball for body, 1/2-inch ball for head, 4 (1/4-inch) balls for arms and legs, and 2 smaller balls for ears. Arrange balls to resemble teddy bear shape on ungreased cookie sheet. Repeat with remaining pieces of dough, placing cookies 2 inches apart on cookie sheets.

**3.** Bake 10 to 13 minutes or until set. Cool 2 minutes; remove from cookie sheets. Decorate as desired with icing.

**High Altitude (3500–6500 ft): No change.**

**1 Cookie:** Calories 120 (Calories from Fat 50); Total Fat 6g (Saturated Fat 1.5g; Trans Fat 0g); Cholesterol 10mg; Sodium 70mg; Total Carbohydrate 16g (Dietary Fiber 0g; Sugars 10g); Protein 1g

% Daily Value: Vitamin A 0%; Vitamin C 0%; Calcium 0%; Iron 0%

Exchanges: 1 Other Carbohydrate, 1 Fat

Carbohydrate Choices: 1

> **BAKING TIP:**
> *If using chocolate chips, cinnamon candies or candy-coated chocolate candies to decorate these cookies, place them on the cookies while warm from the oven so the decorations stick. Add other decorations when the cookies are cool; attach with vanilla frosting or use the frosting recipe on the gingerbread cookie label.*

# CINNAMON POLAR BEARS

→ **PREP TIME: 1 hr 20 mins**
**START TO FINISH: 2 hrs 20 mins**

**4 dozen cookies**

1 cup granulated sugar
1 cup butter or margarine, softened
1 egg
2 1/4 cups all-purpose flour
1 teaspoon ground cinnamon
Powdered sugar
1 tablespoon (96) miniature semisweet chocolate chips
48 red cinnamon candies

**1.** In large bowl, beat granulated sugar and butter with electric mixer on medium speed until light and fluffy, scraping bowl occasionally. Beat in egg until well blended. On low speed, beat in flour and cinnamon until well combined, scraping bowl occasionally. Cover dough with plastic wrap; refrigerate 1 hour for easier handling.

**2.** Heat oven to 350°F. For each cookie, shape dough into 1-inch ball; place on ungreased cookie sheet and flatten ball slightly. Shape dough into 3 (1/4-inch) balls; place 2 of the balls above and touching larger ball for ears. Place 1 ball on top to resemble snout; flatten slightly. Repeat with remaining dough, placing cookies 2 inches apart on cookie sheets.

**3.** Bake 11 to 15 minutes or until firm to the touch. Immediately remove from cookie sheets; lightly sprinkle cookies with powdered sugar. Press 2 chocolate chips into each cookie for eyes and 1 cinnamon candy for nose.

**High Altitude (3500–6500 ft): Increase flour to 2 1/3 cups.**

**1 Cookie:** Calories 80 (Calories from Fat 35); Total Fat 4g (Saturated Fat 2g; Trans Fat 0g); Cholesterol 15mg; Sodium 25mg; Total Carbohydrate 10g (Dietary Fiber 0g; Sugars 5g); Protein 0g

% Daily Value: Vitamin A 4%; Vitamin C 0%; Calcium 0%; Iron 0%

Exchanges: 1/2 Other Carbohydrate, 1 Fat

Carbohydrate Choices: 1/2

# COOKIE ICE CREAM-A-ROUNDS

→ **PREP TIME: 1 hr**
**START TO FINISH: 4 hrs**

**9 ice cream sandwiches**

~~~~~~~~~~~~~~~~~~~~~~~~

1 roll (18 oz.) refrigerated
   chocolate chip cookies
1/2 cup miniature semisweet
   chocolate chips or candy
   sprinkles
2 1/4 cups any flavor ice cream,
   slightly softened

**1.** Heat oven to 350°F. Shape cookie dough into 18 balls; place 3 inches apart on ungreased cookie sheets.

**2.** Bake 10 to 15 minutes or until light golden brown. Cool 1 minute; remove from cookie sheets. Cool completely, about 15 minutes.

**3.** Meanwhile, cut 9 (12x9-inch) sheets of plastic wrap or waxed paper. Place chocolate chips in small shallow bowl.

**4.** For each sandwich, spoon about 1/4 cup ice cream onto bottom of 1 cooled cookie. Top with second cookie, bottom side down; press together gently. Roll outer edge of ice cream in chocolate chips. Quickly wrap each sandwich in plastic wrap. Freeze until firm, about 3 hours (for longer storage, place wrapped sandwiches in resealable freezer plastic bag). Let stand 10 minutes before serving.

**High Altitude (3500–6500 ft): No change.**

**1 Ice Cream Sandwich:** Calories 400 (Calories from Fat 190); Total Fat 21g (Saturated Fat 8g; Trans Fat 2g); Cholesterol 25mg; Sodium 210mg; Total Carbohydrate 48g (Dietary Fiber 2g; Sugars 31g); Protein 4g

% Daily Value: Vitamin A 4%; Vitamin C 0%; Calcium 4%; Iron 8%

Exchanges: 1 1/2 Starch, 1 1/2 Other Carbohydrate, 4 Fat

Carbohydrate Choices: 3

# CHOCOLATE HALLOWEEN PRETZELS

→ PREP TIME: 50 mins
START TO FINISH: 50 mins

**24 cookies**

〰〰〰〰〰〰〰〰〰〰〰

## PRETZELS
3/4 cup sugar
1/2 cup butter
1/2 teaspoon almond extract
1 egg
1 3/4 cups all-purpose flour
1/4 cup unsweetened baking
   cocoa

## ICING
3/4 cup semisweet chocolate
   chips
1 1/2 teaspoons shortening
Assorted Halloween candy
   sprinkles

**1.** Heat oven to 325°F. In large bowl, beat sugar and butter with electric mixer on medium speed until well blended, scraping bowl occasionally. Beat in almond extract and egg until blended. On low speed, beat in flour and cocoa until well mixed, scraping bowl occasionally.

**2.** Shape dough into 6-inch-long roll. Cut roll into 6 slices; cut each slice into quarters. For each pretzel, shape 1 dough quarter into 10-inch-long rope. Shape rope into U-shape; cross ends and place over bottom of U to form pretzel. Place 1 inch apart on ungreased cookie sheets.

**3.** Bake 8 to 10 minutes or until set and firm to the touch. Cool 1 minute; remove from cookie sheets. Cool completely, about 10 minutes.

**4.** In small microwavable bowl, microwave chocolate chips and shortening on High 30 seconds. Stir; continue microwaving, stirring every 10 seconds, until chocolate is melted and can be stirred smooth. Dip tops of pretzels in chocolate. Sprinkle with candy sprinkles. Refrigerate until chocolate is set before storing.

**High Altitude (3500–6500 ft): Heat oven to 350°F.**

**1 Cookie:** Calories 140 (Calories from Fat 60); Total Fat 7g (Saturated Fat 3.5g; Trans Fat 0g); Cholesterol 20mg; Sodium 30mg; Total Carbohydrate 18g (Dietary Fiber 0g; Sugars 10g); Protein 2g

% Daily Value: Vitamin A 4%; Vitamin C 0%; Calcium 0%; Iron 4%

Exchanges: 1 Other Carbohydrate, 1 1/2 Fat

Carbohydrate Choices: 1

# VALENTINE ROLLED COOKIES

→ PREP TIME: 1 hr 15 mins
START TO FINISH: 2 hrs 15 mins

**5 dozen cookies**

~~~~~~~~~~~~~~~~~~~~~~~~~~~

1 cup sugar
1 cup butter or margarine,
    softened
3 tablespoons milk
1 teaspoon vanilla
1 egg
3 cups all-purpose flour
1 1/2 teaspoons baking powder
1/2 teaspoon salt
1/4 to 1/2 teaspoon red food
    color
Sugar, if desired

**1.** In large bowl, beat 1 cup sugar, the butter, milk, vanilla and egg with electric mixer on medium speed until well blended, scraping bowl occasionally. On low speed, beat in flour, baking powder and salt until well mixed, scraping bowl occasionally.

**2.** Divide dough in half. To one half of dough, stir or knead in red food color until desired pink color. Cover with plastic wrap; refrigerate at least 1 hour for easier handling.

**3.** Heat oven to 400°F. Work with 1/3 of white dough at a time; keep remaining dough refrigerated. On lightly floured work surface, roll out white dough with rolling pin to 1/8-inch thickness. Cut with floured 2 1/2-inch heart-shaped canapé or cookie cutter; place 1 inch apart on ungreased cookie sheets. Repeat with 1/3 of pink dough, keeping remaining pink dough refrigerated.

**4.** Using floured 1-inch heart-shaped canapé or cookie cutter, cut center from each pink and white cookie. Remove centers; replace each center of cookie with cutout of opposite colored dough. Sprinkle with sugar if desired.

**5.** Bake 5 to 9 minutes or until edges are light golden brown. Cool 1 minute; remove from cookie sheets.

**High Altitude (3500–6500 ft): Increase flour to 3 cups plus 2 tablespoons.**

**1 Cookie:** Calories 70 (Calories from Fat 30); Total Fat 3g (Saturated Fat 1.5g; Trans Fat 0g); Cholesterol 10mg; Sodium 55mg; Total Carbohydrate 8g (Dietary Fiber 0g; Sugars 3g); Protein 0g

% Daily Value: Vitamin A 2%; Vitamin C 0%; Calcium 0%; Iron 0%

Exchanges: 1/2 Other Carbohydrate, 1/2 Fat

Carbohydrate Choices: 1/2

**BAKING TIP:**
*For a sweet finish, use purchased decorating icing to pipe the initials of your favorite valentines on individual cookies. Let the kids cut dough into shapes for any season or holiday—stars, eggs or flowers—with a corresponding small shape cut in the center of each.*

KIDS BAKE ●

# LITTLE JACK HORNER PIES

→ PREP TIME: 25 mins
START TO FINISH: 35 mins

**10 pies**

Pastry for Two-Crust Pie (page 142) or 1 box (15 oz.) refrigerated pie crusts, softened as directed on box
2/3 cup plum, strawberry or peach preserves
2 tablespoons sugar
1/4 teaspoon ground cinnamon

**1.** Heat oven to 400°F. Make pastry as directed in recipe for Two-Crust Pie (do not place in pie plate) or unroll pie crusts on work surface (if necessary, roll pie crusts with rolling pin until 11 inches in diameter).

**2.** With 4-inch round cookie cutter, cut each pastry into 5 rounds. Spoon about 1 tablespoon preserves onto half of each pastry round. Fold pastry over filling; press edges with fork to seal.

**3.** In small bowl, mix sugar and cinnamon; sprinkle over pies. Place on ungreased large cookie sheet.

**4.** Bake 8 to 10 minutes or until light golden brown. Immediately remove from cookie sheets. Serve warm or cool.

**High Altitude (3500–6500 ft): No change.**

**1 Pie:** Calories 260 (Calories from Fat 110); Total Fat 13g (Saturated Fat 3g; Trans Fat 2g); Cholesterol 0mg; Sodium 220mg; Total Carbohydrate 34g (Dietary Fiber 0g; Sugars 13g); Protein 2g
% Daily Value: Vitamin A 0%; Vitamin C 0%; Calcium 0%; Iron 6%
Exchanges: 1 Starch, 1 Other Carbohydrate, 2 1/2 Fat
Carbohydrate Choices: 2

> **BAKING TIP:**
> *You can make pie crust cookies from the trimmings—just cut the pastry into shapes and sprinkle with any remaining sugar and cinnamon. Bake on an ungreased cookie sheet at 400°F for 5 to 8 minutes or until light golden brown.*

**P**ull out the stops! It's the holidays, the perfect time to meet your family in the kitchen and bake something wonderful.

# CHOCOLATE-HAZELNUT BREAKFAST RING

→ **PREP TIME: 25 mins**
**START TO FINISH: 40 mins**

**8 servings**

~~~~~~~~~~~~~~~~~~~~~~~~

1 can (13.8 oz.) refrigerated
   pizza crust
2/3 cup hazelnut spread with
   cocoa (from 13-oz. jar), stirred
   to soften
1/2 cup whole hazelnuts
   (filberts), toasted, finely
   chopped
1 egg, beaten
1/2 teaspoon granulated sugar
1 teaspoon powdered sugar

**1.** Heat oven to 350°F. Line cookie sheet with cooking parchment paper. On lightly floured work surface, unroll dough; press into 13x10-inch rectangle. Gently spread hazelnut spread to within 1/2 inch of edges. Sprinkle with toasted hazelnuts.

**2.** Fold long sides of dough over filling to meet in center. Starting with 1 long side, loosely roll up dough. Shape dough roll into ring on cookie sheet; pinch ends together to seal. Cut 5 (1-inch-deep) slits in top of dough. Brush with beaten egg; sprinkle with granulated sugar.

**3.** Bake 20 to 25 minutes or until golden brown. Remove from cookie sheet; place on serving platter. Cool 10 minutes before serving. Sprinkle with powdered sugar; serve warm.

**High Altitude (3500–6500 ft): Heat oven to 375°F.**

**1 Serving:** Calories 320 (Calories from Fat 130); Total Fat 14g (Saturated Fat 1.5g; Trans Fat 0g); Cholesterol 25mg; Sodium 370mg; Total Carbohydrate 41g (Dietary Fiber 2g; Sugars 18g); Protein 8g

% Daily Value: Vitamin A 0%; Vitamin C 0%; Calcium 6%; Iron 10%

Exchanges: 2 Starch, 1/2 Other Carbohydrate, 2 1/2 Fat

Carbohydrate Choices: 3

> **BAKING TIP:**
> *To toast whole hazelnuts, spread them on a cookie sheet and bake at 375°F for 5 to 8 minutes or until golden brown. To remove the skins, roll the warm nuts in a clean kitchen towel.*

# WHITE CHOCOLATE–ICED CRANBERRY BREAD

**1 loaf; 12 slices**

## BREAD

2 1/4 cups all-purpose flour
3/4 cup granulated sugar
1 1/2 teaspoons baking powder
1/2 teaspoon baking soda
1/2 teaspoon salt
1/2 cup coarsely chopped
    sweetened dried cranberries
3/4 cup half-and-half
2 teaspoons grated orange peel
2 eggs
1/2 cup butter or margarine,
    melted
1/4 cup orange juice

## ICING

1 oz. white chocolate baking bar,
    chopped
1 to 2 tablespoons half-and-half
1/2 cup powdered sugar

**1.** Heat oven to 350°F. Grease bottom only of 8x4-inch loaf pan with shortening or cooking spray. In large bowl, mix flour, granulated sugar, baking powder, baking soda and salt. Stir in cranberries.

**2.** In small bowl, beat 3/4 cup half-and-half, the orange peel and eggs with wire whisk until well blended. Add half-and-half mixture, melted butter and orange juice to flour mixture; stir with spoon just until dry ingredients are moistened. Pour batter into pan.

**3.** Bake 50 to 60 minutes or until deep golden brown and toothpick inserted in center comes out clean. Cool in pan 10 minutes. Run knife around edges of pan to loosen. Remove loaf from pan; place on wire rack. Cool completely, about 1 hour.

**4.** In small microwavable bowl, microwave baking bar and 1 tablespoon of the half-and-half on High 30 seconds. Stir until melted and smooth (if necessary, microwave 10 to 20 seconds longer). With wire whisk, beat in powdered sugar until smooth (if necessary, add additional half-and-half, 1/2 teaspoon at a time, until desired spreading consistency). Spoon and spread icing over cooled loaf, allowing some to run down sides.

**High Altitude (3500–6500 ft): Bake 8x4-inch pan 1 hour to 1 hour 10 minutes. Bake mini loaf pans 40 to 50 minutes.**

**1 Slice:** Calories 290 (Calories from Fat 100); Total Fat 12g (Saturated Fat 6g; Trans Fat 0.5g); Cholesterol 60mg; Sodium 280mg; Total Carbohydrate 43g (Dietary Fiber 1g; Sugars 24g); Protein 4g
% Daily Value: Vitamin A 8%; Vitamin C 2%; Calcium 6%; Iron 8%
Exchanges: 1 Starch, 2 Other Carbohydrate, 2 Fat
Carbohydrate Choices: 3

**BAKING TIP:**

*For mini loaves, grease bottoms only of three 5 3/4x3 1/4x2-inch foil loaf pans. Divide the batter evenly into the pans, using about 1 cup batter for each. Place the filled pans on a cookie sheet and bake in a preheated 350°F oven for 35 to 45 minutes or until golden brown and toothpick inserted in center comes out clean.*

# CANDY CANE COFFEE CAKE

→ PREP TIME: 20 mins
START TO FINISH: 1 hr 15 mins

**12 servings**

## COFFEE CAKE

1 package (3 oz.) cream cheese,
    softened
2 tablespoons granulated sugar
1 teaspoon almond extract
1/4 cup sliced almonds
1/4 cup chopped maraschino
    cherries, well drained
1 can (8 oz.) refrigerated crescent
    dinner rolls

## GLAZE

1/2 cup powdered sugar
2 teaspoons milk

**1.** Heat oven to 375°F. Grease cookie sheet with shortening or cooking spray. In small bowl, beat cream cheese and granulated sugar with electric mixer on medium speed until light and fluffy, scraping bowl occasionally. With spoon, stir in almond extract, almonds and cherries; set aside.

**2.** Unroll dough onto cookie sheet; press into 13x7-inch rectangle, firmly pressing perforations to seal. Spoon cream cheese mixture down center 1/3 of rectangle.

**3.** On each long side of dough rectangle, make cuts 1 inch apart to edge of filling. Fold opposite strips of dough over filling and cross strips in center to form a braided appearance; seal ends. Curve one end to form candy cane shape.

**4.** Bake 18 to 22 minutes or until golden brown. Remove from cookie sheet; place on wire rack. Cool completely, about 30 minutes.

**5.** In small bowl, mix glaze ingredients with spoon until smooth; drizzle over coffee cake. If desired, garnish with additional sliced almonds and cherries. Store in refrigerator.

**High Altitude (3500–6500 ft): Bake 20 to 24 minutes.**

**1 Serving:** Calories 140 (Calories from Fat 70); Total Fat 8g (Saturated Fat 3g; Trans Fat 1g); Cholesterol 10mg; Sodium 170mg; Total Carbohydrate 17g (Dietary Fiber 0g; Sugars 10g); Protein 2g

% Daily Value: Vitamin A 2%; Vitamin C 0%; Calcium 0%; Iron 4%

Exchanges: 1 Other Carbohydrate, 1 1/2 Fat

Carbohydrate Choices: 1

> **BAKING TIP:**
> *You can cut maraschino cherries easily by snipping them with kitchen scissors. Drain cherries on paper towels to absorb the moisture.*

# STRAWBERRY PRETZEL DELIGHT

→ PREP TIME: 30 mins
START TO FINISH: 2 hrs 30 mins

**16 servings**

~~~~~~~~~~~~~~~~~~~~~~~

## CRUST
2 cups crushed pretzel sticks
1/4 cup sugar
1/2 cup butter or margarine,
   melted

## FILLING
1 can (12 oz.) sweetened condensed milk (not evaporated)
1/2 cup water
1 box (4-serving size) vanilla
   instant pudding and pie filling
   mix
1 container (4 oz.) frozen
   whipped topping, thawed
   (1 1/2 cups)

## TOPPING
1 can (21 oz.) strawberry pie
   filling

**1.** Heat oven to 350°F. In large bowl, mix crust ingredients; press in bottom of ungreased 13x9-inch pan. Bake 8 minutes. Cool 10 minutes.

**2.** Meanwhile, in same large bowl, beat condensed milk and water with electric mixer on low speed until well blended. Add pudding mix; beat 2 minutes on medium speed. Refrigerate 5 minutes.

**3.** Fold whipped topping into thickened pudding mixture. Spread over cooled baked crust. Refrigerate until filling is firm, about 1 hour.

**4.** Spoon strawberry pie filling over filling. Cover; refrigerate at least 1 hour or until serving time. If desired, garnish individual servings with tree-shaped pretzels. Store in refrigerator.

**High Altitude (3500–6500 ft): No change.**

**1 Serving:** Calories 240 (Calories from Fat 80); Total Fat 9g (Saturated Fat 5g; Trans Fat 0g); Cholesterol 20mg; Sodium 290mg; Total Carbohydrate 37g (Dietary Fiber 0g; Sugars 29g); Protein 3g
% Daily Value: Vitamin A 6%; Vitamin C 0%; Calcium 6%; Iron 2%
Exchanges: 1/2 Starch, 2 Other Carbohydrate, 2 Fat
Carbohydrate Choices: 2 1/2

**BAKING TIP:**
*Trim each serving with a small tree-shaped pretzel dipped in melted chocolate chips or candy coating.*

# BRAIDED PUMPKIN WREATHS

**2 wreaths; 24 slices each**

### BREAD
5 3/4 to 6 1/2 cups all-purpose
    flour
1/3 cup sugar
1 1/2 teaspoons salt
2 packages regular active dry
    yeast
1 cup canned pumpkin
    (not pie filling mix)
1/4 cup butter or margarine
1 1/2 cups apple cider or apple
    juice

### TOPPING
1 egg
1 tablespoon water
2 teaspoons sesame seed,
    if desired
2 teaspoons poppy seed,
    if desired

**1.** In large bowl, mix 2 cups of the flour, the sugar, salt and yeast. In 2-quart saucepan, heat pumpkin, butter and cider over medium heat until 120°F to 130°F. Add to flour mixture; beat with electric mixer on medium speed 3 minutes, scraping bowl occasionally. With spoon, stir in enough of the remaining 3 3/4 to 4 1/2 cups flour to make a soft dough.

**2.** On floured work surface, knead dough until smooth and elastic, 3 to 5 minutes. Grease large bowl with shortening or cooking spray. Place dough in bowl, turning to grease top; cover with plastic wrap and cloth towel. Let rise in warm place (80°F to 85°F) about 1 hour or until doubled in size.

**3.** Grease large cookie sheet with shortening or cooking spray. Gently push fist into dough to deflate; divide in half, then divide each half into 3 pieces. On lightly floured work surface, with hands, roll each piece into 24-inch-long rope. On cookie sheet, place 3 ropes close together; braid loosely and shape into ring, pinching ends together to seal. Repeat with remaining dough. Cover; let rise in warm place 20 to 30 minutes or until almost doubled in size.

**4.** Heat oven to 375°F. In small bowl, beat egg and water with fork until well blended. Uncover dough; brush egg mixture over braids. If desired, sprinkle with sesame and poppy seed. Bake 18 to 24 minutes or until golden brown. Remove from cookie sheet; place on wire racks. Cool completely, about 1 hour.

**High Altitude (3500–6500 ft): Use 1 package regular active dry yeast. Bake 22 to 26 minutes.**

**1 Slice:** Calories 80 (Calories from Fat 10); Total Fat 1.5g (Saturated Fat 0.5g; Trans Fat 0g); Cholesterol 5mg; Sodium 80mg; Total Carbohydrate 14g (Dietary Fiber 0g; Sugars 2g); Protein 2g

% Daily Value: Vitamin A 15%; Vitamin C 0%; Calcium 0%; Iron 4%

Exchanges: 1 Starch

Carbohydrate Choices: 1

# PEAR AND GINGER CREAM TART

→ PREP TIME: 45 mins
START TO FINISH: 2 hrs

**8 servings**

~~~~~~~~~~~~~~~~~~~~~~~

## PASTRY CREAM
1 1/2 cups milk
1 tablespoon grated gingerroot
4 egg yolks
3/4 cup sugar
1/2 cup all-purpose flour
2 tablespoons butter
1 1/2 teaspoons vanilla

## CRUST
Pastry for One-Crust Tart
  (page 142)
or 1 refrigerated pie crust (from
  15-oz. box), softened as
  directed on box

## TOPPING
2 cans (15 oz. each) pear halves
  in juice, drained
1 oz. white chocolate baking bar
  (from 6-oz. box)
1 teaspoon shortening

**1.** In 3-quart saucepan, heat milk and gingerroot over low heat about 5 minutes, stirring frequently, until very hot but not boiling.

**2.** In medium bowl, beat egg yolks and sugar with electric mixer on medium speed 4 to 6 minutes or until pale yellow, scraping bowl occasionally. On low speed, beat in flour until combined. Gradually beat in warm milk mixture until well blended, scraping bowl occasionally.

**3.** Return mixture to saucepan; cook over medium-low heat about 5 minutes, stirring constantly, until mixture is very thick and begins to boil. Boil 1 minute, stirring constantly. Remove from heat. Stir in butter and vanilla. Pour into medium bowl. Place plastic wrap on surface of pastry cream; refrigerate until completely cooled, about 1 hour.

**4.** Meanwhile, heat oven to 450°F. Using 9-inch tart pan with removable bottom or 9-inch glass pie plate, make pastry as directed in recipe or place pie crust in pan as directed on box for One-Crust Baked Shell. Bake 9 to 11 minutes or until lightly browned. Cool completely, about 30 minutes.

**5.** Spoon pastry cream into cooled baked shell. Cut pear halves into thin slices; arrange over pastry cream.

**6.** In small microwavable bowl, microwave baking bar and shortening on High 45 to 60 seconds, stirring once halfway through microwaving, until melted. If necessary, continue to microwave on High in 15-second increments, stirring until smooth. Drizzle over tart. Store in refrigerator.

**High Altitude (3500–6500 ft): No change.**

**1 Serving:** Calories 370 (Calories from Fat 150); Total Fat 17g (Saturated Fat 6g; Trans Fat 2g); Cholesterol 120mg; Sodium 200mg; Total Carbohydrate 50g (Dietary Fiber 2g; Sugars 30g); Protein 6g
% Daily Value: Vitamin A 8%; Vitamin C 0%; Calcium 8%; Iron 10%
Exchanges: 1 1/2 Starch, 2 Other Carbohydrate, 3 Fat
Carbohydrate Choices: 3

> **BAKING TIP:**
> *If you have fresh gingerroot left over, wrap and freeze it for up to 6 months. Grate what you need from the frozen gingerroot, re-wrap and return it to the freezer.*

# HOLIDAY MOMENTS

→ PREP TIME: 1 hr
START TO FINISH: 2 hrs

**3 dozen cookies**

~~~~~~~~~~~~~~~~~~~~

## COOKIES
1 cup butter, softened
3/4 cup cornstarch
1/3 cup powdered sugar
1 cup all-purpose flour

## COATING
3 tablespoons powdered sugar
2 tablespoons red sugar
2 tablespoons green sugar

**1.** In large bowl, beat butter with electric mixer on medium speed until light and fluffy, scraping bowl occasionally. On low speed, beat in cornstarch and 1/3 cup powdered sugar until moistened; beat on high speed until light and fluffy, scraping bowl occasionally. On low speed, beat in flour until well combined, scraping bowl occasionally. Cover with plastic wrap; refrigerate at least 1 hour for easier handling.

**2.** Meanwhile, in small bowl, mix coating ingredients; set aside.

**3.** Heat oven to 350°F. Shape dough into 1-inch balls; place 1 inch apart on ungreased cookie sheets.

**4.** Bake 9 to 15 minutes or until cookies are very light golden brown. Cool 1 minute; remove from cookie sheets. Carefully roll warm cookies in coating.

**High Altitude (3500–6500 ft): Increase flour to 1 1/4 cups. Bake 14 to 17 minutes.**

**1 Cookie:** Calories 80 (Calories from Fat 45); Total Fat 5g (Saturated Fat 2.5g; Trans Fat 0g); Cholesterol 15mg; Sodium 35mg; Total Carbohydrate 8g (Dietary Fiber 0g; Sugars 3g); Protein 0g

% Daily Value: Vitamin A 4%; Vitamin C 0%; Calcium 0%; Iron 0%

Exchanges: 1/2 Other Carbohydrate, 1 Fat

Carbohydrate Choices: 1/2

> **BAKING TIP:**
> *Be sure the cookies are still warm when rolled in the sugar mixture. When warm, the butter in the cookies is soft and helps the sugar stick to the cookies.*

# CHOCOLATE-DRIZZLED WALNUT COOKIES

→ **PREP TIME:** 1 hr 15 mins
**START TO FINISH:** 1 hr 15 mins

**3 dozen cookies**

1 cup butter, softened
1/2 cup powdered sugar
1 teaspoon vanilla
2 1/4 cups all-purpose flour
1/4 teaspoon salt
3/4 cup finely chopped walnuts
2 oz. semisweet baking chocolate, chopped

**1.** Heat oven to 375°F. In medium bowl, beat butter and powdered sugar with electric mixer on medium speed until creamy, scraping bowl occasionally. Beat in vanilla. On low speed, beat in flour and salt until mixture is crumbly, scraping bowl occasionally. With spoon, stir in 1/2 cup of the walnuts.

**2.** Shape dough into 1 1/4-inch balls; roll each into 3x3/4-inch-long log. Place on ungreased cookie sheets.

**3.** Bake 9 to 12 minutes or until set and bottoms are golden brown. Immediately remove from cookie sheets; place on wire racks. Cool completely, about 10 minutes.

**4.** Meanwhile, in small microwavable bowl, microwave chocolate on High 30 seconds; stir until smooth.

**5.** Place cooled cookies on sheet of waxed paper. Drizzle chocolate over cookies; sprinkle with remaining 1/4 cup walnuts. Let stand until chocolate is set before storing.

**High Altitude (3500–6500 ft): No change.**

**1 Cookie:** Calories 110 (Calories from Fat 70); Total Fat 7g (Saturated Fat 3g; Trans Fat 0g); Cholesterol 15mg; Sodium 50mg; Total Carbohydrate 9g (Dietary Fiber 0g; Sugars 3g); Protein 1g

% Daily Value: Vitamin A 4%; Vitamin C 0%; Calcium 0%; Iron 2%

Exchanges: 1/2 Other Carbohydrate, 1 1/2 Fat

Carbohydrate Choices: 1/2

> **BAKING TIP:**
> *Nuts will taste fresh for up to 5 months if they're stored in the freezer.*

# PISTACHIO SHORTBREAD TREES

→ PREP TIME: 40 mins
START TO FINISH: 1 hr 15 mins

**32 cookies**

~~~~~~~~~~~~~~~~~~~~~~~~~~~

## COOKIES

1 cup butter, softened
1/2 cup granulated sugar
1/2 cup finely chopped pistachio
  nuts
2 1/4 cups all-purpose flour
1 teaspoon vanilla
16 pretzel spindles or sticks,
  broken in half

## ICING

1 cup powdered sugar
1 to 3 tablespoons milk

**1.** Heat oven to 325°F. Grease 2 cookie sheets with shortening or cooking spray. In large bowl, beat butter and granulated sugar with electric mixer on medium speed until light and fluffy, scraping bowl occasionally. Reserve 2 tablespoons of the pistachio nuts for garnish; beat remaining nuts, the flour and vanilla into butter mixture until combined (dough will be stiff).

**2.** Divide dough evenly into 4 pieces; shape into balls. On lightly floured work surface, pat each ball into 6-inch round; place on cookie sheets. With table knife, lightly make indentations on surface of dough, dividing each round into 8 wedges. In outside edge of each wedge, insert 1 pretzel half for tree trunk.

**3.** Bake 16 to 21 minutes or until edges are light golden brown (if baking both cookie sheets at one time, switch positions halfway through baking). Cool 2 minutes; remove rounds from cookie sheets. Cut each into 8 wedges; place on wire racks. Cool completely, about 15 minutes.

**4.** Very finely chop reserved 2 tablespoons pistachio nuts. In small bowl, mix icing ingredients until smooth, adding enough milk for desired drizzling consistency. Drizzle icing in zigzag design over each cooled cookie. Before icing sets, sprinkle cookies with reserved pistachio nuts.

**High Altitude (3500–6500 ft): No change.**

**1 Cookie:** Calories 120 (Calories from Fat 60); Total Fat 7g (Saturated Fat 3g; Trans Fat 0g); Cholesterol 15mg; Sodium 50mg; Total Carbohydrate 14g (Dietary Fiber 0g; Sugars 7g); Protein 1g

% Daily Value: Vitamin A 4%; Vitamin C 0%; Calcium 0%; Iron 2%

Exchanges: 1 Other Carbohydrate, 1 1/2 Fat

Carbohydrate Choices: 1

# CHRISTMAS TREE COOKIES

→ PREP TIME: 1 hr
START TO FINISH: 1 hr

**2 dozen cookies**

~~~~~~~~~~~~~~~~~~~~~~~~~~~

## GREEN DOUGH

1/4 cup all-purpose flour
1/4 cup butter, softened
1 tablespoon green crème de
  menthe liqueur or crème de
  menthe syrup
2 drops green food color
Decorating bag fitted with small
  writing tip

## COOKIES

1 roll (18 oz.) refrigerated sugar
  cookies
Candy sprinkles or miniature
  candy-coated chocolate
  baking bits

**1.** Heat oven to 350°F. In small bowl, mix green dough ingredients until well blended. Place dough in decorating bag fitted with small writing tip; set aside.

**2.** Work with half of dough at a time; keep remaining dough refrigerated. On lightly floured work surface, roll out dough with rolling pin to 1/4-inch thickness. Cut with 2 1/2- to 3 1/2-inch tree-shaped cookie cutter; place 2 inches apart on ungreased cookie sheets.

**3.** Squeeze decorating bag to pipe green dough around outer edge of each tree cookie; pipe dots randomly in center. Top each dot with candy sprinkle.

**4.** Bake 9 to 11 minutes or until light golden brown. Cool 1 minute; remove from cookie sheets.

**High Altitude (3500–6500 ft): No change.**

**1 Cookie:** Calories 110 (Calories from Fat 50); Total Fat 6g (Saturated Fat 2g; Trans Fat 1g); Cholesterol 10mg; Sodium 70mg; Total Carbohydrate 14g (Dietary Fiber 0g; Sugars 7g); Protein 0g

% Daily Value: Vitamin A 0%; Vitamin C 0%; Calcium 0%; Iron 2%

Exchanges: 1 Other Carbohydrate, 1 Fat

Carbohydrate Choices: 1

> **BAKING TIP:**
> *A small resealable food-storage plastic bag can be used in place of the decorating bag. Place the green dough in the bag and seal it. Cut a small hole in one bottom corner of the bag. Squeeze the bag to pipe the dough as directed in the recipe.*

# CREAM CHEESE SUGAR COOKIES

→ **PREP TIME: 1 hr**
**START TO FINISH: 2 hrs**

**6 dozen cookies**

1 cup sugar
1 cup butter, softened
1 package (3 oz.) cream cheese,
    softened
1/2 teaspoon salt
1/2 teaspoon almond extract
1/2 teaspoon vanilla
1 egg yolk
2 cups all-purpose flour
Colored sugar or decorator icing,
    if desired

**1.** In large bowl, beat all ingredients except flour and colored sugar with electric mixer on medium speed until light and fluffy, scraping bowl occasionally. On low speed, beat in flour until well mixed, scraping bowl occasionally. Shape dough into 3 disks and wrap each in plastic wrap; refrigerate 1 hour for easier handling.

**2.** Heat oven to 375°F. Work with 1 disk of dough at a time; keep remaining dough refrigerated. On floured work surface, roll out dough with rolling pin to 1/8-inch thickness. Cut with lightly floured 2 1/2-inch round or desired shape cookie cutters; place 1 inch apart on ungreased cookie sheets. If desired, sprinkle with colored sugar (or leave cookies plain to be decorated with icing after baking).

**3.** Bake 6 to 10 minutes or until light golden brown. Immediately remove from cookie sheets. If desired, decorate plain cookies with icing.

**High Altitude (3500–6500 ft): Increase flour to 2 1/4 cups. Bake 6 to 8 minutes. Cool on cookie sheet 1 minute; remove from cookie sheet.**

**1 Undecorated Cookie:** Calories 50 (Calories from Fat 30); Total Fat 3g (Saturated Fat 1.5g; Trans Fat 0g); Cholesterol 10mg; Sodium 35mg; Total Carbohydrate 5g (Dietary Fiber 0g; Sugars 3g); Protein 0g

% Daily Value: Vitamin A 2%; Vitamin C 0%; Calcium 0%; Iron 0%

Exchanges: 1/2 Other Carbohydrate, 1/2 Fat

Carbohydrate Choices: 1/2

# MINT-KISSED MERINGUES

→ PREP TIME: 20 mins
START TO FINISH: 2 hrs 25 mins

**4 dozen cookies**

~~~~~~~~~~~~~~~~~~~~~~~

2 egg whites
1/4 teaspoon cream of tartar
1/8 teaspoon salt
1/2 cup sugar
1/4 teaspoon mint extract
3 to 5 drops green food color
Multicolored candy sprinkles,
   if desired

**1.** Heat oven to 200°F. Grease 2 large cookie sheets with shortening or cooking spray. In small bowl, beat egg whites, cream of tartar and salt with electric mixer on medium speed until foamy. On high speed, add sugar, 1 tablespoon at a time, beating until sugar is dissolved, meringue is glossy and very stiff peaks form. Beat in mint extract. With rubber spatula, fold in food color, 1 drop at a time, until well blended and desired color.

**2.** Use disposable decorating bag or gallon-size food storage plastic bag with 1/2-inch hole cut in one bottom corner of bag (if desired, fit large star tip in decorating bag or in hole of plastic bag). Spoon meringue into bag; twist top of bag to seal. Squeeze bag to pipe meringue into 1-inch puffs onto cookie sheets. If desired, sprinkle each with candy sprinkles.

**3.** Bake on middle oven rack 2 hours. Immediately remove cookies from cookie sheets; place on wire racks. Cool completely, about 5 minutes.

**High Altitude (3500–6500 ft):** When making meringue, beat until sugar is dissolved, meringue is glossy and soft peaks form.

**1 Cookie:** Calories 10 (Calories from Fat 0); Total Fat 0g (Saturated Fat 0g; Trans Fat 0g); Cholesterol 0mg; Sodizum 10mg; Total Carbohydrate 2g (Dietary Fiber 0g; Sugars 2g); Protein 0g

% Daily Value: Vitamin A 0%; Vitamin C 0%; Calcium 0%; Iron 0%

Exchanges: Free

Carbohydrate Choices: 0

●

# FESTIVE TWO-IN-ONE BARS

→ **PREP TIME: 25 mins**
**START TO FINISH: 2 hrs 45 mins**

**36 bars**

~~~~~~~~~~~~~~~~~~~~~~~~~~~

1 roll (18 oz.) refrigerated sugar
   cookies
1/4 cup unsweetened baking
   cocoa
1 cup semisweet chocolate chips
   (6 oz.)
1/4 cup chopped salted peanuts
1/2 cup chopped mixed candied
   red and green cherries
1/2 cup chopped pecans
1 oz. vanilla-flavored candy
   coating or almond bark
2 teaspoons vegetable oil

**1.** Heat oven to 350°F (325°F for dark pan). In medium bowl, break up cookie dough. Stir or knead in cocoa until well blended. With floured fingers, press dough evenly in bottom of ungreased 13x9-inch pan.

**2.** Sprinkle half of dough with chocolate chips and peanuts; sprinkle remaining half with cherries and pecans.

**3.** Bake 15 to 20 minutes or until edges are set. Cool completely on wire rack, about 1 hour 30 minutes.

**4.** In 1-quart saucepan, heat candy coating and oil over low heat about 2 minutes, stirring constantly, until coating is melted and smooth. Drizzle over cooled cherry-topped bars. Let stand until set, about 30 minutes. Cut into 6 rows by 6 rows.

**High Altitude (3500–6500 ft): No change.**

**1 Bar:** Calories 120 (Calories from Fat 60); Total Fat 6g (Saturated Fat 2g; Trans Fat 0.5g); Cholesterol 0mg; Sodium 45mg; Total Carbohydrate 15g (Dietary Fiber 0g; Sugars 9g); Protein 1g

% Daily Value: Vitamin A 0%; Vitamin C 0%; Calcium 0%; Iron 4%

Exchanges: 1 Other Carbohydrate, 1 Fat

Carbohydrate Choices: 1

> **BAKING TIP:**
> *You can use leftover candy coating to make candy-coated pretzels. Melt the coating and dip pretzel shapes into it. Let them stand until set. Look for tree- and bell-shaped pretzels around the holidays.*

# STRING O' LIGHTS ALMOND WAFERS

→ **PREP TIME: 1 hr**
**START TO FINISH: 1 hr 30 mins**

**2 dozen cookies**

~~~~~~~~~~~~~~~~~~~~~~~

1 cup all-purpose flour
1/2 cup coarsely chopped slivered almonds
1/4 cup sugar
3/4 cup butter, softened
1/4 teaspoon almond extract
1/3 cup chocolate creamy
   ready-to-spread frosting
   (from 1-lb. can)
Assorted decorating gel or icing

**1.** In small bowl, beat flour, almonds, sugar, butter and almond extract with electric mixer on low speed until dough clings together, scraping bowl occasionally. Divide dough in half; shape each half into rectangle. Wrap dough with plastic wrap; refrigerate 30 minutes for easier handling.

**2.** Heat oven to 375°F. Work with 1 rectangle of dough at a time; keep remaining dough refrigerated. On floured work surface, roll dough with rolling pin to 1/4-inch thickness. With fluted pastry cutter or pizza cutter, cut into 4x1-inch rectangles; place 1 inch apart on ungreased cookie sheets.

**3.** Bake 9 to 13 minutes or until bottoms are light golden brown. Cool 1 minute; remove from cookie sheets. Cool completely, about 5 minutes.

**4.** In small resealable food-storage plastic bag, place frosting; seal bag. Cut small hole in one bottom corner of bag. Squeeze bag to pipe frosting across cookies in wavy line to resemble wire. With decorating gel, place about 5 (1/4-inch) dots along wire for light bulbs.

**High Altitude (3500–6500 ft): No change.**

**1 Cookie:** Calories 110 (Calories from Fat 70); Total Fat 8g (Saturated Fat 3.5g; Trans Fat 0g); Cholesterol 15mg; Sodium 40mg; Total Carbohydrate 9g (Dietary Fiber 0g; Sugars 4g); Protein 1g

% Daily Value: Vitamin A 4%; Vitamin C 0%; Calcium 0%; Iron 2%

Exchanges: 1/2 Other Carbohydrate, 1 1/2 Fat

Carbohydrate Choices: 1/2

●

# HANUKKAH RUGELACH

→ PREP TIME: 1 hr 25 mins
START TO FINISH: 2 hrs 55 mins

**64 cookies**

〰〰〰〰〰〰〰〰〰

## COOKIES
2 tablespoons granulated sugar
1 cup butter, softened
1 package (8 oz.) cream cheese, softened
2 cups all-purpose flour

## FILLING
1/2 cup finely chopped dates
1/2 cup finely chopped pistachio nuts
1/3 cup granulated sugar
2 teaspoons ground cinnamon
1/4 cup butter, softened

## TOPPING
1 tablespoon powdered sugar

**1.** In large bowl, beat all cookie ingredients except flour with electric mixer on medium speed until light and fluffy, scraping bowl occasionally. On low speed, beat in flour until well mixed, scraping bowl occasionally. Shape dough into ball; divide into 4 pieces. Shape each piece into ball; flatten into 1/2-inch-thick disk. Wrap each disk in plastic wrap; refrigerate 1 hour for easier handling.

**2.** Heat oven to 375°F. Grease 2 cookie sheets with shortening or cooking spray. In small bowl, mix filling ingredients until well blended.

**3.** Work with 1 disk of dough at a time; keep remaining dough refrigerated. On floured work surface, roll out dough with floured rolling pin to 1/8-inch thickness, forming 12-inch round. Sprinkle one-quarter of date-nut mixture onto round; press into dough slightly. Cut round into 16 wedges. Starting with curved edge, roll up each wedge; place point side down on cookie sheets.

**4.** Bake 13 to 18 minutes or until light golden brown. Immediately remove from cookie sheets; place on wire racks. Cool completely, about 30 minutes. Sprinkle with powdered sugar.

**High Altitude (3500–6500 ft): Bake 14 to 17 minutes.**

**1 Cookie:** Calories 80 (Calories from Fat 50); Total Fat 5g (Saturated Fat 2.5g; Trans Fat 0g); Cholesterol 15mg; Sodium 40mg; Total Carbohydrate 6g (Dietary Fiber 0g; Sugars 3g); Protein 0g

% Daily Value: Vitamin A 4%; Vitamin C 0%; Calcium 0%; Iron 0%

Exchanges: 1/2 Other Carbohydrate, 1 Fat

Carbohydrate Choices: 1/2

# WHITE CHOCOLATE BREAD PUDDING WITH RED BERRY SAUCE

→ **PREP TIME:** 30 mins
**START TO FINISH:** 1 hr 50 mins

**8 servings (2/3 cup pudding and 3 tablespoons sauce each)**

~~~~~~~~~~~~~~~~~~~~~

## BREAD PUDDING

1 box (6 oz.) white chocolate
   baking bar (6 bars), coarsely
   chopped
3 cups milk
6 cups cubed (1-inch) French
   bread (about 6 oz.)
2 eggs
1/4 cup sugar
1 teaspoon ground cinnamon
1 teaspoon vanilla

## SAUCE

1 package (10 oz.) frozen sweetened raspberries in syrup,
   thawed
3/4 cup cranberry juice cocktail
2 tablespoons sugar
2 tablespoons cornstarch

**1.** Heat oven to 350°F. Grease 2-quart casserole with shortening or cooking spray. In 3-quart saucepan, cook white chocolate and milk over medium heat about 5 minutes, stirring frequently, until white chocolate is melted (do not boil). Stir in bread cubes; set aside.

**2.** In large bowl, beat eggs with fork. Stir in remaining bread pudding ingredients until well blended. Stir in bread mixture. Pour into casserole.

**3.** Bake 45 to 55 minutes or until knife inserted in center comes out clean. Cool on wire rack 30 minutes.

**4.** Meanwhile, in 2-quart saucepan, mix sauce ingredients. Cook over medium heat about 4 minutes, stirring constantly, until mixture boils and thickens. Place strainer over 2-cup serving bowl; pour raspberry mixture into strainer. Press mixture with back of spoon through strainer to remove seeds; discard seeds. Serve sauce with warm bread pudding.

**High Altitude (3500–6500 ft): No change.**

**1 Serving:** Calories 370 (Calories from Fat 120); Total Fat 13g (Saturated Fat 6g; Trans Fat 0g); Cholesterol 165mg; Sodium 230mg; Total Carbohydrate 52g (Dietary Fiber 2g; Sugars 39g); Protein 11g

% Daily Value: Vitamin A 8%; Vitamin C 10%; Calcium 20%; Iron 8%

Exchanges: 3 Starch, 1/2 Other Carbohydrate, 2 Fat

Carbohydrate Choices: 3 1/2

> **BAKING TIP:**
> *White chocolate is sensitive to heat and can scorch and clump easily when melted. Melting the white chocolate with milk prevents both scorching and clumping.*

# FUDGY PEPPERMINT TRUFFLE CHOCOLATE CAKE

→ Prep Time: 30 mins
Start to Finish: 2 hrs 20 mins

**12 servings**

~~~~~~~~~~~~~~~~~~~~~~~

### FILLING

1 cup semisweet chocolate chips
(6 oz.)
2/3 cup sweetened condensed
milk (not evaporated)
1/2 teaspoon peppermint extract

### CAKE

1 box (1 lb. 2.25 oz.) devil's food
cake mix with pudding
1 container (8 oz.) fat-free sour
cream
1/3 cup vegetable oil
3 eggs

### ICING

3/4 cup powdered sugar
1 1/2 oz. cream cheese, softened
1 to 2 tablespoons milk
6 hard peppermint candies,
finely crushed

**1.** Heat oven to 350°F. Grease 12-cup fluted tube cake pan with shortening; lightly flour. In medium microwavable bowl, microwave filling ingredients on High 30 seconds. Stir until melted and smooth (if necessary, microwave 10 to 20 seconds longer); set aside.

**2.** In large bowl, beat cake ingredients with electric mixer on low speed until combined; beat 2 minutes on medium speed. Spoon batter evenly into pan. Drop spoonfuls of filling over batter, keeping filling away from side of pan.

**3.** Bake 35 to 45 minutes or until toothpick inserted near center comes out clean and edge begins to pull away from side of pan. Cool in pan on wire rack 10 minutes. Place wire rack upside down over pan; turn rack and pan over. Remove pan. Cool completely, about 1 hour (center of cake may sink slightly during cooling).

**4.** In medium bowl, beat powdered sugar, cream cheese and 1 tablespoon of the milk with wire whisk until smooth, adding additional milk until desired drizzling consistency. Drizzle icing over cooled cake; sprinkle with crushed candies. Store in refrigerator.

**High Altitude (3500–6500 ft): Heat oven to 375°F. For cake, add 2 tablespoons flour to dry cake mix, decrease oil to 1/4 cup and increase eggs to 4.**

**1 Serving:** Calories 450 (Calories from Fat 160); Total Fat 17g (Saturated Fat 7g; Trans Fat 0.5g); Cholesterol 65mg; Sodium 410mg; Total Carbohydrate 66g (Dietary Fiber 2g; Sugars 48g); Protein 6g
% Daily Value: Vitamin A 4%; Vitamin C 0%; Calcium 15%; Iron 15%
Exchanges: 1 1/2 Starch, 3 Other Carbohydrate, 3 Fat
Carbohydrate Choices: 4 1/2

> **BAKING TIP:**
> *A pastry brush is ideal for greasing the grooves of a fluted tube pan.*

# SAUCY CENTER CHOCOLATE CAKES

→ PREP TIME: 20 mins
START TO FINISH: 40 mins

**7 servings**

~~~~~~~~~~~~~~~~~~~~~~~~~

1/2 cup butter
8 oz. semisweet baking
   chocolate, chopped
4 eggs
2 tablespoons hazelnut coffee
   drink syrup
1/2 cup granulated sugar
2 tablespoons all-purpose flour
Powdered sugar

**1.** Heat oven to 400°F. Generously grease 7 (6-oz.) custard cups with shortening; lightly flour. In 2-quart saucepan, melt butter and chocolate over low heat, stirring frequently, until smooth; set aside.

**2.** In medium bowl, beat eggs and syrup with electric mixer on high speed until foamy. Gradually beat in granulated sugar. Beat on high speed 2 minutes or until light and thickened, scraping bowl occasionally. On low speed, beat in flour and chocolate mixture just until blended, scraping bowl occasionally. Divide batter evenly among custard cups, filling each about 3/4 full. Place cups on cookie sheet.

**3.** Bake 11 to 15 minutes or until cakes have formed top crust, but are still soft in center. Cool 5 minutes. Place individual dessert plate over each custard cup; turn plate and cup over. Remove cup. Sift powdered sugar over cakes; serve warm.

**High Altitude (3500–6500 ft): Bake 13 to 15 minutes.**

**1 Serving:** Calories 420 (Calories from Fat 230); Total Fat 26g (Saturated Fat 13g; Trans Fat 1g); Cholesterol 155mg; Sodium 125mg; Total Carbohydrate 41g (Dietary Fiber 2g; Sugars 37g); Protein 5g

% Daily Value: Vitamin A 15%; Vitamin C 0%; Calcium 2%; Iron 8%

Exchanges: 1 Starch, 2 Other Carbohydrate, 5 Fat

Carbohydrate Choices: 3

# CHOCOLATE-GLAZED FUDGE CAKE

→ **PREP TIME: 30 mins**
**START TO FINISH: 2 hrs 5 mins**

**16 servings**

~~~~~~~~~~~~~~~~~~~~~~~

**C A K E**
1 cup butter
16 oz. semisweet baking
chocolate, chopped
2 teaspoons vanilla
6 eggs, lightly beaten

**G L A Z E**
1/4 cup whipping (heavy) cream
1 tablespoon light corn syrup
1 teaspoon vanilla
3 oz. semisweet baking
chocolate, chopped

**G A R N I S H**
2 tablespoons chopped toasted
hazelnuts (filberts)

**1.** Heat oven to 350°F. Grease 8-inch round cake pan with shortening or cooking spray. In 2-quart saucepan, melt butter and 16 oz. chocolate over medium-low heat, stirring frequently, until smooth. Remove from heat. Stir in 2 teaspoons vanilla. Gently stir in eggs until well combined. Pour batter evenly into pan. Place cake pan in 13x9-inch pan.

**2.** Place pans in oven on middle rack; add warm water to larger pan until 1 inch deep. Bake 35 to 40 minutes or until center is set. Remove cake pan from water bath; place on wire rack. Cool 40 minutes.

**3.** Carefully run knife around edge of pan. Place wire rack upside down over pan; turn rack and pan over. Remove pan. Cool 20 minutes longer.

**4.** Meanwhile, in 1-quart saucepan, heat whipping cream, corn syrup and 1 teaspoon vanilla to boiling over medium heat, stirring occasionally. Remove from heat. Stir in 3 oz. chocolate until melted and smooth.

**5.** Place cake on serving platter. Place pieces of waxed paper under cake to catch drips. Slowly pour glaze over top and side of cake to cover. With narrow metal spatula, smooth glaze over cake. Sprinkle hazelnuts around top edge of cake. When glaze is set, remove waxed paper. Store in refrigerator.

**High Altitude (3500–6500 ft): Bake 45 to 50 minutes.**

**1 Serving:** Calories 340 (Calories from Fat 230); Total Fat 25g (Saturated Fat 13g; Trans Fat 0.5g); Cholesterol 115mg; Sodium 105mg; Total Carbohydrate 23g (Dietary Fiber 2g; Sugars 19g); Protein 4g

% Daily Value: Vitamin A 10%; Vitamin C 0%; Calcium 2%; Iron 8%

Exchanges: 1 Starch, 1/2 Other Carbohydrate, 5 Fat

Carbohydrate Choices: 1 1/2

**BAKING TIP:**
*To toast hazelnuts, see page 200.*

# WHITE CHOCOLATE–FUDGE TORTE

→ PREP TIME: 55 mins
START TO FINISH: 5 hrs 40 mins

**16 servings**

### CAKE
16 oz. semisweet baking
   chocolate, chopped
1 cup unsalted butter
6 eggs

### TOPPING
1 cup white chocolate chunks or
   white vanilla baking chips,
   melted
1 cup whipping (heavy) cream
1 package (8 oz.) cream cheese,
   softened
1/3 cup powdered sugar
2 tablespoons white crème de
   cacao, if desired
1/2 cup miniature semisweet
   chocolate chips, if desired

### RASPBERRY SAUCE
1 package (10 oz.) frozen
   raspberries in light syrup,
   thawed
1 tablespoon cornstarch
1/3 cup red currant jelly

**1.** Heat oven to 400°F. Grease 9-inch springform pan with shortening or cooking spray. In 3-quart saucepan, melt semisweet chocolate and butter over medium-low heat, stirring constantly, until smooth. Cool completely, about 35 minutes.

**2.** Meanwhile, in small bowl, beat eggs with electric mixer on high speed 5 minutes or until triple in volume.

**3.** Fold eggs into cooled chocolate mixture until well blended. Pour batter evenly into pan.

**4.** Bake 15 to 20 minutes (cake edges will be set but center will jiggle when moved). Cool completely in pan on wire rack, about 1 hour 30 minutes. Refrigerate until firm, about 1 hour 30 minutes.

**5.** In heavy 1-quart saucepan, heat white chocolate and 3 tablespoons of the whipping cream over low heat, stirring frequently, until chocolate is melted. In large bowl, beat cream cheese, powdered sugar and, if desired, crème de cacao with electric mixer on medium speed until smooth. While beating, slowly add white chocolate mixture, beating until smooth, scraping bowl occasionally.

**6.** In small bowl, beat remaining whipping cream with electric mixer on high speed until stiff peaks form. With rubber spatula, fold into white chocolate mixture; if desired, fold in miniature chocolate chips. Spread topping over cake. Refrigerate until firm, at least 1 hour.

**7.** To prepare sauce, drain raspberries, reserving syrup. Add water to syrup to make 3/4 cup. In 1-quart saucepan, mix syrup mixture and cornstarch. Stir in jelly. Cook over medium heat, stirring frequently, until thickened and clear. Stir in raspberries. Refrigerate until cold.

**8.** Remove side of pan; leave torte on pan bottom. Serve dessert with sauce. Store in refrigerator.

**High Altitude (3500–6500 ft): Use 10-inch springform pan. Bake 20 minutes.**

**1 Serving:** Calories 490 (Calories from Fat 320); Total Fat 35g (Saturated Fat 21g; Trans Fat 1g); Cholesterol 145mg; Sodium 85mg; Total Carbohydrate 37g (Dietary Fiber 3g; Sugars 32g); Protein 6g

% Daily Value: Vitamin A 15%; Vitamin C 4%; Calcium 6%; Iron 8%

Exchanges: 1 1/2 Starch, 1 Other Carbohydrate, 7 Fat

Carbohydrate Choices: 2 1/2

# CHOCOLATE-CARAMEL TARTLETS

→ **PREP TIME: 40 mins**
**START TO FINISH: 1 hr 5 mins**

**24 tartlets**

~~~~~~~~~~~~~~~~~~~~~~~~~~

**CRUST**
1/2 cup butter, softened
1 package (3 oz.) cream cheese,
   softened
1 1/4 cups all-purpose flour
1 tablespoon sugar

**FILLING**
1/2 cup sugar
4 teaspoons water
1 tablespoon butter
1/3 cup whipping (heavy) cream
1/4 cup semisweet chocolate
   chips

**GARNISH**
1 oz. vanilla-flavored candy
   coating or almond bark,
   if desired

**1.** Heat oven to 450°F. In large bowl, mix crust ingredients with electric mixer on low speed until well combined and dough forms. Divide dough into 24 equal pieces; roll each into ball. Press ball in bottom and up side of each of 24 ungreased mini muffin cups.

**2.** Bake 7 to 9 minutes or until edges are light golden brown. Remove crusts from pan; place on wire racks. Cool completely, about 15 minutes.

**3.** Meanwhile, in heavy 1 1/2-quart saucepan, mix 1/2 cup sugar and the water. With pastry brush dipped in water, brush any sugar down sides of saucepan. Without stirring, cook over medium-high heat 10 to 12 minutes or until mixture turns dark golden brown (if sugar mixture is not cooking, gently swirl mixture in saucepan). Remove from heat. While stirring constantly, add 1 tablespoon butter and the whipping cream, stirring until bubbling stops. Return saucepan to low heat; cook and stir until mixture is smooth.

**4.** Spoon 1/2 teaspoon caramel mixture into each cooled baked crust. Stir chocolate chips into remaining caramel mixture until melted and smooth (if mixture thickens, cook and stir over low heat until smooth). Spoon about 1 teaspoon chocolate filling into each crust.

**5.** If desired, chop candy coating; place in small microwavable bowl. Microwave on High 30 seconds. Stir until melted and smooth (if necessary, microwave 10 seconds longer). Place melted candy coating in resealable freezer plastic bag; partially seal bag. Cut tiny hole in one bottom corner of bag. On sheet of waxed paper, pipe 24 (1-inch) tree shapes; let stand until set. Before serving, garnish each tartlet with tree.

**High Altitude (3500–6500 ft): Bake 8 to 10 minutes.**

**1 Tartlet:** Calories 110 (Calories from Fat 60); Total Fat 7g (Saturated Fat 4g; Trans Fat 0g); Cholesterol 20mg; Sodium 40mg; Total Carbohydrate 11g (Dietary Fiber 0g; Sugars 6g); Protein 1g

% Daily Value: Vitamin A 6%; Vitamin C 0%; Calcium 0%; Iron 2%

Exchanges: 1/2 Other Carbohydrate, 1 1/2 Fat

Carbohydrate Choices: 1

# CRÈME DE MENTHE CHEESECAKE

→ **PREP TIME:** 20 mins
**START TO FINISH:** 6 hrs

**16 servings**

~~~~~~~~~~~~~~~~~~~~~~~~

**CRUST**
1 3/4 cups chocolate cookie
  crumbs (from 9-oz. package)
1/4 cup butter, melted

**FILLING**
3 packages (8 oz. each) cream
  cheese, softened
3/4 cup granulated sugar
3 eggs
3/4 cup whipping (heavy) cream
1/4 cup green crème de menthe

**GARNISH**
1/2 cup whipping (heavy) cream
1 tablespoon powdered sugar
8 thin rectangular crème de
  menthe chocolate candies,
  coarsely chopped

**1.** Heat oven to 300°F. In medium bowl, mix crust ingredients; press in bottom and up side of ungreased 9-inch springform pan.

**2.** In large bowl, beat cream cheese with electric mixer on medium speed until fluffy. Gradually add granulated sugar, beating until smooth and scraping bowl occasionally. Add eggs, one at a time, beating well and scraping bowl after each addition. With spoon, stir in 3/4 cup whipping cream and the crème de menthe until well blended. Pour into crust-lined pan.

**3.** Bake 1 hour to 1 hour 10 minutes or until edges are set but center still jiggles slightly when gently shaken. Turn oven off; open oven door at least 4 inches. Let cheesecake sit in oven until center is set, about 30 minutes.

**4.** Remove cheesecake from oven; place on wire rack. Cool completely, about 1 hour. Cover; refrigerate at least 3 hours before serving.

**5.** Just before serving, carefully run knife around side of pan to loosen. Remove side of pan; leave cheesecake on pan bottom. In small bowl, beat 1/2 cup whipping cream and the powdered sugar with electric mixer on high speed until stiff peaks form. Pipe or spoon whipped cream around edge of cheesecake. Garnish with chopped candies. Store in refrigerator.

**High Altitude (3500–6500 ft): To help prevent cracking, place pan filled with 1 to 1 1/2 inches water on oven rack below cheesecake during baking.**

**1 Serving:** Calories 360 (Calories from Fat 240); Total Fat 27g (Saturated Fat 16g; Trans Fat 1g); Cholesterol 115mg; Sodium 240mg; Total Carbohydrate 23g (Dietary Fiber 0g; Sugars 17g); Protein 6g

% Daily Value: Vitamin A 20%; Vitamin C 0%; Calcium 6%; Iron 6%

Exchanges: 1 1/2 Starch, 5 Fat

Carbohydrate Choices: 1 1/2

# FROSTED CRANBERRY-CHERRY PIE

→ **PREP TIME: 15 mins**
**START TO FINISH: 2 hrs**

**8 servings**

~~~~~~~~~~~~~~~~~~~~~~~

**CRUST**
Pastry for Two-Crust Pie (page 142)
or 1 box (15 oz.) refrigerated pie crusts, softened as directed on box

**FILLING**
1 can (21 oz.) cherry pie filling
1 can (16 oz.) whole berry cranberry sauce
3 tablespoons cornstarch
1/4 teaspoon ground cinnamon

**GLAZE**
1/2 cup powdered sugar
1 tablespoon light corn syrup
2 to 3 teaspoons water

**GARNISH**
1/4 cup sliced almonds, if desired

**1.** Heat oven to 425°F. Using 9-inch glass pie plate, make pastry as directed in recipe or place 1 pie crust as directed on box for Two-Crust Pie.

**2.** In large bowl, mix filling ingredients; spoon into pastry-lined pie plate. Top with second pastry; seal edge and flute. Cut slits or shapes in several places in top of pie. Cover edge with 2- to 3-inch-wide strips of foil to prevent excessive browning; remove foil during last 15 minutes of baking.

**3.** Bake 35 to 45 minutes or until crust is golden brown.

**4.** Remove pie from oven. Immediately, in small bowl, mix powdered sugar, corn syrup and enough water until smooth and desired drizzling consistency; drizzle glaze over hot pie. If desired, decorate or sprinkle with almonds. Cool at least 1 hour before serving.

**High Altitude (3500–6500 ft): No change.**

**1 Serving:** Calories 480 (Calories from Fat 160); Total Fat 18g (Saturated Fat 4.5g; Trans Fat 3g); Cholesterol 0mg; Sodium 310mg; Total Carbohydrate 76g (Dietary Fiber 3g; Sugars 46g); Protein 4g

% Daily Value: Vitamin A 0%; Vitamin C 4%; Calcium 0%; Iron 10%

Exchanges: 1 Starch, 4 Other Carbohydrate, 3 1/2 Fat

Carbohydrate Choices: 5

# APPLE-CRANBERRY CRISP WITH EGGNOG SAUCE

→ **PREP TIME: 25 mins**
**START TO FINISH: 1 hr 5 mins**

**10 servings**

**SAUCE**
2 containers (3.5 to 4 oz. each)
   refrigerated vanilla pudding
1 cup eggnog

**FRUIT MIXTURE**
5 cups sliced peeled apples
   (5 medium)
2 cups fresh or frozen
   cranberries
3/4 cup granulated sugar
2 tablespoons all-purpose flour

**TOPPING**
2/3 cup all-purpose flour
1 cup quick-cooking oats
3/4 cup packed brown sugar
1/2 teaspoon ground cinnamon
1/2 cup butter or margarine,
   cut into pieces

**1.** Place pudding in medium bowl. With wire whisk, gradually stir in eggnog until blended. Cover; refrigerate.

**2.** Heat oven to 375°F. In large bowl, mix fruit mixture ingredients; spread evenly in ungreased 12x8-inch (2-quart) glass baking dish.

**3.** In another medium bowl, mix 2/3 cup flour, the oats, brown sugar and cinnamon. With pastry blender or fork, cut in butter until mixture resembles fine crumbs. Spoon evenly over fruit mixture.

**4.** Bake 35 to 40 minutes or until deep golden brown and bubbly. Serve warm with chilled sauce. Store sauce in refrigerator.

**High Altitude (3500–6500 ft): Bake 50 to 55 minutes.**

**1 Serving:** Calories 380 (Calories from Fat 110); Total Fat 13g (Saturated Fat 6g; Trans Fat 0.5g); Cholesterol 40mg; Sodium 110mg; Total Carbohydrate 62g (Dietary Fiber 3g; Sugars 45g); Protein 4g

% Daily Value: Vitamin A 10%; Vitamin C 4%; Calcium 8%; Iron 8%

Exchanges: 1 Starch, 3 Other Carbohydrate, 2 1/2 Fat

Carbohydrate Choices: 4

# ORANGE CRÈME DESSERT WITH RUBY CRANBERRY SAUCE

**12 servings**

12 chocolate-covered graham crackers, finely crushed (about 1 cup)

2 cups fresh or frozen cranberries

3/4 cup sugar

1 teaspoon cornstarch

3/4 cup water

1 package unflavored gelatin

1/4 cup orange juice

4 containers (6 oz. each) fat-free orange crème yogurt (2 cups)

2 teaspoons grated orange peel

2 cups frozen (thawed) reduced-fat whipped topping

**1.** Heat oven to 375°F. Grease 9-inch springform pan with shortening or cooking spray. Press cracker crumbs evenly in bottom of pan. Bake 7 minutes. Refrigerate or place in freezer until completely cooled.

**2.** Meanwhile, in 2-quart saucepan, mix cranberries, sugar, cornstarch and water. Heat to boiling over medium heat, stirring constantly. Reduce heat to low; simmer uncovered 10 to 15 minutes, stirring occasionally, until cranberries pop. Cool 15 minutes. Refrigerate.

**3.** In 1-quart saucepan, sprinkle gelatin over orange juice; let stand 2 minutes to soften gelatin. Place saucepan over low heat; heat and stir until gelatin is dissolved.

**4.** In blender, blend yogurt and orange peel until smooth. With blender running, add gelatin mixture. Cover; blend on high speed 15 to 20 seconds or until well combined. Spoon into medium bowl. Gently stir in whipped topping. Spoon and gently spread over cooled crust. Refrigerate until set, about 3 hours.

**5.** Remove side of pan; leave dessert on pan bottom. Serve 2 tablespoons cranberry mixture over each individual serving. Store in refrigerator.

**High Altitude (3500–6500 ft): No change.**

**1 Serving:** Calories 190 (Calories from Fat 35); Total Fat 4g (Saturated Fat 3.5g; Trans Fat 0g); Cholesterol 0mg; Sodium 65mg; Total Carbohydrate 34g (Dietary Fiber 1g; Sugars 28g); Protein 4g

% Daily Value: Vitamin A 0%; Vitamin C 4%; Calcium 10%; Iron 0%

Exchanges: 1 Starch, 1 Other Carbohydrate, 1 Fat

Carbohydrate Choices: 2

**BAKING TIP:**
*You can make this lower-fat dessert a day ahead of time. After preparing, just cover and refrigerate.*

*G*ot to have it right now? Jump in and start baking—
you'll have something yummy before you know it!

# BREADSTICK FOCACCIA

→ **PREP TIME:** 15 mins
**START TO FINISH:** 40 mins

**6 servings**

1 can (11 oz.) refrigerated
   breadsticks (12 breadsticks)
1 teaspoon olive oil
2 teaspoons chopped fresh
   rosemary
1/2 teaspoon coarse salt
1 tablespoon slivered pitted
   ripe olives
6 thin red bell pepper strips

**1.** Heat oven to 375°F. Unroll dough; separate into 12 strips. Starting at center of ungreased cookie sheet, coil strips loosely into a spiral, pinching ends together securely as strips are added. Press down very firmly on tops of dough strips to form 1/2-inch-thick round of dough.

**2.** Drizzle olive oil over dough. Sprinkle with rosemary, salt and olives. Arrange bell pepper strips in spoke-fashion on top.

**3.** Bake 20 to 25 minutes or until edges are deep golden brown. Cut into wedges; serve warm.

**High Altitude (3500–6500 ft): No change.**

**1 Serving:** Calories 150 (Calories from Fat 30); Total Fat 3.5g (Saturated Fat 0.5g; Trans Fat 0.5g); Cholesterol 0mg; Sodium 580mg; Total Carbohydrate 25g (Dietary Fiber 0g; Sugars 3g); Protein 4g

% Daily Value: Vitamin A 4%; Vitamin C 4%; Calcium 0%; Iron 8%

Exchanges: 1 1/2 Starch, 1/2 Fat

Carbohydrate Choices: 1 1/2

# CHEDDAR TWISTERS

→ PREP TIME: 10 mins
START TO FINISH: 35 mins

**8 rolls**

~~~~~~~~~~~~~~~~~~~~

2 cans (8 oz. each) refrigerated
  crescent dinner rolls
1 1/2 cups finely shredded sharp
  Cheddar cheese (6 oz.)
1/4 cup chopped green onions
  (4 medium)
1 egg
1 teaspoon water
2 teaspoons sesame seed
1/2 teaspoon garlic salt with
  parsley blend (from 4.8-oz. jar)

**1.** Heat oven to 375°F. Lightly grease large cookie sheet with shortening or cooking spray. Unroll both cans of the dough. Separate into 8 rectangles; firmly press perforations to seal.

**2.** In small bowl, mix cheese and onions. Spoon scant 1/4 cup cheese mixture in 1-inch-wide strip lengthwise down center of each rectangle to within 1/4 inch of each end. Fold dough in half lengthwise to form long strip; firmly press edges to seal. Twist each strip 4 or 5 times; bring ends together to form ring and pinch to seal. Place on cookie sheet.

**3.** In another small bowl, beat egg and water until well blended; brush over dough. Sprinkle with sesame seed and garlic salt blend.

**4.** Bake 15 to 20 minutes or until golden brown. Immediately remove from cookie sheet; cool 5 minutes. Serve warm.

**High Altitude (3500–6500 ft): No change.**

**1 Roll:** Calories 310 (Calories from Fat 180); Total Fat 20g (Saturated Fat 9g; Trans Fat 3g); Cholesterol 50mg; Sodium 640mg; Total Carbohydrate 23g (Dietary Fiber 0g; Sugars 5g); Protein 10g

% Daily Value: Vitamin A 6%; Vitamin C 0%; Calcium 15%; Iron 8%

Exchanges: 1 1/2 Starch, 1 High-Fat Meat, 2 Fat

Carbohydrate Choices: 1 1/2

**BAKING TIP:**
*You can substitute 1/2 teaspoon garlic salt and a dash of parsley flakes for the garlic salt with parsley blend.*

# ONION-GARLIC LOAF

→ **PREP TIME: 15 mins**
**START TO FINISH: 55 mins**

**5 servings**

~~~~~~~~~~~~~~~~~~~~~~~~

1 tablespoon butter
1/2 cup thinly sliced green
   onions, including tops
1 clove garlic, minced
1 can (11 oz.) refrigerated French
   loaf
1/4 cup grated Parmesan cheese

**1.** Heat oven to 350°F. Grease cookie sheet with shortening or cooking spray. In 7-inch skillet, melt butter over medium heat. Add onions and garlic; cook and stir 2 to 3 minutes or until tender.

**2.** Carefully unroll dough. Spread with onion mixture. Reserve 1 teaspoon of the cheese for topping; sprinkle remaining cheese evenly over onion mixture. Roll up dough; place seam side down on cookie sheet.

**3.** With sharp or serrated knife, make 4 or 5 diagonal slashes on top of loaf. Sprinkle with reserved 1 teaspoon cheese.

**4.** Bake 26 to 30 minutes or until deep golden brown. Immediately remove from cookie sheet; cool 10 minutes. Cut diagonally into slices with serrated knife; serve warm.

**High Altitude (3500–6500 ft): No change.**

**1 Serving:** Calories 190 (Calories from Fat 50); Total Fat 6g (Saturated Fat 2.5g; Trans Fat 0.5g); Cholesterol 10mg; Sodium 480mg; Total Carbohydrate 28g (Dietary Fiber 1g; Sugars 3g); Protein 7g

% Daily Value: Vitamin A 4%; Vitamin C 0%; Calcium 8%; Iron 10%

Exchanges: 2 Starch, 1 Fat

Carbohydrate Choices: 2

> **BAKING TIP:**
> *Sprinkle your favorite herbs over the filling before rolling up the loaf—try fresh basil or dried oregano. Crumble dried herbs as you sprinkle them to release their aroma and flavor.*

●

# BLUEBERRY-LEMON TART

→ **PREP TIME:** 20 mins
**START TO FINISH:** 1 hr 15 mins

**16 servings**

1 box (15 oz.) refrigerated pie
  crusts, softened as directed on
  box
2 containers (6 oz. each) low-fat
  lemon burst yogurt
1 package (8 oz.) cream cheese,
  softened
1 can (21 oz.) blueberry pie filling
  with more fruit
1 cup fresh blueberries

**1.** Heat oven to 375°F. Remove pie crusts from pouches; unroll 1 crust on center of ungreased large cookie sheet. Unroll second pie crust and place over first crust, matching edges and pressing to seal. With rolling pin, roll out into 14-inch round.

**2.** Fold 1/2 inch of crust edge under, forming border; press to seal seam (if desired, flute edge). Prick crust generously with fork.

**3.** Bake 20 to 25 minutes or until golden brown. Cool completely, about 30 minutes.

**4.** In medium bowl, beat yogurt and cream cheese with electric mixer on medium speed until blended. Spread evenly over cooled baked crust. Spread pie filling evenly over yogurt mixture. Top with blueberries. Cut into wedges. Store in refrigerator.

**High Altitude (3500–6500 ft): Bake 17 to 22 minutes.**

**1 Serving:** Calories 230 (Calories from Fat 110); Total Fat 12g (Saturated Fat 6g; Trans Fat 0g); Cholesterol 20mg; Sodium 170mg; Total Carbohydrate 28g (Dietary Fiber 0g; Sugars 13g); Protein 3g

% Daily Value: Vitamin A 6%; Vitamin C 0%; Calcium 4%; Iron 0%

Exchanges: 1 Starch, 1 Other Carbohydrate, 2 Fat

Carbohydrate Choices: 2

# FRESH STRAWBERRY TARTS

→ PREP TIME: 45 mins
START TO FINISH: 1 hr 15 mins

**6 tarts**

1 refrigerated pie crust (from
15-oz. box), softened as
directed on box
3/4 teaspoon sugar
2 1/2 cups sliced fresh
strawberries
1/2 cup strawberry pie glaze
6 tablespoons hot fudge
topping, heated
1/3 cup frozen (thawed) whipped
topping

**1.** Heat oven to 450°F. Spray back of 12-cup regular-size muffin pan with cooking spray. Remove pie crust from pouch; unroll on work surface. Sprinkle crust with sugar; press in lightly.

**2.** Cut 6 rounds from crust with 4-inch round cookie cutter or trace 6 rounds with top of large drinking glass and cut out with sharp knife (if necessary, piece pie crust scraps together for sixth round).

**3.** Fit rounds, sugared side up, alternately over backs of muffin cups. Pinch 5 equally spaced pleats around side of each cup. Prick each generously with fork.

**4.** Bake 5 to 7 minutes or until lightly browned. Cool 5 minutes. Carefully remove tart shells from muffin cups. Cool completely, about 30 minutes.

**5.** Meanwhile, in large bowl, gently mix strawberries and pie glaze. Refrigerate until thoroughly chilled, about 30 minutes.

**6.** Just before serving, spoon 1 tablespoon warm fudge topping into each tart shell. Spoon about 1/3 cup berry mixture over topping in each; top with whipped topping.

**High Altitude (3500–6500 ft): Bake 5 to 6 minutes.**

**1 Tart:** Calories 330 (Calories from Fat 110); Total Fat 12g (Saturated Fat 4.5g; Trans Fat 0g); Cholesterol 5mg; Sodium 220mg; Total Carbohydrate 54g (Dietary Fiber 3g; Sugars 29g); Protein 2g

% Daily Value: Vitamin A 0%; Vitamin C 35%; Calcium 4%; Iron 4%

Exchanges: 3 1/2 Other Carbohydrate, 2 1/2 Fat

Carbohydrate Choices: 3 1/2

> **BAKING TIP:**
> *It's best to use strawberries soon after you purchase them. To store for a day or two, arrange unwashed berries in a single layer on a baking pan with sides lined with paper towels. Cover the berries with paper towels and refrigerate; wash just before use.*

# ELEGANT FRUIT WEDGES

→ PREP TIME: 15 mins
START TO FINISH: 50 mins

**10 servings**

~~~~~~~~~~~~~~~~~~~~~~~~

1 refrigerated pie crust (from 15-oz. box), softened as directed on box
1 package (8 oz.) cream cheese, softened
2 tablespoons milk
1/4 cup powdered sugar
1/2 teaspoon grated orange peel
2 to 3 cups assorted cut-up fresh fruit

**1.** Heat oven to 450°F. Remove pie crust from pouch; unroll on ungreased cookie sheet (if desired, flute edge). Generously prick crust with fork. Bake 9 to 11 minutes or until lightly browned. Cool completely, about 30 minutes.

**2.** Meanwhile, in small bowl, beat cream cheese, milk, powdered sugar and orange peel with electric mixer on medium speed until smooth.

**3.** Place cooled baked crust on serving plate. Spread cream cheese mixture over crust to within 1/2 inch of edge. Arrange fruit on cream cheese mixture. Cut into wedges. Store in refrigerator.

**High Altitude (3500–6500 ft): No change.**

**1 Serving:** Calories 210 (Calories from Fat 120); Total Fat 14g (Saturated Fat 7g; Trans Fat 0g); Cholesterol 30mg; Sodium 160mg; Total Carbohydrate 19g (Dietary Fiber 0g; Sugars 7g); Protein 3g
% Daily Value: Vitamin A 8%; Vitamin C 15%; Calcium 2%; Iron 0%
Exchanges: 1 Starch, 1/2 Other Carbohydrate, 2 1/2 Fat
Carbohydrate Choices: 1

> **BAKING TIP:**
> *Select the most colorful, finest fruit for a stunning dessert. Fresh strawberries, blueberries, peaches and kiwifruit add a rainbow of color.*

# MINI FRUIT PIZZAS

➜ PREP TIME: 25 mins
START TO FINISH: 40 mins

**20 fruit pizzas**

~~~~~~~~~~~~~~~~~~~~~~~~~

1 package (18 oz.) refrigerated
   ready-to-bake sugar cookies
   (20 cookies)
1 package (8 oz.) cream cheese,
   softened
2 tablespoons frozen limeade
   concentrate
1/2 cup powdered sugar
10 fresh strawberries, quartered
1 kiwifruit, peeled, cut in half
   lengthwise and cut into 10
   slices
1/2 cup fresh blueberries
1/2 cup fresh raspberries

**1.** Bake cookies as directed on package. Cool completely, about 10 minutes.

**2.** Meanwhile, in medium bowl, beat cream cheese, limeade concentrate and powdered sugar with electric mixer on medium speed until smooth.

**3.** Spread each cooled cookie with 1 tablespoon cream cheese mixture. Arrange fruit on top of each. Serve immediately, or cover and refrigerate up to 2 hours before serving.

**High Altitude (3500–6500 ft): No change.**

**1 Fruit Pizza:** Calories 170 (Calories from Fat 80); Total Fat 9g (Saturated Fat 3.5g; Trans Fat 1.5g); Cholesterol 20mg; Sodium 100mg; Total Carbohydrate 21g (Dietary Fiber 0g; Sugars 13g); Protein 2g

% Daily Value: Vitamin A 4%; Vitamin C 15%; Calcium 0%; Iron 4%

Exchanges: 1 1/2 Other Carbohydrate, 2 Fat

Carbohydrate Choices: 1 1/2

# COFFEE SHOP COOKIES

→ PREP TIME: 20 mins
START TO FINISH: 40 mins

**9 large cookies**

~~~~~~~~~~~~~~~~~~~~~~~~

1 roll (18 oz.) refrigerated sugar
  cookies
1/3 cup packed brown sugar
1 teaspoon vanilla
3/4 cup old-fashioned oats
1/2 cup butterscotch chips
2 milk chocolate candy bars (1.55
  oz. each), unwrapped,
  chopped

**1.** Heat oven to 350°F. Grease 1 large or 2 small cookie sheets with shortening or cooking spray. In large bowl, break up cookie dough. Stir or knead in brown sugar and vanilla until well mixed. Stir or knead in oats, butterscotch chips and chocolate (dough will be stiff).

**2.** Drop dough by rounded 1/4 cupfuls 2 inches apart onto cookie sheets. Flatten each with fingers to 1/2-inch thickness.

**3.** Bake 13 to 18 minutes or until cookies are slightly puffed and edges are golden brown. Cool 1 minute; remove from cookie sheets.

**High Altitude (3500–6500 ft): Bake 15 to 18 minutes.**

**1 Large Cookie:** Calories 400 (Calories from Fat 150); Total Fat 17g (Saturated Fat 7g; Trans Fat 2.5g); Cholesterol 20mg; Sodium 170mg; Total Carbohydrate 58g (Dietary Fiber 2g; Sugars 37g); Protein 4g
% Daily Value: Vitamin A 0%; Vitamin C 0%; Calcium 4%; Iron 10%
Exchanges: 1 Starch, 3 Other Carbohydrate, 3 Fat
Carbohydrate Choices: 4

# PEANUTTY CHOCOLATE CANDY COOKIES

→ PREP TIME: 45 mins
START TO FINISH: 45 mins

**3 dozen cookies**

~~~~~~~~~~~~~~~~~~~~~~~~~~~

1 box (1 lb. 2.25 oz.) chocolate
   fudge cake mix with pudding
1/2 cup butter or margarine,
   softened
2 eggs
1 bag (14 oz.) candy-coated
   peanut butter pieces
1 cup coarsely chopped salted
   peanuts

**1.** Heat oven to 350°F. Grease cookie sheets with shortening or cooking spray. In large bowl, beat cake mix, butter and eggs with electric mixer on low speed just until moistened. With spoon, stir in peanut butter pieces and peanuts.

**2.** Drop dough by rounded tablespoonfuls 2 inches apart onto cookie sheets.

**3.** Bake 7 to 10 minutes or until edges are set and tops appear dry. Cool 2 minutes; remove from cookie sheets.

**High Altitude (3500–6500 ft): Heat oven to 375°F. Flatten cookies slightly before baking. Bake 10 to 13 minutes.**

**1 Cookie:** Calories 160 (Calories from Fat 70); Total Fat 8g (Saturated Fat 2.5g; Trans Fat 0g); Cholesterol 20mg; Sodium 170mg; Total Carbohydrate 19g (Dietary Fiber 1g; Sugars 13g); Protein 4g

% Daily Value: Vitamin A 2%; Vitamin C 0%; Calcium 4%; Iron 4%

Exchanges: 1 Starch, 1 1/2 Fat

Carbohydrate Choices: 1

# CHERRY–CHOCOLATE CHIP COOKIES

**20 cookies**

1 roll (18 oz.) refrigerated oat-
    meal chocolate chip cookies
1/4 cup chopped maraschino
    cherries, well drained
1 tablespoon all-purpose flour
2 cups Wheaties® cereal,
    coarsely crushed

**1.** Heat oven to 350°F. In large bowl, break up cookie dough. Pat cherries dry with paper towels. Stir or knead cherries and flour into dough until well mixed.

**2.** Drop dough by heaping teaspoonfuls into cereal crumbs; coat well, pressing cereal into dough. Shape into balls; place 2 inches apart on ungreased cookie sheets.

**3.** Bake 12 to 15 minutes or until golden brown. Immediately remove from cookie sheets.

**High Altitude (3500–6500 ft): No change.**

**1 Cookie:** Calories 130 (Calories from Fat 50); Total Fat 6g (Saturated Fat 2g; Trans Fat 0g); Cholesterol 0mg; Sodium 110mg; Total Carbohydrate 19g (Dietary Fiber 0g; Sugars 10g); Protein 1g

% Daily Value: Vitamin A 0%; Vitamin C 0%; Calcium 0%; Iron 6%

Exchanges: 1 1/2 Other Carbohydrate, 1 Fat

Carbohydrate Choices: 1

> **BAKING TIP:**
> *Simply pour the cereal into a bowl and crush it until the pieces are broken or place the cereal in a resealable plastic bag and flatten it slightly with a rolling pin. To keep these moist cookies from drying out, seal them in an airtight container.*

# CHOCOLATE TOFFEE BARS

→ PREP TIME: 20 mins
START TO FINISH: 1 hr 35 mins

**36 bars**

## CRUST
1 cup all-purpose flour
1/2 cup packed brown sugar
1/2 cup butter or margarine,
   softened

## TOPPING
1 cup packed brown sugar
2 tablespoons all-purpose flour
1 teaspoon baking powder
2 eggs
1 cup semisweet chocolate chips
   (6 oz.)
1/2 cup chopped nuts

**1.** Heat oven to 350°F. In small bowl, mix crust ingredients; press in bottom of ungreased 13x9-inch pan. Bake 8 to 10 minutes or until lightly browned. Cool slightly, about 5 minutes. Increase oven temperature to 375°F.

**2.** Meanwhile, in medium bowl, mix 1 cup brown sugar, 2 tablespoons flour, the baking powder and eggs until well blended. Stir in chocolate chips and nuts.

**3.** Pour topping evenly over partially baked crust; spread slightly if necessary. Bake 13 to 18 minutes longer or until deep golden brown and center is set. Cool completely, about 1 hour. Cut into 6 rows by 6 rows.

**High Altitude (3500–6500 ft): In crust, decrease butter to 1/3 cup. In topping, increase flour to 3 tablespoons.**

1 **Bar:** Calories 110 (Calories from Fat 50); Total Fat 5g (Saturated Fat 2.5g; Trans Fat 0g); Cholesterol 20mg; Sodium 40mg; Total Carbohydrate 15g (Dietary Fiber 0g; Sugars 11g); Protein 1g

% Daily Value: Vitamin A 2%; Vitamin C 0%; Calcium 2%; Iron 4%

Exchanges: 1 Other Carbohydrate, 1 Fat

Carbohydrate Choices: 1

# MAPLE-WALNUT PIE BARS

→ PREP TIME: 10 mins
START TO FINISH: 2 hrs 25 mins

**36 bars**

〜〜〜〜〜〜〜〜〜〜〜〜

1 roll (18 oz.) refrigerated sugar
  cookies
3 eggs
1/3 cup packed brown sugar
2 tablespoons all-purpose flour
1 1/3 cups maple-flavored syrup
1 1/2 cups chopped walnuts
Powdered sugar, if desired

**1.** Heat oven to 350°F (325°F for dark pan). In ungreased 13x9-inch pan, break up cookie dough. With floured fingers, press dough evenly in bottom of pan. Bake 13 to 15 minutes or until edges are golden brown.

**2.** Meanwhile, in large bowl, beat eggs with wire whisk. Stir in brown sugar, flour and syrup until well blended. Stir in walnuts.

**3.** Pour egg mixture evenly over partially baked crust; bake 30 to 35 minutes longer or until filling is set. Cool completely on wire rack, about 1 hour 30 minutes. If desired, sprinkle with powdered sugar. Cut into 6 rows by 6 rows.

**High Altitude (3500–6500 ft): No change.**

**1 Bar:** Calories 150 (Calories from Fat 60); Total Fat 6g (Saturated Fat 1g; Trans Fat 0.5g); Cholesterol 20mg; Sodium 60mg; Total Carbohydrate 20g (Dietary Fiber 0g; Sugars 11g); Protein 2g

% Daily Value: Vitamin A 0%; Vitamin C 0%; Calcium 0%; Iron 4%

Exchanges: 1 1/2 Other Carbohydrate, 1 Fat

Carbohydrate Choices: 1

**BAKING TIP:**
*A small tea strainer works perfectly for sprinkling powdered sugar over the bars.*

# ZEBRA BROWNIES

→ PREP TIME: 15 mins
START TO FINISH: 2 hrs 50 mins

**36 bars**

~~~~~~~~~~~~~~~~~~~~~~~~

## FILLING
2 packages (3 oz. each) cream
   cheese, softened
1/4 cup sugar
1/2 teaspoon vanilla
1 egg

## BROWNIES
1 box (1 lb. 6.5 oz.) supreme
   brownie mix with pouch of
   chocolate flavor syrup
1/3 cup vegetable oil
1/4 cup water
2 eggs

**1.** Heat oven to 350°F. Generously grease bottom only of 13x9-inch pan with shortening or cooking spray. In small bowl, beat filling ingredients with electric mixer on medium speed until smooth; set aside.

**2.** In large bowl, beat brownie ingredients 50 strokes with spoon. Spread half of brownie batter evenly in pan. Pour filling mixture over brownie batter, spreading to cover. Top with spoonfuls of remaining brownie batter. To marble, lightly pull knife through batter in wide curves; turn pan and repeat.

**3.** Bake 30 to 35 minutes or until set. DO NOT OVERBAKE. Cool completely, about 1 hour. Refrigerate at least 1 hour before serving. Cut into 6 rows by 6 rows. Store in refrigerator.

**High Altitude (3500–6500 ft):** Follow High Altitude brownie mix directions for 13x9-inch pan.

**1 Bar:** Calories 120 (Calories from Fat 45); Total Fat 5g (Saturated Fat 1.5g; Trans Fat 0g); Cholesterol 25mg; Sodium 75mg; Total Carbohydrate 17g (Dietary Fiber 0g; Sugars 12g); Protein 1g

% Daily Value: Vitamin A 0%; Vitamin C 0%; Calcium 0%; Iron 4%

Exchanges: 1 Other Carbohydrate, 1 Fat

Carbohydrate Choices: 1

# DULCE DE LECHE BARS

→ PREP TIME: 30 mins
START TO FINISH: 3 hrs 10 mins

**48 bars**

~~~~~~~~~~~~~~~~~~~~~~~~~~~~~~

2 rolls (18 oz. each) refrigerated
    sugar cookies
1 3/4 cups oats
2/3 cup packed brown sugar
2 teaspoons vanilla
1 bag (14 oz.) caramels,
    unwrapped
1/2 cup butter
1 can (14 oz.) sweetened con-
    densed milk (not evaporated)
3 tablespoons caramel topping

**1.** Heat oven to 350°F. In large bowl, break up 1 roll of cookie dough. Stir or knead in 3/4 cup of the oats, 1/3 cup of the brown sugar and 1 teaspoon of the vanilla. With floured fingers, press dough evenly in bottom of ungreased 15x10x1-inch pan. Bake 13 to 18 minutes or until light golden brown.

**2.** Meanwhile, in same bowl, break up remaining roll of cookie dough. Stir or knead in remaining cup of oats, 1/3 cup brown sugar and 1 teaspoon vanilla. In 3-quart heavy saucepan, heat caramels, butter and sweetened condensed milk over medium-low heat, stirring frequently, until caramels are melted and mixture is smooth.

**3.** Spread caramel mixture evenly over partially baked crust; crumble remaining dough mixture evenly over caramel. Bake 18 to 22 minutes longer or until light golden brown. Cool 15 minutes. Run knife around sides of pan to loosen. Cool completely, about 2 hours.

**4.** With small spoon, drizzle caramel topping over bars. Cut into 8 rows by 6 rows.

**High Altitude (3500–6500 ft): Bake crust 15 to 20 minutes.**

**1 Bar:** Calories 190 (Calories from Fat 70); Total Fat 7g (Saturated Fat 3g; Trans Fat 1g); Cholesterol 15mg; Sodium 105mg; Total Carbohydrate 29g (Dietary Fiber 0g; Sugars 19g); Protein 2g

% Daily Value: Vitamin A 2%; Vitamin C 0%; Calcium 4%; Iron 4%

Exchanges: 2 Other Carbohydrate, 1 1/2 Fat

Carbohydrate Choices: 2

# SO-EASY LEMON BARS

→ PREP TIME: 15 mins
START TO FINISH: 1 hr 35 mins

**36 bars**

1 roll (18 oz.) refrigerated sugar
   cookies
4 eggs
1 1/2 cups granulated sugar
2 tablespoons all-purpose flour
2 tablespoons butter or margarine, melted
2 tablespoons grated lemon peel
   (2 medium)
1/3 cup fresh lemon juice
   (2 medium)
1 to 2 tablespoons powdered
   sugar

**1.** Heat oven to 350°F. In ungreased 13x9-inch pan, break up cookie dough. With floured fingers, press dough evenly in bottom of pan. Bake 15 to 20 minutes or until light golden brown.

**2.** Meanwhile, in large bowl, beat eggs with wire whisk or fork until blended. Beat in granulated sugar, flour and butter until well blended. Stir in lemon peel and lemon juice.

**3.** Pour egg mixture over partially baked crust; bake 20 to 30 minutes longer or until edges are light golden brown. Cool completely, about 30 minutes. Sprinkle with powdered sugar. With knife dipped in hot water, cut into 6 rows by 6 rows.

**High Altitude (3500–6500 ft): Bake crust 18 to 21 minutes. After topping crust, bake 25 to 30 minutes.**

**1 Bar:** Calories 110 (Calories from Fat 35); Total Fat 4g (Saturated Fat 1g; Trans Fat 0.5g); Cholesterol 30mg; Sodium 50mg; Total Carbohydrate 18g (Dietary Fiber 0g; Sugars 13g); Protein 1g

% Daily Value: Vitamin A 0%; Vitamin C 0%; Calcium 0%; Iron 2%

Exchanges: 1 Other Carbohydrate, 1 Fat

Carbohydrate Choices: 1

# WHITE CHOCOLATE–RASPBERRY BARS

→ PREP TIME: 20 mins
START TO FINISH: 2 hrs 10 mins

**36 bars**

〜〜〜〜〜〜〜〜〜〜〜〜〜

1 roll (18 oz.) refrigerated sugar
    cookies
1 1/4 cups white chocolate
    chunks or white vanilla baking
    chips
1 jar (12 oz.) raspberry jam or
    preserves (3/4 cup)
1 teaspoon oil

**1.** Heat oven to 350°F. In ungreased 13x9-inch pan, break up cookie dough. With floured fingers, press dough evenly in bottom of pan. Sprinkle 1 cup of the white chocolate chunks over crust; press firmly into dough.

**2.** Bake 16 to 20 minutes or until light golden brown.

**3.** Spread jam evenly over partially baked crust; bake 10 minutes longer. Cool completely, about 1 hour.

**4.** In small resealable food-storage plastic bag, place remaining 1/4 cup white chocolate chunks and the oil; partially seal bag. Microwave on High 30 seconds. Squeeze bag until chunks are smooth (if necessary, microwave 15 to 30 seconds longer).

**5.** Cut small hole in one bottom corner of bag; squeeze bag gently to drizzle white chocolate over bars. Refrigerate until chocolate is set, about 20 minutes. Cut into 6 rows by 6 rows. Serve bars at room temperature.

**High Altitude (3500–6500 ft): In step 2, bake crust 18 to 21 minutes.**

**1 Bar:** Calories 120 (Calories from Fat 40); Total Fat 4.5g (Saturated Fat 2g; Trans Fat 0.5g); Cholesterol 0mg; Sodium 45mg; Total Carbohydrate 18g (Dietary Fiber 0g; Sugars 13g); Protein 0g

% Daily Value: Vitamin A 0%; Vitamin C 0%; Calcium 0%; Iron 2%

Exchanges: 1 Other Carbohydrate, 1 Fat

Carbohydrate Choices: 1

# CHOCOLATE CHIP–COCONUT CHEESECAKE BARS

→ **PREP TIME: 10 mins**
**START TO FINISH: 2 hrs 20 mins**

**16 bars**

〜〜〜〜〜〜〜〜〜〜〜〜〜

1 package (8 oz.) cream cheese,
  softened
1/2 cup sugar
1 egg
1/2 cup coconut
1 roll (18 oz.) refrigerated
  chocolate chip cookies

**1.** Heat oven to 350°F. In small bowl, beat cream cheese, sugar and egg with electric mixer on medium speed until smooth. With spoon, stir in coconut.

**2.** Remove half of cookie dough from wrapper; place in ungreased 9- or 8-inch square pan. With floured fingers, press dough evenly in bottom of pan. Spoon and spread cream cheese mixture evenly over dough. Crumble and sprinkle remaining half of cookie dough over cream cheese mixture.

**3.** Bake 35 to 40 minutes or until golden brown and firm to the touch. Cool 30 minutes. Refrigerate at least 1 hour or until chilled before serving. Cut into 4 rows by 4 rows. Store in refrigerator.

**High Altitude (3500–6500 ft): Bake 40 to 45 minutes.**

**1 Bar:** Calories 240 (Calories from Fat 130); Total Fat 14g (Saturated Fat 6g; Trans Fat 1.5g); Cholesterol 35mg; Sodium 150mg; Total Carbohydrate 27g (Dietary Fiber 0g; Sugars 19g); Protein 3g

% Daily Value: Vitamin A 4%; Vitamin C 0%; Calcium 0%; Iron 6%

Exchanges: 1 Starch, 1 Other Carbohydrate, 2 1/2 Fat

Carbohydrate Choices: 2

**BAKING TIP:**

*For easy cutting, line the pan with foil and prepare the bars as directed. When they're cool, use the foil to lift the bars from the pan. Peel away the foil and cut the bars with a long, sharp knife. Chilling the uncut bars makes them easier to cut and so does wiping the knife clean between cuts.*

# CHERRY CHEESECAKE DESSERT

→ PREP TIME: 15 mins
START TO FINISH: 1 hr 15 mins

**12 servings**

〜〜〜〜〜〜〜〜〜〜〜〜〜〜

## FILLING
1 package (8 oz.) cream cheese, softened
1/4 cup sugar
1 tablespoon all-purpose flour
1/2 teaspoon vanilla
1 egg

## CRUST
1 roll (18 oz.) refrigerated sugar cookies

## TOPPING
2 cans (21 oz. each) cherry pie filling
1/2 teaspoon almond extract

**1.** Heat oven to 375°F. In medium bowl, beat filling ingredients with electric mixer on medium speed until well blended; set aside.

**2.** Remove cookie dough from wrapper; place in ungreased 13x9-inch pan. With floured fingers, press dough evenly in bottom of pan. Spoon and spread filling evenly over crust.

**3.** Bake 17 to 20 minutes or until edges begin to brown. Cool completely, about 40 minutes.

**4.** In another medium bowl, mix topping ingredients; spread over top. Store in refrigerator.

**High Altitude (3500–6500 ft):** In step 2, before pressing dough into pan, stir or knead in 1 tablespoon flour. Pre-bake crust 8 to 10 minutes or until light golden but still soft to the touch. In step 3, bake 17 to 20 minutes.

**1 Serving:** Calories 380 (Calories from Fat 140); Total Fat 16g (Saturated Fat 6g; Trans Fat 2g); Cholesterol 50mg; Sodium 170mg; Total Carbohydrate 55g (Dietary Fiber 2g; Sugars 40g); Protein 4g

% Daily Value: Vitamin A 6%; Vitamin C 4%; Calcium 4%; Iron 8%

Exchanges: 1 Starch, 2 1/2 Other Carbohydrate, 3 Fat

Carbohydrate Choices: 3 1/2

# BLACK FOREST CHERRY CAKE

→ PREP TIME: 25 mins
START TO FINISH: 55 mins

**12 servings**

〜〜〜〜〜〜〜〜〜〜〜〜

### CAKE
1 box (1 lb. 2.25 oz.) devil's food
 cake mix with pudding
2 tablespoons all-purpose flour
1 3/4 cups water
3 eggs

### FILLING AND TOPPING
1 can (21 oz.) cherry or cherry-
 cranberry pie filling
3/4 teaspoon almond extract
1 container (8 oz.) frozen
 reduced-fat whipped topping,
 thawed
Maraschino or candied cherry
 and chocolate curls, if desired

**1.** Heat oven to 350°F. Grease 15x10x1-inch pan with shortening or cooking spray. Line with foil, extending foil over short sides of pan; grease foil. In large bowl, beat cake mix, flour, water and eggs with electric mixer on low speed until moistened, scraping bowl occasionally. Beat on high speed 2 minutes, scraping bowl occasionally. Spread batter evenly in pan.

**2.** Bake 18 to 20 minutes or until cake springs back when touched lightly in center. Remove cake from pan by lifting foil; place on wire rack. Cool completely, about 15 minutes.

**3.** Meanwhile, in small bowl, mix pie filling and 1/2 teaspoon of the almond extract.

**4.** Cut cooled cake in half crosswise to make 2 (10x7-inch) layers; remove foil. Place 1 cake layer on serving platter or tray; spread pie filling mixture over top. Top with remaining cake layer.

**5.** Stir remaining 1/4 teaspoon almond extract into whipped topping. Spread mixture over sides and top of cake. Serve immediately, or loosely cover and refrigerate until serving time. If desired, garnish each serving with maraschino or candied cherry and chocolate curls. Store in refrigerator.

**High Altitude (3500–6500 ft): Heat oven to 375°F.**

**1 Serving:** Calories 290 (Calories from Fat 60); Total Fat 7g (Saturated Fat 4g; Trans Fat 0g); Cholesterol 55mg; Sodium 360mg; Total Carbohydrate 53g (Dietary Fiber 2g; Sugars 35g); Protein 5g

% Daily Value: Vitamin A 2%; Vitamin C 2%; Calcium 8%; Iron 10%

Exchanges: 1 1/2 Starch, 2 Other Carbohydrate, 1 Fat

Carbohydrate Choices: 3 1/2

# GINGER-BLUEBERRY CRISP

**4 servings (3/4 cup each)**

## FRUIT

4 cups frozen blueberries (do not thaw)
1/4 cup all-purpose flour
2 tablespoons sugar

## TOPPING

1/2 cup sugar
1/2 cup old-fashioned oats
1/4 cup all-purpose flour
2 tablespoons grated orange peel
2 tablespoons chopped crystallized ginger
1/4 cup butter or margarine, cut into small pieces

**1.** Heat oven to 375°F. In 2 1/2- to 3-cup soufflé or casserole dish, mix fruit ingredients.

**2.** In medium bowl, mix topping ingredients with fork until crumbly; sprinkle evenly over fruit mixture.

**3.** Bake 45 to 50 minutes or until topping is light golden brown and mixture is bubbly. Cool at least 30 minutes before serving.

**High Altitude (3500–6500 ft): In topping, decrease butter to 1 tablespoon.**

**1 Serving:** Calories 490 (Calories from Fat 120); Total Fat 13g (Saturated Fat 6g; Trans Fat 0.5g); Cholesterol 30mg; Sodium 95mg; Total Carbohydrate 88g (Dietary Fiber 8g; Sugars 52g); Protein 5g
% Daily Value: Vitamin A 10%; Vitamin C 30%; Calcium 4%; Iron 8%
Exchanges: 1 1/2 Starch, 4 1/2 Other Carbohydrate, 2 1/2 Fat
Carbohydrate Choices: 6

**BAKING TIP:**
*Top each serving of warm crisp with whipped cream or ice cream and a sprinkle of chopped candied ginger.*

# BROWN SUGAR SHORTBREAD PUFFS

→ **PREP TIME: 1 hr**
**START TO FINISH: 1 hr**

**4 dozen cookies**

~~~~~~~~~~~~~~~~~~~

1 cup packed brown sugar
1 1/4 cups butter, softened
1 teaspoon vanilla
1 egg yolk
2 1/4 cups all-purpose flour

**1.** Heat oven to 350°F. In large bowl, beat brown sugar and butter with electric mixer on medium speed until light and fluffy, scraping bowl occasionally. Beat in vanilla and egg yolk until blended. On low speed, beat in flour until mixture forms a smooth dough.

**2.** Drop dough by rounded teaspoonfuls 2 inches apart onto ungreased cookie sheets.

**3.** Bake 10 to 15 minutes or until light golden brown and set. Immediately remove from cookie sheets.

**High Altitude (3500–6500 ft): No change.**

**1 Cookie:** Calories 80 (Calories from Fat 45); Total Fat 5g (Saturated Fat 2.5g; Trans Fat 0g); Cholesterol 15mg; Sodium 35mg; Total Carbohydrate 9g (Dietary Fiber 0g; Sugars 4g); Protein 0g

% Daily Value: Vitamin A 4%; Vitamin C 0%; Calcium 0%; Iron 2%

Exchanges: 1/2 Other Carbohydrate, 1 Fat

Carbohydrate Choices: 1/2

# Metric Conversion Guide

## Volume

| U.S. Units | Canadian Metric | Australian Metric |
|---|---|---|
| 1/4 teaspoon | 1 mL | 1 ml |
| 1/2 teaspoon | 2 mL | 2 ml |
| 1 teaspoon | 5 mL | 5 ml |
| 1 tablespoon | 15 mL | 20 ml |
| 1/4 cup | 50 mL | 60 ml |
| 1/3 cup | 75 mL | 80 ml |
| 1/2 cup | 125 mL | 125 ml |
| 2/3 cup | 150 mL | 170 ml |
| 3/4 cup | 175 mL | 190 ml |
| 1 cup | 250 mL | 250 ml |
| 1 quart | 1 liter | 1 liter |
| 1 1/2 quarts | 1.5 liters | 1.5 liters |
| 2 quarts | 2 liters | 2 liters |
| 2 1/2 quarts | 2.5 liters | 2.5 liters |
| 3 quarts | 3 liters | 3 liters |
| 4 quarts | 4 liters | 4 liters |

## Weight

| U.S. Units | Canadian Metric | Australian Metric |
|---|---|---|
| 1 ounce | 30 grams | 30 grams |
| 2 ounces | 55 grams | 60 grams |
| 3 ounces | 85 grams | 90 grams |
| 4 ounces (1/4 pound) | 115 grams | 125 grams |
| 8 ounces (1/2 pound) | 225 grams | 225 grams |
| 16 ounces (1 pound) | 455 grams | 500 grams |
| 1 pound | 455 grams | 1/2 kilogram |

## Measurements

| Inches | Centimeters |
|---|---|
| 1 | 2.5 |
| 2 | 5.0 |
| 3 | 7.5 |
| 4 | 10.0 |
| 5 | 12.5 |
| 6 | 15.0 |
| 7 | 17.5 |
| 8 | 20.5 |
| 9 | 23.0 |
| 10 | 25.5 |
| 11 | 28.0 |
| 12 | 30.5 |
| 13 | 33.0 |

## Temperatures

| Fahrenheit | Celsius |
|---|---|
| 32° | 0° |
| 212° | 100° |
| 250° | 120° |
| 275° | 140° |
| 300° | 150° |
| 325° | 160° |
| 350° | 180° |
| 375° | 190° |
| 400° | 200° |
| 425° | 220° |
| 450° | 230° |
| 475° | 240° |
| 500° | 260° |

NOTE: The recipes in this cookbook have not been developed or tested using metric measures. When converting recipes to metric, some variations in quality may be noted.

# Helpful Nutrition and Cooking Information

## Nutrition Guidelines

We provide nutrition information for each recipe that includes calories, fat, cholesterol, sodium, carbohydrate, fiber and protein. Individual food choices can be based on this information.

### Recommended intake for a daily diet of 2,000 calories as set by the Food and Drug Administration

| | |
|---|---|
| Total Fat | Less than 65g |
| Saturated Fat | Less than 20g |
| Cholesterol | Less than 300mg |
| Sodium | Less than 2,400mg |
| Total Carbohydrate | 300g |
| Dietary Fiber | 25g |

### Criteria Used for Calculating Nutrition Information

- The first ingredient was used wherever a choice is given (such as 1/3 cup sour cream or plain yogurt).

- The first ingredient amount was used wherever a range is given (such as 3- to 3 1/2-pound cut-up broiler-fryer chicken).

- The first serving number was used wherever a range is given (such as 4 to 6 servings).

- "If desired" ingredients and recipe variations were not included (such as sprinkle with brown sugar, if desired).

- Only the amount of a marinade or frying oil that is estimated to be absorbed by the food during preparation or cooking was calculated.

### Ingredients Used in Recipe Testing and Nutrition Calculations

- Ingredients used for testing represent those that the majority of consumers use in their homes: large eggs, 2% milk, 80%-lean ground beef, canned ready-to-use chicken broth and vegetable oil spread containing not less than 65 percent fat.

- Fat-free, low-fat or low-sodium products were not used, unless otherwise indicated.

- Solid vegetable shortening (not butter, margarine, nonstick cooking sprays or vegetable oil spread as they can cause sticking problems) was used to grease pans, unless otherwise indicated.

We use equipment for testing that the majority of consumers use in their homes. If a specific piece of equipment (such as a wire whisk) is necessary for recipe success, it is listed in the recipe.

- Cookware and bakeware without nonstick coatings were used, unless otherwise indicated.

- No dark-colored, black or insulated bakeware was used.

- When a pan is specified in a recipe, a metal pan was used; a baking dish or pie plate means oven-proof glass was used.

- An electric hand mixer was used for mixing only when mixer speeds are specified in the recipe directions. When a mixer speed is not given, a spoon or fork was used.

## Cooking Terms Glossary

**Beat:** Mix ingredients vigorously with spoon, fork, wire whisk, hand beater or electric mixer until smooth and uniform.

**Boil:** Heat liquid until bubbles rise continuously and break on the surface and steam is given off. For rolling boil, the bubbles form rapidly.

**Chop:** Cut into coarse or fine irregular pieces with a knife, food chopper, blender or food processor.

**Cube:** Cut into squares 1/2 inch or larger.

**Dice:** Cut into squares smaller than 1/2 inch.

**Grate:** Cut into tiny particles using small rough holes of grater (citrus peel or chocolate).

**Grease:** Rub the inside surface of a pan with shortening, using pastry brush, piece of waxed paper or paper towel, to prevent food from sticking during baking (as for some casseroles).

**Julienne:** Cut into thin, matchlike strips, using knife or food processor (vegetables, fruits, meats).

**Mix:** Combine ingredients in any way that distributes them evenly.

**Sauté:** Cook foods in hot oil or margarine over medium-high heat with frequent tossing and turning motion.

**Shred:** Cut into long thin pieces by rubbing food across the holes of a shredder, as for cheese, or by using a knife to slice very thinly, as for cabbage.

**Simmer:** Cook in liquid just below the boiling point on top of the stove; usually after reducing heat from a boil. Bubbles will rise slowly and break just below the surface.

**Stir:** Mix ingredients until uniform consistency. Stir once in a while for stirring occasionally, often for stirring frequently and continuously for stirring constantly.

**Toss:** Tumble ingredients (such as green salad) lightly with a lifting motion, usually to coat evenly or mix with another food.